THE YORKSHIRE DALES

Hollybush Spout, Ingleton Glens

THE
YORKSHIRE DALES

A WALKERS' GUIDE
TO THE NATIONAL PARK

by

GLADYS SELLERS

Drawings by R.B.Evans
Colour photographs by Walt Unsworth

CICERONE PRESS,
MILNTHORPE, CUMBRIA

© Gladys Sellers 1984, 1992
ISBN 1 85254 097 8
First published 1984
Reprinted 1986
Revised Edition 1992

British Library Cataloguing-in-Publication Data. A catalogue record for this book
is available from the British Library.

ACKNOWLEDGEMENTS

I should like to thank the following staff at the headquarters of the
Yorkshire Dales National Park Authority for their assistance with
certain aspects of this book: Susie Arnott, Footpath Officer, for
help with right of way path changes. Simon Rose, Project Officer
for the Three Peaks Footpath Project, for discussing the aims and
methods used with me. Robert White, archaeologist, for a resumé
of the conservation work both completed and proposed on the
many former lead mining sites within the Park.

In addition I should like to thank Miss A.H.Pilkington for her
forbearance in accompanying me on much of the check-walking
needed, not all of it of great interest to her but essential to me, and
not all in good weather.

Gladys Sellers

Advice to Readers

Readers are advised that whilst every effort is taken by the author
to ensure the accuracy of this guidebook, changes can occur
which may affect the contents. It is advisable to check locally on
transport, accommodation, shops etc but even rights-of-way can
be altered and, more especially overseas, paths can be eradicated
by landslip, forest fires or changes of ownership.

The publisher would welcome notes of any such changes

Front Cover : Walkers approaching Catrigg Force, with Pen-y-ghent
in the distance   (Walt Unsworth)

PREFACE TO THE SECOND EDITION

In the last ten years or so the number of visitors walking in the Dales has increased greatly. Their very numbers have brought about considerable changes to the network of paths since work was started on the first edition of this book. Around the popular places such as Malham Cove and Aysgarth Falls improvements to paths have made the old route descriptions erroneous if not downright libellous. A great many paths are now easier to follow and better signposted. However, some farm tracks that are not rights of way but give access to the fells are now marked 'Private' and in this second edition some walks have had to be deleted or hedged about with warnings of trespass. New barbed wire fences have proliferated on some fells and caused changes to routes to be made. Parking difficulties have increased. From bitter experience the writer urges walkers not to park on lonely roads: theft from cars is rife in the Dales, particularly from cars parked in that sort of place. As many walks as possible start from car parks, though there is no guarantee of safety in numbers.

Guidebook authors are necessarily influenced by the maps at their disposal and the 1984 editions of the 1:25,000 Outdoor Leisure maps give more complete coverage of the eastern edge of the Park than the older ones used for the first edition of this book. In addition, the Northern Areas sheet, a double-sided horror, gives Wensleydale and Swaledale - for the first time - the great benefits of this calibre of map. It has made possible a reappraisal of the walking in upper Swaledale. In total much new material has been added to the second edition, and in order to keep the book's size within moderation, a number of short walks of little importance have been deleted and others have been telescoped.

It is to be hoped that moderate walkers who like something they can get their teeth into will find much more of use to them in this second edition than in the first. Considering the rate at which the countryside is changing, it is sheer speculation to hope even that this edition will have as long a life as its predecessor.

Gladys Sellers, 1992

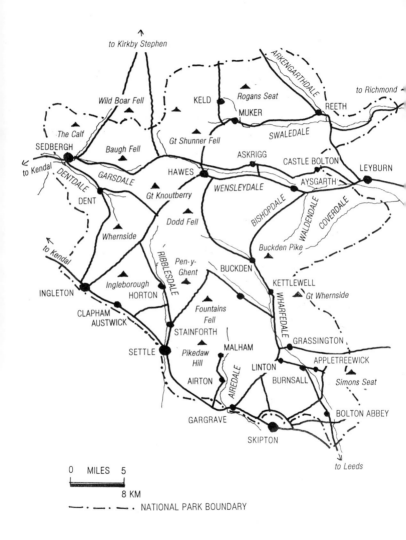

CONTENTS

Introducing the Yorkshire Dales National Park 9

The evolution of guidebooks 12

Getting the best out of this book 14

The Three Peaks Footpath Project 19

The contribution of geology to the scenery of The Dales 23

Man's contribution to the scenery of The Dales 31

The Settle-Carlisle Railway 38

Lead mining and smelting in The Dales 42

Caving and potholing in the Yorkshire Dales 53

1.   Lower Wharfedale - Bolton Abbey to Burnsall 58

2.   Wharfedale - Burnsall to Grassington 83

3.   Upper Wharfedale 108

4.   Airedale 126

5.   Ribblesdale 143

6.   Ingleton and Clapham 174

7.   Dentdale and Garsdale 201

8.   Sedbergh and the Howgills 221

9.   Lower Wensleydale - West Witton to Aysgarth 239

10. Upper Wensleydale and Mallerstang 261

11. Swaledale 285

*Attractive waterfalls are a feature of the Yorkshire Dales. This one
is Cotter Force near the head of Wensleydale.*

INTRODUCING
THE YORKSHIRE DALES NATIONAL PARK

England and Wales have ten national parks between them, established under the provisions of the 1949 Access to the Countryside Act. The Yorkshire Dales National Park was designated in 1954 and some 96 per cent of it is privately owned, for the Act did not transfer land to public ownership. Many of the features making up the Dales landscape are unique: its hay meadows, hamlets and villages, its limestone scars above the valley and its sombre moorlands. The main task of the county council sub-committee that manages the Park is to protect and conserve this landscape whilst encouraging its use for quiet recreation. Protection must be done with restraint lest parks become museums. The people who live there have to move with the times to earn a living and protection of the landscape is often at some social cost to them. Today the Yorkshire Dales National Park is under pressure as never before. The leisure explosion and the motor car have brought tourism to the fore and tourism's insatiable appetite does little to foster conservation and protection. The Park sub-committee's powers of conservation are limited. It can control building developments and resist pressure to create theme parks and the like, but it has no powers to control forestry and only limited power to control quarrying, two activities that ruin the traditional landscape of the Dales. On the plus side it can influence farmers to use methods that maintain the traditional landscape. Today much thought is being given to a new National Parks Act that would give the parks more clout to handle the pressures upon them, including extra funding for rights of way and for tackling the increasing problem of footpath erosion.

As part of its brief to protect the landscape the Park's Committee attempts to educate visitors in the way they should use their environment. With this in mind it has established National Park Centres at the following places:

Aysgarth Falls	(0969 663424)
Clapham	(04685 419)
Grassington	(0756 752748)
Hawes	(0969 667450)
Malham	(07293 363)
Sedbergh	(05396 20125)

Only Grassington is open throughout the week in winter, the others at weekends only. At all the centres, large car parks are provided, today often not big enough, which cost £1 a day, less for shorter periods. In addition the Park provides car parks with toilets at Horton in Ribblesdale, Stainforth, Dent, Kettlewell and Buckden. There are other car parks within the Park provided by local authorities.

The Park sub-committee has done a great deal to fulfil its obligation to provide access to the countryside. There are some 1,067 miles of right of way paths and every right of way path is now signposted where it leaves the road. Waymarking and siting of auxiliary signposts is much better than it was ten years ago. Paths are maintained and stiles repaired so that a vast network of paths and bridleways that were sinking into obscurity through lack of use have been restored. A major task has been the repair of the rights of way paths in the Three Peaks area, a task spread over several years and costing the best part of £1M.

In the last six or seven years the Park has handled over 100 changes to rights of way paths, some proposed by farmers who offer an alternative to passing through their stock yards, or who wish to divert a path to build a new barn or the like; others to make better routes available to walkers - for example, the route up Whernside from Ribblehead. In addition work is in hand to legalise paths on the fells that have been used for years and years on an *ipso facto* basis. This is not a cut-and-dried affair, for the vast number of walkers has turned some landowners against them and recourse to a public enquiry has to be made. Some fine new walks have been made possible by the creation of new rights of way paths, for example, that up Pen-y-ghent Gill.

The area of the Park is vast: 680 square miles. Its boundaries enclose the finest of the Pennine Dales, but exclude the towns and villages on the fringe and pay more attention to the county boundary than to natural ones. Tracing the boundary from Tan Hill, almost its most northerly point, it follows the county boundary as it was in 1954 west-wards all the way to Mason Gill. As it happens this part of the county boundary does not include the head of the Vale of Eden which is very characteristic Dales country and does include a part of the Howgills which is quite out of character. From Mason Gill the boundary roughly follows the line of the A65 road to Skipton, excluding Ingleton, Settle and Gargrave. Naturally it skirts Skipton, then follows very approximately the boundary of Barden Moor to Bolton Abbey. Here it turns south to encompass Beamsley Beacon and Moor, and then turns north roughly following the watersheds of Wharfedale and the lower part of Coverdale. Nidderdale was therefore omitted - but what a task to set standards of excellence for scenery! Skirting Middleham the boundary now moves westwards following the River Ure and its principal tributary Apedale Beck, across the mouth of Wensleydale. It then runs north-east almost to the outskirts of Richmond, where true to principle it omits that little gem of a town and turns west again following the road through Marske almost to Reeth, then back by the county boundary to Tan Hill.

THE EVOLUTION OF GUIDEBOOKS

There have been guidebooks of one sort or another for walkers in the Craven Dales for many more years than one would imagine. These early guidebooks were a far cry from today's, which, if they contain the word 'Ramble' or 'Walk' in the title give quite detailed instructions as to how to find the way. The early ones are vague yet verbose accounts of walks complete with botanical notes, accounts of 'natural curiosities', and historical associations, written to be enjoyed in the armchair.

One of the very earliest of these was Dobson's *Rambles by the Ribble* reprinted in 1846 from a set of newspaper articles in the Preston Chronicle. It is an account, in the style of the times, of his walks. There are few indications of his routes, though he made good use of the railway network to get to his starting point, For example, he took an evening train from Preston to Lancaster, stayed the night and got an early train next morning to Hornby in order to walk to the source of the Ribble, though not, let it be said, in one day. And he includes a fair measure of 'natural curiosities'.

The development of the railway network played a surprising part in the writing of the early guidebooks for walkers. Harker's *Rambles in Upper Wharfedale* 1869, expresses concern that the railway would bring 'a larger influx of visitors than the district has ever seen', and Thompson's 1879 *Guide to the District of Craven and the Settle and Carlisle Railway* specifically sets out to cater for rail travellers. Most of his walks, like Harker's, were along the roads and he very handily gives a list of the pubs.

By 1920 the Victorian interest in the railways was long past and with it went much of the verbose romanticism of the early guides. Crowther's *Rambles round Grassington* of that year is a much more down to earth guidebook, with, at least, some walking detail. So too, is Edmund Bogg's slim pocket-sized guide of 1921. He was a botanist and writer who led parties of walkers from Leeds. By 1930 the Youth Hostels Association had come into being and attitudes to walking were changing. In literary style A.J.Brown's *Moorland Tramping in West Yorkshire* is a throw-back to Victorian times, in attitude a great step forward. He abjured the car-ridden lanes and made long distance walks, from Settle to Bainbridge, for example, mostly along the old drove roads. For the first time there are good sketch maps of the routes but the reader is left to work out the details for himself. It was still a book for the armchair. Guidebook styles were far removed from today's even in 1954. That year the Y.H.A. published its *Guide to Ingleton, Dent and Stainforth.* Mainly a collection of most readable specialist articles about the area, the cross country routes are merely sketched in around the place names with instructions to supplement Sheet No. 90 of the Ordnance Survey. However, ten years later their *Guide to the Yorkshire Dales* had a very different approach, giving much more route detail and some historical associations. This approach has been developed by most present-day writers, and their books are essentially for use in the field rather than the armchair. Yet it is all too easy for the walker to lose his/her place in the instruction because of the amount of material based on natural history or historical associations that may be included. The poor author is between the Scylla of bald instructions and the Charybdis of imparting information. The Yorkshire Dales National Park Authority has produced a series of leaflets describing walks and its authors tackle this problem by writing separate paragraphs of instructions entitled 'The Route' and 'Viewpoint' at the appropriate points. Necessarily the choice of walk is limited: they are usually short and none venture on the high fells.

Today many more people than Harker dreamed of visit and walk in the Dales, the vast majority arriving by car. Leaflets, stiles, waymarks and all too often crowds of people, all help to guide the walker along his chosen route. An informative guidebook will help him/her to choose a walk that gives the maximum pleasure and increase his knowledge of the countryside.

On the limestone shelf above Cray (Walk 3.6)

GETTING THE BEST OUT OF THIS BOOK

This book introduces you to the pleasures of walking in the Yorkshire Dales. Pleasure soon becomes pain if walks prove to be longer or more demanding than you expected, so they are divided into three categories. The easiest, category C, are short easy walks with not much uphill, suitable for those with young families. Category B, the majority, are half day or short day walks. Though some of them go onto the high ground they don't stay there long. Category A are more demanding in every way. They are longer, are mostly on the high ground where the going will be wet and hard and if the weather deteriorates will need map and compass work to get down from or continue. Sometimes a party may be slower than expected and have only limited time at its disposal, or the weather will deteriorate, so whenever possible a short return is given for the longer walks. Occasionally a much shorter walk can be done using the same starting and finishing paths. All this information is summarised in the introductory paragraph of a walk, but the detail of the shorter route is given at the end as a separate paragraph.

One of a guidebook writer's tasks is to select routes of character, quality and of the right length. In some places, Wharfedale in particular, there is such a network of good paths that the task becomes invidious, and on some routes the walker has been left to make his own choice of the alternatives. The times given are for the average walker. Others, especially those with children, will need to modify them. The times do not include rests except where this is stated on the longer walks. Almost all of the valley walks are on right of way paths. Wherever this is not the case, the fact is stated. On the open fell, above the intake wall, a freedom to wander has been assumed for more than thirty years to the author's knowledge and has produced many well-used paths. However, some of these paths are not rights of way and access may in future be contested. An exception is Barden Fell and Moor for which access rights have been negotiated and which are closed on certain days in the shooting season.

Remember that a guidebook does not replace a map: it clarifies and supplements it over the narrow band of country covered by each walk. The map supplies the wider background, but accurate map reading is a refined skill that needs much practice. It is much easier to read a book.

Finally remember that the land in the Dales Park is not owned by the state but by private individuals many of whom farm their own land. Age-old rights of way give us access to it, but it behoves us to treat it with respect. Do nothing that will hinder the efforts of farmers who make a living from the land you enjoy visiting. Do nothing that will injure your environment - leave nothing but footprints, take nothing but photographs. To be a bit more specific:

1. Take all your litter home with you.
2. When picnicking use a gas stove, not a fire.
3. Be careful with matches and cigarettes. Moorland fires are devastating.
4. Enjoy the flowers and trees where they are growing.
5. Take care not to pollute any stream. It may be the source of a farm's drinking water.
6. Close all gates so that animals cannot stray on to the road.
7. In lambing time keep your dog on a lead. A sheep in lamb, chased by a dog even if not touched by it, is liable to lose that lamb.
8. Take care not to block farm gates and access roads, if you park other than in Y.D.N.P. car parks.
9. Avoid climbing walls if at all possible. Only on a very few of the category A walks is it necessary.

Another of a guidebook writer's traditional tasks is to provide some historical and botanical background to the walks. Today there is a much greater interest in our environment than ever before and the writer must do more than just list his buildings and his flowers. He must look at the landscape with the eye of the geologist, botanist, archaeologist, historian and industrial archaeologist and interpret it in a way which is both understandable and enjoyable. Too many snippets of information fitted into the text breaks the thread of a set of instructions, so you will find only a number at the appropriate point referring to the 'Things of Interest' section where such material is collected. Some subjects are too big and too wide in their application to be covered there, so in addition there is a series of articles about them. Anyone with an especial interest in the subjects below may like to do these recommended walks:

(Chapters are shown in Bold type)

Geology: **4**.1 to **4**.6; **6**.1; **6**.2; **6**.8; **6**.9; **7**.7; **9**.1; **11**.3
Botany: **1**.1; **2**.4; **5**.1; **6**.1; **6**.7; **9**.6; **11**.2; **11**.4; **11**.8; **11**.9
Churches: **1**.1; **1**.4; **2**.3; **3**.6
Lead Mining: **2**.6; **2**.7; **3**.3; **4**.9; **9**.6; **11**.4 to **11**.6; **11**.9; **11**.10; **11**.11
Industrial Archaelogy: **4**.4; **5**.1; **9**.11; **10**.7
Caving: **5**.2; **5**.8b; **5**.11 to **5**.15; **6**.2b; **6**.5; **6**.6

EQUIPMENT

Category C All you need for these are trainers, and bearing in mind the weather here may be more liable to showers than where you live, a light waterproof. Otherwise, wear what you would wear for a walk in the local park that day.

Category B

Light boots, windproof jacket, pullover, waterproofs.

Category A

Good boots are highly desirable. Breeches or trousers unless there is a heat wave. Windproof jacket, extra pullover, waterproof and over trousers, woolly cap

Map and compass and some knowledge of their use.

Some extra food over and above the day's normal food.

In winter all walks go up a category and a torch must always be carried. Add to the Category A walks the following: long gaiters, scarf, windproof gloves, thermos with hot drink, bivvy bag.

GETTING AROUND

Most of the walks in this guide are based on the assumption that the walker arrives by car, needs somewhere to park it, and a circular route. This is not necessarily so and in any case some walks are natural through routes, not circuits.

Many bus companies operate in the Dales: it is quite a complicated matter to check in advance which goes where. However, the Y.D.N.P. offers a free booklet entitled *Dales Connections* which covers all bus services and the Settle-Carlisle railway together with its connecting bus services. No walker needing public transport should be without one.

ACCOMMODATION IN THE DALES

There is a wealth of hospitality in the Dales: pubs, bed and breakfast establishments and farmhouses. These days self-catering accommodation is popular and there is a wide choice. Caravanning or camping suits many people and there are campsites at the following places:

Appletreewick	Arncliffe	Barden
Cracoe	Kettlewell	Gargrave
Malham	Stirton	Ingleton
Little Stainforth	Aysgarth	Horton in Ribblesdale
Hawes	Dent	Newbiggin in Bishopdale
Kirkby Stephen	Ravenstonedale	Sedbergh
Muker	Richmond	

For people doing the long distance walks youth hostels may be more suitable than camping. There are hostels at:

Kettlewell	Ingleton	Aysgarth	Richmond
Linton	Malham	Hawes	Keld
Dentdale	Stainforth	Grinton	Kirkby Stephen

Bunkhouses are a relatively new development and they may vary from very basic to quite luxurious. The Parks committee started them some twelve to fifteen years ago by converting disused barns into simple accommodation for walkers. The Park's Dales Barns usually hold twelve to twenty people in three or four rooms, and have toilets, showers, drying rooms and self-catering facilities. Privately owned ones may offer less. Charges vary from £2 to £6 a night according to the standard. It is advisable to book bed space in advance by letter or phone. In 1991 the list was as follows:

Dales Barns:

Barden Tower, Barden: Mr I.H.Leak, High Gamsworth Cottage, Barden. (0756 720630)

Cam Farm, Langstrothdale: Mrs D.Smith, Cam Houses, Buckden. (0860 648045)

Catholes Farm, Sedbergh: Mrs J.Handley, Catholes Farm, Sedbergh. (05396 20334)

Dub Cote Farm, Horton in Ribblesdale: Mrs J.Glasgow, Dub Cote Farm, Horton in Ribblesdale. (07296 238)

Grange Farm, Hubberholme: Mrs A.Falshaw, Grange Farm, Hubberholme. (0756 760259)

Hill Top Farm, Malham: J. and A.Heseltine, Hill Top Farm,

Malham. (0729 830320)

Skirfare Bridge, Kinsley: Mrs J.L.Foster, Northcote, Kilnsey. (0756 752465)

Privately owned bunkhouses

Airton Quaker Hostel: Mr & Mrs G.Parker, Airton, Skipton. (0729 830263)

The Old School Bunkhouse, Mr T.C.Lambert (05242 41477) Chapel-le-Dale:

Halton Gill: J. & A.Cowan, Manor Farm, Halton Gill. (0756 770241)

Ingleton: J.A. & M.Charlton, Stacksteads Farm, Ingleton. (05242 41386)

Oughtershaw: Mrs S.V.Bentley, Hazelbank Farm, Oughtershaw, Buckden. (0756 760312)

Ravenstonedale: Mr & Mrs Hamer, Bowber Head, Ravenstonedale, Kirkby Stephen. (05873 254)

The Y.D.N.P. offers a cheap booklet, available by post that gives details of all types of accommodation.

MAPS

The Outdoor Leisure Maps Nos. 2, 10, and 30 cover the greater part of the Y.D.N.P. and most of the walks in this book, but do not cover Mallerstang or the Howgills. The latter are nicely covered by the Pathfinder Map No. 617, SD 69/79, except for the one walk starting from the northern side, and as this map also covers Baugh Fell, Swarth Fell and part of Wild Boar Fell as well as Grisedale and part of Mallerstang, it is well worth having if you are a regular visitor to the Dales. For those who are not so fortunate, Stile Maps, by Stile Publications, Mercury House, Otley, LS21 3HE, are excellent alternatives. They are small, cheap, footpath maps of remarkable clarity on the familiar scale of 1:25,000 and are available for the following areas: Bolton Abbey, Grassington, Malhamdale, The Three Peaks, Sedbergh (Dent), Sedbergh (Howgills), Aysgarth Area, Hawes and District, and Upper Swaledale. They are usually obtainable in the appropriate National Park Centre.

THE THREE PEAKS FOOTPATH PROJECT

Fifteen years ago there was little or no erosion of the most popular paths in the Three Peaks area. Ten years ago, when the walking for the first edition of this book was being done, it was quite noticeable and then rapidly worsened. Vast erosion scars developed on the steep escarpments and the paths over the boggy moorlands widened and worsened to a degree that was unacceptable to walkers, local farmers, and all who loved the landscape of the Yorkshire Dales. Here and there something had been done quickly, for example, the wooden walkways on the Brackenbottom route up Pen-y-ghent: liked by many walkers but environmentally quite unsatisfactory.

In 1987 the Yorkshire Dales National Park Authority produced a five-year plan to restore all the main rights of way paths (not all the paths are rights of way) to a firm, pleasant-to-walk-on, environmentally acceptable state in such a way that they would require little maintenance. The cost was estimated at £750,000 spread over the five years and various bodies connected with the countryside contributed the money. Several walking clubs even chipped in. In the event, another £180,000 was needed to complete the work. A project officer was appointed and a community programme set up to start the job.

Nothing like this had ever been done before and there were no ready made solutions to the assorted problems. Because of the geological structure of the Three Peaks area, the rock in the valley bottoms and some little way up the flanks of the fells is limestone, and there the ground drains quickly. Then comes a long stretch of peat moorland, badly drained, slow drying. Finally there is a cap of millstone grit, with very stony, thin, easily damaged soils and turf. Clearly very different methods would be needed, and in effect the whole project was one vast environmental experiment. Methods and materials were chosen according to their availability and the nature of the ground. Vast amounts of material were required so machinery had to be used, and this meant that paths had to be made up to 2.5 metres wide, much wider than walkers need. Hire of specialist machines has been the biggest single expense of the project, costing more than either wages or the materials used.

A start was made on some of the paths on the peaty ground. One of the first lengths of path to be tackled was the Pennine Way path across the peat moor below the escarpment on Pen-y-ghent using crushed limestone from nearby quarries. It wasn't just a simple matter of spreading it on the ground, for peat of that type and depth would just swallow it up. First the peat had to be excavated, then a trough of plastic mesh put in. This was then filled with the crushed limestone which was consolidated with a vibrator machine and rolled firm so that it would be stable, not wash away in the rain, and be pleasant to walk upon. Finally grasses and the local heath rush were encouraged to grow into the edges to soften the considerable visual impact of this white worm creeping up the moor. At first modest amounts of fertiliser were applied, turves tucked into the edges, and plastic matting used to reinforce weak bits of turf, but this was not enough. In the autumn of 1990 some major reseeding was done in an attempt to hasten what might be called the ageing process to make the path less obtrusive to the eye and by the next spring it was clearly successful.

Another method was used on the path from Horton-in-Ribblesdale to Ingleborough. A considerable length of path just above Horton is on the limestone strata and did not need any attention, but above Nick Pot where the peat moorlands start, another technique was used, borrowed from Scotland where it had been used on the West Highland Way. A big digger first made a drainage ditch on the top side of the path to be, then removed the surface peat, here not so deep as on Pen-y-ghent, and brought the subsoil to the surface. Spread in a neat ridge, it then needed time to consolidate, helped by walker's feet. At first it was an unpleasant slippery, soggy mess, but then it improved and in the dry summer of 1990 was excellent to walk upon. Winter rain saw a return to the wet and slippery state, and the Project Officer admits that it could be better. Environmentally it blends well with the landscape.

Yet another method was used on the path to Ingleborough from the Old Hill Inn, the use of 'Flexiboard', which is strips of oak board held together by iron bands, tarred and gritted to prevent a slippery surface from developing. It is flexible enough to bend to the contour of the ground and to make gentle curves so that the path does not have to be laid in a straight line. This footpath passes over the Nature Conservancy Council's National Nature Reserve, Ingleborough High Lot, where path widening to avoid the bad parts had become extreme. The Nature Conservancy Council was very concerned that irreversible damage was being done to a wide area of its reserve and in 1989/90 asked that something should be done immediately to contain the situation. A Flexiboard path was chosen as the quick answer. It is easy to walk on, too easy; it gets boring and is unkind to the feet especially in descent. Visually it is quite unsatisfactory, and eventually will be replaced with a stone-based track similar to the one on Pen-y-ghent.

A different type of area is the top 300 feet or so of the summits, each of them different. A start was made on Whernside with a set of steps made out of old railway sleepers up the badly eroded steep escarpment that leads to the ridge. These steps are far too big for anybody less than about 6 foot 3 inches in height and already an escape route has been trodden out by unwilling feet. Steps are no real answer to the problem because of people's very different leg lengths, and stone pitching, a traditional technique used in the Lake District to repair many paths, is a far better solution, which at some future date will replace these steps. From the top of them it is about ¾ mile to the summit, most of the ground kicked to pieces by the vast number of feet that have passed this way. The whole of this length has been remade and a lot of landscaping has been done, much of it by volunteer labour provided by the British Trust for Conservation Volunteers.

A big landscape restoration plan was built into the entire project because the big machines disturb a wider area of ground than they actually work on. Reseeding trials using our native grasses were started on the top of Whernside in the early stages of the work, and some have grown amazingly well even though they were sown on virtually soil-less ground. However, it was found that the amounts of seed that would be needed were so big that they were not available in this country, so perennial rye grass, normally used to reseed lowland hay fields was used. It will not survive more than a few years in the winter weather on the top of Whernside, but the small amounts of native grass that remain will increase and will take over as the rye grass fades away. Reseeding is a very large scale operation and was done using a machine which sprays a mixture of seeds, fertiliser, clay and wood pulp. This helps to stabilise the soil and provides a good start for the seeds. Unfortunately the melting of the winter snows of 1990/91 washed away considerable areas of young grass, and the job had to be done again.

The tops of both Ingleborough and Pen-y-ghent pose rather different problems and there work was delayed. The summit plateau of Ingleborough is the site of a Brigantian hill fort and is a scheduled ancient monument. Nothing can be done there without the sanction of

English Heritage and nothing is planned at present. There used to be an appallingly steep, rough piece of path from the end of the Flexiboard to the start of the summit plateau. It now has a pitched stone staircase, only made good at the second attempt. Again, the melting snows of 1990/91 did the damage, undermining and collapsing the considerable length that was already built. Underground springs whose presence were formerly unsuspected had to be diverted with buried plastic drains before the work of pitching could be redone.

Pen-y-ghent's summit problem will surprise most people. The way everybody goes from the end of the new path up the moor is not the right of way path as marked on the map, and as the remit for the project is to repair and remake the right of way paths, not the several unofficial paths, nothing could be done to improve it. Fortunately there is one quite elegant solution - to make the path that people use the right of way path. A legal procedure had to be followed to do this and work did not start until the summer of 1991, virtually completing the project.

The autumn of 1992, when I go to press, is too soon to assess fully the environmental effect of the remade paths. The earliest length to be done, that on Pen-y-ghent, has mellowed very considerably. Even a length of Flexiboard used on the Ribblehead to Whernside route gets lost in long grass in summer. Given time, even that on Ingleborough will merge into the moor. The recovery of the former 'paths' alongside the remade ones has been quite remarkable. Walkers who never experienced their earlier appalling state may be tempted to say 'Waste of money, 'Downgrading the hills', and so on. I agree; up to a point the new paths do downgrade the hills: route finding is less of a problem, fatigue is diminished, though there is still the weather to contend with. Some of the challenge has been taken out of the Three Peaks circuit but for most walkers it is now a pleasure, not a filthy wallow.

THE CONTRIBUTION OF GEOLOGY
TO THE SCENERY OF THE DALES

Every walker realises, however vaguely, that the nature of the rocks and the forces of Nature have shaped our hills and valleys. More specifically, the type of rock strata immediately below the surface, earth movements, glaciation and weathering are the four main agents that mould scenery and of these, the underlying rocks strata and faulting are the most important. The difference between the dramatic limestone scenery around Settle and Ingleton and the gentle, rounded hills of the Howgill Fells could scarcely be more marked and it stems from these two causes. Beautiful scenery is more than a collection of shapes however well assembled. Natural vegetation, modified by man's usage, is an integral part of it. The type of vegetation is partly determined by climate, partly by man's usage, but in the Dales the biggest factor that influences vegetation is that of rock structure. Vegetation plays a big part in the range of colours in the landscape especially in autumn, from the fresh greens of the limestone pastures to the russets of the hill grasses, tawny bracken and sombre heather.

Most of the surface rock strata in the Dales belong to the Carboniferous group which was laid down horizontally and has not subsequently been folded. This is the basic reason for the gentle horizontal lines of the moors and fells compared with the more rugged lines of the mountains of say, Snowdonia, where the rocks are older and much contorted by earth movements.

In the valleys of Ribblesdale, Airedale, Wharfedale and around Chapel-le-Dale, Great Scar or Mountain Limestone, as it is also called, predominates. This extensive block of Great Scar limestone, tilted slightly upwards to the south-west, is terminated by the South Craven Fault (which can be clearly seen along the line of the A65 below Giggleswick Scar), and together with the Mid and North Craven Faults is the reason for the many massive limestone scars to be seen in the Malham-Settle-Ingleton areas. This pale grey limestone is around 200 metres (600 feet) thick and its effect on scenery extends from the valley floors to well up the hillsides. This Great Scar limestone was formed in a warm tropical sea as a series of layers or beds of slightly differing properties. Some beds are rich in fossils, others are not; some contain more impurities than others. These differences, whatever their nature, impart different resistances to weathering, particularly frost action. Freeze/thaw cycles fracture some types of limestone very readily and cause the short steep cliffs that extend for many hundreds of yards along some valley sides. These cliffs or scars and their slopes of rock fragments (scree) are very well seen on the hillsides above Chapel-le-Dale and in upper Wharfedale.

In many places round Ingleborough and Malham there are considerable areas of level bare rock. These are the upper surfaces of some of the beds of limestone. It is deeply weathered into clefts, some of which are a metre or more deep and up to half a metre wide, and is known as limestone pavement or sometimes as clint fields. Clints are the level parts, grikes the clefts which provide suitable homes for lime and shade loving plants such as harts tongue ferns, herb robert and many others normally found in woodland. It is not clear just how they came to be formed. Glaciation played a part, for they are not found in either the Mendips or the Peak District, two limestone areas that were not ice-covered during the last Ice Age. The surface soil that was scraped off by the glaciers has been replaced, but on the limestone pavements it has been lost again. It is thought that small changes in climate and grazing patterns may be the cause, but nobody really knows why, though there is archaeological evidence that it has happened in post glacial times.

Streams are almost entirely absent in the limestone uplands. The cause is the permeability of the limestone and its solubility in rain water. This is so slight it is measured in terms of parts per million, from around twenty five to 200 or even more in some circumstances; slow in human terms, but no slower than other geological processes. It means very minute cracks will be enlarged and eventually water will drain away through the surface rocks leaving considerable areas such as that above Malham Tarn and Settle without streams. Even sizeable rivers like the Skirfare in Littondale disappear in summer. Indeed, one might safely say that unless a valley has either been cut down to the lower impervious rocks or has been lined with glacial drift (see later) it is unlikely to have a stream.

This extensive block of Great Scar limestone whose special properties of bedding and water solubility contribute so much to Dales scenery has a slightly downward tilt to the north-east which has brought its top surface down from a height of about 365 metres (1,200 feet) around Ingleborough to about 182 metres (600 feet) on the floor of

Wensleydale around Aysgarth. In the normal succession of rock strata, the Yoredale beds lie on top of the Great Scar limestone. The name Yoredale is taken from the River Ure, the principal river of Wensleydale, where their effect on the landscape was first noted. The Yoredale beds are a repeating sequence of limestone, shale, (which may contain thin coal seams) then sandstone. Unlike the Great Scar limestone this limestone is rather impure and the beds of it are only about 10 metres (30 feet) thick, and the other rocks even thinner. The series is easily seen on the steep-sided cone of Ingleborough above the clint fields of Chapel-le-Dale where it is 300 metres (1,000 feet) thick. This thick band lies on top of the Great Scar limestone across all the western fells but in Wharfedale the Yoredale beds have been almost eroded away in geological times and around Grassington the Millstone Grit which, in the normal sequence of rock strata, lies on top of the Yoredales, lies almost on top of the Great Scar limestone.

This characteristic sequence of different rocks contributes a great deal to the scenery of Wensleydale simply because of the different way they weather. The limestone beds are harder and more weather resistant than the others, so they have been left as a series of rocky steps running for miles along the valley sides separated by grass-grown slopes where the readily eroded shale bands have crumbled away. These resistant bands of limestone are the reason for the many fine waterfalls in Wensleydale. Some notable ones are Hardraw Force, Whitfield and Mill Gills, but all three Aysgarth falls are formed in three different beds of Great Scar limestone, which are, as often, separated by shale beds. The undercutting of the shales has produced the set of three falls. In the north-west of the Dales the Yoredale series extend as far as the Dent Fault which cuts off this vast area of assorted Carboniferous rocks from the Howgill Fells which are of totally different and much older rocks. Like Wensleydale, the floors of Dentdale and Garsdale are of Great Scar limestone.

On the highest fells (except the Howgills) the Yoredale series is topped with a thin band of millstone grit. Like the Great Scar limestone it is horizontally bedded; unlike it, it is impervious to water. Its streams drain first onto the Yoredales at whose foot they reach the Great Scar limestone where they are engulfed forming caves and pot holes. Below the Great Scar limestone is a basement layer of very much older Lower Palaeozoic rocks, Silurian and Ordovician slates and grits, and here the water that sank below ground when it reached the Great Scar limestone is forced to the surface to reappear as springs, some of them quite large such as Keld Head in Kingsdale, others small enough to escape notice.

The Silurian slates and grits appear at the surface in the Austwick and Horton-in-Ribblesdale areas as a result of faulting. Because these rocks are so much older they have been folded and contorted; often the layers are stood on end, in great contrast with the carboniferous limestone which is normally level. This change can be most strikingly seen in Foredale Quarry, Horton-in-Ribblesdale. In Crummackdale the valley floor is of Silurian slate and has a stream, whilst the walls are of Great Scar limestone. Associated with Silurian rocks are the Ordovician rocks made up of shales and mudstones as well as slates and grits. Between them they make the Howgill Fells, rounded grassy hills to the north-west of Sedbergh, much more like the eastern part of the Lake District than the Craven Dales because of their similar rock structure. Part of the Howgills lie within the boundaries of the park simply because they are within the former county boundary.

The difference in scenery between the Howgills on the one side of the River Rawthey, and Dentdale and Garsdale on the other is due to the position of the Dent Fault. This runs roughly from north-east of Kirkby Stephen across the mouth of Dentdale through Barbondale to Leck, which is north-west of Ingleton. The mighty upthrusting forces of this fault raised the land north-west of it and weathering in the aeons of time that have passed since then has removed all the rock strata deposited above them.

More of these contorted, ancient rocks form the scenery of the Ingleton glens. Both these rocks and the Silurian slates at Austwick and Horton have been brought near to the surface by the Craven Faults, a complex set of them that run very roughly parallel to each other. The three main ones are the North, Mid and South Craven Faults, and together with their cross faults they are responsible for some of the most spectacular Dales scenery. Giggleswick Scar, just above the A65 road north of Settle is made of Great Scar limestone raised by the upthrust of the South Craven Fault. On the other side of the road the surface rock is Millstone Grit, seen in the stone walls, and very different from the white limestone of the scar above.

Cross faulting has produced many of the small scars above and behind Settle. The Mid Craven Fault produced Malham Cove and Gordale Scar. The North Craven Fault produced the cliffs behind Malham Tarn, and further east, the waterfall of Catrigg Force, in

Reef knolls near Cracoe - Elbolton Hill, Stebden Hill and Carden Hill

Ribblesdale, and Linton Falls on the Wharfe. Let it not be thought that this faulting was a sudden cataclysmic affair. It was a slow process taking place over hundreds of years and producing many minor faults. Its crude direct effects are now very much modified by weathering.

Immediately south of the Mid Craven Fault is an irregular line of smooth rounded hills some 200-300 feet high extending from Appletreewick to Settle. They are particularly well seen along the northern edge of Barden Moor where their colour is in sharp contrast with the sombre shades of the moorland. These hills are known as reef knolls from their probable method of formation and are made of a limestone that is different from both the Great Scar or the Yoredale limestones. They are very rich in fossils of several types and are thought to have been mounds or hillocks rising above the general level of the sea in which the Great Scar Limestone was laid down.

Although geological structure is the foundation of scenery, the last Ice Age made some important changes. Already the general pattern of the fells and valleys of the Dales was established when the climatic changes occurred that brought it about. The last Ice Age only took place some 10,000 to 20,000 years ago, a very recent event indeed in the geological time scale. Then an icecap centred on Wild Boar Fell, Baugh Fell and Great Shunner Fell covered the northern Pennines and only a few of the highest summits such as Ingleborough, Pen-y-ghent and Whernside protruded through it. The Vale of York was filled with an enormous glacier and each eastward draining dale provided a long tributary glacier. Apart from removing rock debris and soil and rounding off the hillsides and valleys, the glaciers' greatest contribution to scenery was made when they started to retreat and melt. Soil,

27

pebbles and boulders carried by them were deposited as a layer of stony clay called glacial drift or boulder clay all over the valleys and lower fells up to a height of about 450 metres (1,500 feet). It often masks the minor effects of faulting and the influence of the nature of the underlying rock on vegetation. The layer is not uniformly thick and has been removed or modified in places by weathering.

In some valleys the stones and clay were left as a ridge at the snout of the glacier as it retreated. These terminal moraines are found in a number of places but are not especially obvious, though they had the effect of damming the valleys and causing the meltwaters to form lakes. In these lakes the river sediments which poured in in quantity could settle as a level floor, eventually producing the flat bottomed valleys of Wharfedale above Kettlewell, Littondale, Kingsdale, others near Askrigg and Hawes, and between Reeth and Gunnerside. Other parts of these same dales have the more usual V-shaped profiles. Eventually these lakes were drained by the breaking of their moraine dams, and it is worth noting that in some places this happened in historic times. The evidence is the discovery of man-made implements buried deep in the peat and silt beneath their sites.

Another product of glaciation is the drumlins: egg-shaped hillocks of pebbles and clay under the ice and streamlined by the flow of the glacier. There are any number of them in Ribblesdale - the Three Peaks Walk passes through them twice, once just above Horton and near the head of the valley. They are usually found in large clusters with boggy ground in-between. In Wensleydale they can be seen scattered the length of the dale above Aysgarth. In places the whole landscape is one of hummocks, some so large it is difficult to believe they are drumlins when they are compared with those in Ribblesdale.

Weathering is the slow on-going process that continues to model our scenery. Except in flood time it is an undramatic affair, but it is the process that ultimately produces soil and that soil is usually closely related to the rock beneath it. Soil, climate and man jointly influenced the vegetation. Some plants such as heather won't grow on soils derived from limestone, nor will they grow on the cold wet soils of the highest fells. They need a drier situation, provided by lower ground or by the moors further east where the rainfall is less, such as the moors above Swaledale and Wensleydale, and on Barden Fell and Moor where they are managed for grouse shooting. The contribution they make to the richness of landscape colour in August when all else tends to drab greens is enormous, and contrasts finely with the green of the limestone pastures below.

The soils of the limestone pastures are light and well drained, rich in plant nutrients, and support a wide range of plant species - clover, lady's finger, bird's foot trefoil, horseshoe vetch to name but a few. When close-cropped by man's animals only the general tone of the bright green vegetation can be seen, but given freedom from hard grazing the variety of plants in the limestone pastures in early summer must be amongst the richest in the north of England. A few of the common ones are; mountain pansy, rock rose, primrose, bird's-eye primrose, thyme, scabious, ladies bedstraw, bloody cranesbill. No individual plant species is so common that it swamps the rest and dominates the landscape as does heather.

All these plants are too exacting in their soil requirements to survive on the high moorlands. Here a combination of high rainfall and a rock poor in minerals produces an acidic soil deficient in the nutrients required by the plants of the limestone pastures. Only those that can tolerate poor wet ground can thrive. Few species can do this. Where there is adequate drainage because of the slope, mat grass, bents and fescues are the commonest grasses. Flowers are few - tormentil and heath bedstraw are the commonest. Higher still where the climate is wetter and the drainage poorer only bog plants will grow - cotton grass, wavy-haired grass, heath rush and sphagnum moss. All these plants are a dull browny green and they cover vast areas of the higher ground. The change from one type of plant to the other is always abrupt: there is no mingling of the species. This can be seen on most walks where the limestone is left behind.

Moorland and limestone pastures do not make up the entire picture of the Dales: there is woodland. Wharfedale in particular is well wooded and here there are two distinct types: the woodland on the limestone scars of Littondale and upper Wharfedale and that around Bolton Abbey. The limestone scar woodland is light and open, mainly ash and hazel so it is late coming into leaf. Woodland of this type is full of spring limestone pasture flowers, largely because it is free from grazing animals. Here may be found primroses, violets, woody cranesbill, wood anemone, even lilies of the valley and other rarities. Limestone woodlands are essentially upland woods, though the wind limits their growth to below about the 350 metre (1,200 feet) contour. By contrast the woodland in lower Wharfedale is typical lowland wood. It grows on the valley floor, usually on acid soils derived from the millstone grit, but enriched with humus - and in a drier climate. Oak, sycamore, beech and horse chestnut are the common species and make a dense canopy of leaf in full summer. In spring these woods are richly carpeted with lesser celandine, wood anemone, wood sorrel, garlic and bluebells and are then extraordinarily beautiful. In late October they are no less beautiful when the autumn colours are at their best.

The woods of Swaledale are yet a third type. They are on limestone soils but are not upland woods like those of Littondale. There the oak is conspicuous by its absence, nor is the beech common. Ash, as characteristic of limestone soils as the oak is of acid soils, hazel, sycamore, alder, and the wych-elm are the common trees. Nor do these woods have quite the wealth of carpeting plants. They demonstrate the change of species on a different soil, but their contribution to the landscape is very similar to that of other lowland woods.

The Howgills, those 'odd men out' of the Yorkshire Dales National Park, show none of these contrasts of vegetation. These rounded hills built wholly of Silurian and Ordovician slates and grits, are better drained than the level tops of the Dales and receive rather less rain. Their rocks, like the millstone grit, weather to give a rather poor acid soil, so they are wholly grass mountains, covered with bents, fescues and mat grasses, the plants of poor upland grazing - but good walking.

This is only the broad outline of plants' dependence on soils. Many are exceedingly demanding in their requirements to grow and flower. Besides wanting a lime-rich soil the primrose must have a cool moist one, thyme a dry one, herb robert, shade. The micro climate of any spot influences these plants' choice of site no less than soil. But despite all the rigorous soil requirements, climate has the last word. If it does not allow a plant a sufficient number of days a year for it to grow and set seed, that plant will not succeed in establishing itself on that site. Many plants growing on the high moors do not depend on setting seed to propagate themselves. They spread from the roots. Most obviously grasses are this type of plant. However important this may be to the botanist its effect on landscape is small compared with the overall effect of rock structure.

MAN'S CONTRIBUTION TO THE
SCENERY OF THE DALES

It is not easy to assess man's influence on scenery: we forget that it reflects his agricultural methods and the grazing patterns of his animals. Before about 2000 BC in northern England most of the landscape below the 1,500 foot (300 metre) contour was covered in primeval forest. By this time Neolithic and Bronze Age man had appeared on the scene and they were the first agriculturalists, but too few in number to leave any traces on the landscape except their burial mounds. The earliest agricultural remains today are the so-called prehistoric fields, easily seen above Grassington, at Malham and a few other places. They are not truly prehistoric but Iron Age or Romano-British, those at Grassington dating from the second century AD. These fields, won by clearing the primeval forest are quite small, squarish, and surrounded by low earthy banks. Difficult to detect on the spot they are best seen from some vantage point. See Walks 4.1 and 4.2 for guidance in seeing those at Malham. The best known ones are at Grassington, marked 'Settlement' on the 1:25,000 Outdoor Leisure map, Southern area and they can be seen from Walk 2.5a. There is no public right of way through them as at Malham. These fields, however interesting to the landscape historian, make no impact whatever upon it today. They need a discerning eye even to see them.

Not until the advent of the Anglo-Saxons from the seventh century onwards did widespread changes take place. Their agricultural methods formed the long terraces on the lower slopes of the valleys. They occur widely in Wharfedale and Airedale, in lower Wensleydale and lower Swaledale. The Anglo-Saxons ploughed with ox teams using as many as eight animals, but even then they could not plough uphill. So they ploughed parallel to the contours in one direction only, with the result that, after many, many, years of ploughing, terraces were formed. These terraces are known as lynchets or ranes, are usually at least 200 yards long and may be much more, and from 12 to 20 or more feet wide. They are not enclosed by walls of any kind except to cut them off from the forest and rough grazing. The walls that are such a characteristic feature of the Dales today were built very much later, but were a direct consequence of the farming practices used by the Anglo-Saxons. Their

in large half-open sheds on the farmstead in winter. Most of the dales barns have fallen into disuse and are becoming ruinous. The recent change from mixed arable with animal husbandry to a monocultural one has brought about marked changes to the landscape in many areas, but not in the Dales: here it took place many years ago.

Neverthless new economic pressures operate and the demand for increased production is always present. Hay meadows in June are one of the glories of the upper dales, they seem to grow flowers, not grass, and although this hay is nutritionally very good the yield from a field is not high. If fertilisers are used they favour the growth of the vigorous grasses such as rye grass and meadow foxtail at the expense of the flowers which cannot compete in the changed environment. So those glorious hay fields which may contain up to a hundred different species - the buttercup, globe flower, water avens, meadow cranesbill, pignut, eyebright, to name but a few, are lost, perhaps for ever, for it is not known whether the process brought about by the application of fertiliser is reversible. The Dales hay meadow is sacrificed so that more cows or sheep can be kept per acre on the grass, an economic evil these days unless conservation policies intervene. These hayfields are part of our national heritage of beauty, an inherent part of the Dales scene and a fast disappearing ecological resource.

The villages of the Dales reflect the early agricultural patterns just discussed. In Wharfedale there are compact villages often built around a village green. They were founded by the Anglo-Saxons whose common field system made it essential for people to live in a close community. Many of these villages still have a green - Arncliffe, Litton, Burnsall - relics of the days when man herded his animals into it for safety at night. In Wensleydale some of the villages - Bainbridge, West Burton, West Scrafton are of this type, but others, Carperby, Aysgarth, Castle Bolton are all linear villages, a line of houses up to half a mile long strung along the road. These villages are of Danish origin, and the Danes did not develop the communal field system in the way the Anglo-Saxons did. All are sited on the 'middle ground' well above the valley floor, a clear indication that the lower ground was ill drained, possibly alder swamp. It seems remarkable that such an ancient layout should be retained to this day, except where it had been modified by later industrial development such as the lead mining industry. In Swaledale many villages are packed with houses as new ones were built to keep up with the influx of miners. Gunnerside and

Beamsley Hospital

Muker are fine examples of this, and in Wharfedale Grassington and Hebden show the same sort of change. Today planning control ensures that new buildings are sympathetically sited and in a style that blends with the old. This has been done particularly well at Starbotton, not quite as well in some other villages.

Rebuilding has necessarily taken place throughout the centuries from time to time. In medieval England most houses were built of wood on a stone plinth. They used split tree trunks raised in an inverted V, filled in the bottom part with stone and thatched with heather. None of these cruick built houses survive, but here and there a barn has, as at Drebley. Then came a time of great agricultural prosperity over the whole of England. It reached the Dales in the late years of the seventeenth century. Almost every yeoman farmer could afford to replace his primitive wooden house with a fine stone-built one: the ones that form the heart of the finest villages today. These are the houses with long low mullioned windows, often with mouldings over them and the doorways. Seventy or eighty years later styles changed and windows became more nearly square, and later still became a vertical rectangle. Window style is a good guide to the approximate age of a house.

The finest houses in the Dales belong to one or other of these periods of building activity. Here there are no stately homes, even few large houses, but a wealth of modest ones. Pride of place goes to Friar's

Head, Winterburn. Its fine Elizabethan frontage can be seen very well from the road. Very different in style and reflecting its much earlier ecclesiastical origin is the Gate House at Bolton Abbey, one of the Duke of Devonshire's homes. Close by is the Old Rectory whilst not far away is the Beamsley Hospital founded as early as 1593. At Linton, the Fontaine Alms Houses, built in 1721, are amongst the most remarkable buildings in the Dales.

The contribution of the villages and houses to the total landscape is small, but the aesthetic pleasure they give is very high indeed.

In a modest way the Industrial Revolution came to the Dales just as it did to the rest of north-west England. Amongst the first results was the building of water powered spinning mills in those Dales where hand knitting was an important auxiliary occupation. Considerably later the completion of the Leeds and Liverpool Canal in 1816 meant that cotton could easily be imported to places like Linton, Airton, Langcliffe and Settle, where cotton spinning mills were built on sites used by the traditional water powered corn mills. The population increased because of the fresh employment and rows of cottages were built to accommodate the new work force. Fortunately for the character of the Dales the lack of cheap coal prevented the industry from developing as it did in the nearby Rossendale valley.

In the early part of the nineteenth century there was a boom in the lead mining industry associated with the Industrial Revolution. It brought great changes to the landscape in some dales which can hardly be appreciated today, for time has weathered and healed the scars. It requires some little imagination to visualise the quiet moors and high valleys north of Swaledale as they were then, a hive of industry. There are stony expanses of worked-out veins stretching for miles over the heather moors, punctuated by spoil heaps now grassed over; deeply gouged hushes, so large it is difficult to believe that they are man-made and scattered over the moors are the crumbling relics of the smelt mills. On Grassington Moor the operations were no less intensive, but here the devastation was less widespread. Wensleydale had a rich mining area around East Bolton Moor. Much of it was well scattered and has less impact on the landscape today than either Grassington Moor or Swaledale. In the wake of the Industrial Revolution there came here and there the Victorian industrialists seeking 'estates', such as Walter Morrison who rebuilt Malham Tarn House, now the Field Study Centre, and whose ideas of 'estate' architecture dominated the upper part of the dale for many years.

Inevitably the railways followed and a modest network developed, all derelict today except the Settle-Carlisle line. The direct impact these lines had on the landscape was small, judged by that of the remaining section today, but their secondary effects and their social consequences were much more important. It was no longer necessary to transport beef on the hoof from Scotland via the Dales to the English markets. The drove roads fell into disuse together with the services they required like pubs - Tan Hill was one, Gearstones another and men to handle the gathering groups for fattening the beasts for market. The railways caused an increase in limestone quarrying but the death of many of the small remote collieries as better coal was available cheaply elsewhere. They brought commuting and tourism to the Dales, and this is today's growth industry. The changes to the landscape we are likely to see in the future will be influenced by the current policy of conservation. People realise that our heritage will not stay intact by itself, that positive yet economic measures have to be taken, but this is not the place to discuss these issues.

THE SETTLE - CARLISLE RAILWAY

With the reprieve of the line in April 1989 and the restoration of a regular service, the Settle-Carlisle railway once again serves walkers well, making possible routes that otherwise need two cars or a transport manager. Because of the struggles to keep the line open it has gained an aura of romance, but in reality it is a *tour de force* of Victorian engineering. Its story is told in detail in a number of books, but here a brief account will suffice.

The line was built between 1869 and 1876, considerably later than the building of the main rail network of the country (1830-1850), and was a result of the inter-company hostility and rivalry which was rife at the time. The Derby-based Midland Railway was hell-bent on expansion, and partly by takeovers and partly by building had extended one of its lines as far as Leeds, Skipton, Settle and Ingleton, a coal mining village in those days. Ingleton's Midland station was where the present-day car park is situated, and passengers continuing their journey north had to get a connection at the London and North Western Railway's station on the other side of the River Greta. Many were the connections missed on purpose, it is said. The east and west coast routes from London to Scotland had already been built by the LNW and LNE railways, so there was only one possible way for the Midland to continue independently to the Scottish border - to go right through the heart of the Pennines.

Work was started in November 1869 a couple of miles south of Settle and the line was opened for passenger traffic in May 1876, a tremendous engineering feat with half a dozen major viaducts and tunnels, and many more minor ones. At peak times more than 7,000 navvies were employed, for this was the last major line to be built by traditional pick and shovel methods, though steam locos were used for hauling materials, and steam cranes for hoisting stone to build the viaducts. Local accommodation could not be found for such armies of men and there were a number of construction camps between Settle and Appleby, the largest being at Batty Green, Ribblehead, where some 2,000 men, women, and children were housed in wooden huts in squalid conditions, though all manner of facilities, including a hospital were provided. Drunkenness and brawling were commonplace, outbreaks of smallpox were not unknown, the accident rate was high and the graveyards at Cowgill and Chapel-le-Dale had to be extended to accommodate those who had lost their lives. There is a memorial plaque in St Leonard's, Chapel-le-Dale, to these men. Progress was slow: the ground was a difficult mixture of clay and boulders, the weather, especially the wind, was often appalling, and it was not until May 1876 that the entire line was open for passenger traffic.

From Settle the line climbs up Ribblesdale at a steady gradient of 1 in 100 all the way to Blea Moor, 15 miles away. This stretch was nicknamed the 'Long Drag' by enginemen who struggled not only with the gradient but with fierce winds. During the whole of the next 15 miles the line never drops below the 1,100-foot contour, maintaining a level course by means of viaducts and tunnels. Dent station, at 1,145 feet the highest on any English main line, is 450 feet above the valley floor and almost 5 miles from the village. From Garsdale, the next station along the line, a branch line was built to Hawes which was already on a branch line of the LNER's east coast route. It remained open until 1959. The summit of the line is at Aisgill (1,165 feet), from where it descends the Eden valley to Kirkby Stephen, less steeply than it climbs up Ribblesdale. Having reached the Eden valley the line continues to follow this valley to Carlisle.

The line thrived in its early years, reaching its peak in Edwardian times, when it was incredibly busy, for there were neither buses nor motorcars in significant number in the Dales in those days. After World War II, in common with other railways, a decline set in. A few stations in the Eden valley were closed in 1952 but there was a wholesale closure in 1970, only Settle and Appleby stations remaining open. The line itself remained open because of its usefulness as an alternative route whenever the west coast route had to be closed for maintenance work. This meant that a certain amount of maintenance work had to be done on what was now a mere branch line. In the summer of 1975 the Yorkshire Dales National Park Authority collaborated with British Rail to run a series of specials called Dales Rail trains. Several stations were reopened, connecting bus services to Sedbergh and Hawes were provided, and guided walks laid on. This monthly service was a huge success. Diesel trains had taken over from steam in 1962/3, but British Rail revived steam travel in 1978, providing a limited number of specials which had an enormous following of enthusiastic photographers, 1,000 or even more of them gathering to record a train's sometimes spectacular progress.

However, in 1981 British Rail announced plans to re-route the Nottingham-Glasgow service via the west coast route. A number of local people began to suspect a stealthy closure of the Settle-Carlisle line, despite British Rail's denials of such plans. Two Dales Rail enthusiasts called a public meeting in Settle on June 27, 1981, the outcome of which was the formation of the Friends of the Settle-Carlisle Line. When British Rail announced that it proposed to withdraw all passenger services and close the line between Ribblehead and Appleby in August 1983, there was already the nucleus of a fighting force to keep the line open. Petitions to MPs were organised, some 22,000 written objections were lodged, and campaigns coordinated by the Settle-Carlisle Joint Action Committee. Public hearings were held in five towns in 1986 as a result of which the government was strongly recommended that it should refuse British Rail's application to close the line.

Meanwhile local passenger traffic boomed and railway buffs seized what looked like their last chance to travel on this scenic and historic line. Revenue increased enormously but still did not justify the cost of the major repairs needed in British Rail's eyes. They quoted £6.2M for the repair of the Ribblehead viaduct alone - and there are two other big viaducts, Artengill and Dent Head that required major repairs. The Joint Action Committee commissioned its own survey which produced a figure of £900,000 and English Heritage quoted a figure of £2.5M. In due course British Rail reduced theirs to £2.25M. Financial support was pledged by English Heritage to the tune of £1M, local councils offered £0.5M, leaving British Rail to find the rest. However, in late 1988 the government announced that unless private buyers could be found within six months, the Settle-Carlisle line would be closed. By April 1989 a buyer had not been found but the government backed down from its position and refused permission to close the line. This was indeed a triumph for the local objectors.

By the summer of 1990 British Rail had started repairs all along the line, the major task being the waterproofing of the Ribblehead viaduct. Modern lightweight rolling stock that causes less wear and tear was introduced, and a regular service between Leeds and Carlisle with six trains a day each way was started. Plans included a link from East Lancashire to Hellifield to pick up the trains there, and one to reinstate the northbound platform at Ribblehead. However, the reprieve granted in 1989 did not specify what should happen to the line's stations, most of them in a sorry state. British Rail estimated that full renovation would cost £3.9M, but this would provide safe operational requirements, not a sympathetic restoration. In the spring of 1991 the Yorkshire Dales National Park Authority produced a plan to make the whole line a conservation area in order to preserve a piece of our railway heritage. It was supported by three local authorities and by English Heritage whilst British Rail gave it its blessing. Conservation status will help to raise funds to preserve features such as signal boxes and Victorian semaphore signals that are not needed for railway operations but are an essential feature of this Victorian line. Operation Restoration was inaugurated in May 1991 to help raise funds, aiming at £4M.

Walks utilising the Settle-Carlisle line

There are three outstandingly good walks that can best be done using the rail services and a connecting bus:

1. Walk 7.10. Garsdale to Kirkby Stephen via Swarth Fell, Wild Boar Fell and Little Fell.
2. Walk 5.12. Horton to Settle via Pen-y-ghent.
3. Walk 10.7. Hawes to Horton via Dodd Fell and the Dales Way.

Obviously there are others, not forgetting the medium distance newly devised Settle-Carlisle Way. Walkers from the Leeds area and holidaymakers have a good choice of trains: those from the Manchester/Stockport area are not so lucky and depend on a Sunday special, which gives them a very long day. All the walks from Settle and Horton-in-Ribblesdale can be done using the train. These two places are admirably suited to train users as they both have a cafe and pubs not far from the station: obviously a safe time margin must be allowed. Ingleborough can be done from Horton by the well-marked Three Peaks track direct from the station itself and a descent made to Ribblehead Station by reversing Walk 6.4 over Simon Fell, if a bit of variety is wanted. However, until the north-bound platform at Ribblehead is restored, Whernside (Walk 6.3c), Blea Moor and the walks round upper Ribblesdale (Nos. 5.13, 5.14 and 5.15) are not possible.

mills which were not necessarily at the site of the mine shaft.

The earliest mining was done by working a vein where it could be seen on the surface with heavy hammer and chisels - open cast mining in modern terms. The vein that runs the length of Lea Green (Walk No. 2.5) was worked in that way and the remaining shallow depression makes a long line across the field, grass-grown, but easily seen. Simple picking at the surface followed the vein down and along wherever it seemed richest. By degrees the working became a shallow shaft ringed by the debris thrown out. The vein was worked as far from the shaft as an unsupported roof and the air would allow. This shaft was then abandoned and another started further along the vein. Today these annular spoil heaps are grassed over and can be seen as green rings with a depression in the middle. There's a row of them in the heather on the moor above Slei Gill (Walk No. 11.9) parallel with the big hush there, and there are many around Yarnbury (Walk No. 2.7).

A 'hush' is an artificial ravine made by another mining method used from the early days until the end of the eighteenth century, particularly in Swaledale. Where a vein could be seen on the hillside, or even suspected, a turf dam was made on a stream on the moor above and water allowed to collect there. Then the dam was breeched and the rush of water down the hillside tore away soil and loose rock. The vein was revealed more clearly and its surface was broken up by pick and hammer and the process repeated. The ore in the mixture of rock and soil was washed to the bottom and tended to be separated. This process was known as 'hushing'. It was repeated many, many, times producing huge ravines in the hillsides. They are particularly well seen at the head of Gunnerside Gill, Swaledale, (Walk No. 11.4) and at Slei Gill (Walk No. 11.9), though today they are masked with vegetation. Some of them are so vast they can easily be mistaken for a natural feature.

Up to the start of the eighteenth century most mining was done by groups of men working together and leasing a length of vein from a landowner. Lengths were measured by the 'meer' and marked by stones known as meer stones, crudely carved with the owners' names or initials some of which can still be found today. Even when gunpowder came into use at the end of the seventeenth century, holes for the powder were still made by hand tools. It was not until almost the end of the mining era that rock drills were used. They were driven by compressed air and the compressor was powered by a water-wheel.

The remains of one of these compressor tanks is still visible in

Yarnbury from Beaver Dam

Gunnerside Gill (Walk No. 11.4). As operations became more complex companies such as the London Lead Co. were formed and shaft mining developed. It became common practice to sink a shaft close to the vein and to cut levels to it at sixty-foot intervals so as to work it in several places simultaneously. Ore was removed from the roof not the floor so as to leave a roadway intact. This entailed the building of wooden platforms to reach the ore body as more and more of it was extracted. These wooden platforms constitute one of the major hazards of exploring a disused mine because they are rotten. A party may unwittingly walk upon one, thinking it is a solid floor, with dire consequences. Other hazards are rock falls, deep pools filled with water, partially filled and collapsed shafts. Mine exploration is only for the expert who knows what he is about, not for the walker.

Water has always been a problem in mining. Seepage through the rocks, and active drainage can be considerable. It collects at the lowest point of the mine, a pit at the bottom of the shaft known as a sump. In the early days of mining it was wound up in buckets, either by man or horsepower, slow and ineffective. Later pumps worked by water-wheels were used, but the most effective method of all was to drive a level or adit from the flank of some nearby valley to allow the water to drain away by itself. Even if the adit could not be made to connect with the lowest point of the mine it was still very advantageous as water need only to be pumped up to it instead of all the way to the surface. Underground pumps and water-wheels were installed to do this, the tail race of the wheel discharging into to adit. The best known example of this is the Duke's Level in Hebden Gill (Walk No. 2.7), but there are many other examples.

The water-wheel was the source of power on all the mining fields as mining developed in complexity. The early miners raised their ore body and the water by a jack roller, powered by two men. This was replaced by a horse whim, a winding drum operated by two horses walking round a circular track. As mines became deeper towards the end of the eighteenth century the weight of the rope became disproportionately high and too much for horses, so the water-wheel, by then quite highly developed in Lancashire, came into general use. Wheels were made in sizes to match the water available and the work to be done. They ranged from 10 feet to 50 feet in diameter and up to 6 feet wide. They were overshot to develop maximum power and the giant ones could yield up to 50H.P. Until about 1850 water-wheels were more efficient than steam engines and were used not only to wind the ore body but to pump water, work the crushing and washing plant and to work the bellows at the smelt mills. Where machinery was close to hand the wheel was connected to it by a crank, but power for the winding gear could be transmitted long distances by wire rope. The rope ran over pulleys supported on the top of substantial stone pillars. Today there are no wheels left in our area and only a few of the larger wheel pits remain.

An industry so dependent on water power had to conserve and manage this resource with care. Dams were built in stream beds high on the moors; for example, three were built in Blea Beck above Hebden; and the Moss Dams on Ivelet Moor, Swaledale, were built to conserve and supplement the supply from the streams. Water was brought from them to the wheels by a system of very carefully constructed leats contouring the hillsides, and on Grassington Moor water was re-used many times before going to waste. Most of the system of leats on Grassington Moor can be traced today, even though these are much overgrown by rushes.

The galena content of the mixed material had to be greatly increased before it could be smelted. It also had to be broken down to a small uniform size, about that of a split pea. These two processes are known as dressing the ore. The separation of the galena from the mixture of rock and other minerals of the vein is a complex process depending on the fact that galena is very much heavier than the other minerals and the rock cut from the shafts or levels to reach the vein, but to do it efficiently means the control of a number of other factors, principally the size of the particles. Naturally methods improved over the years. In the early days of mining the bouse, as the material produced at the mine was called, was first washed in a stream flowing just fast enough to carry away the lighter stone and earth leaving the galena-rich material behind, then this was hand sorted to pick out the obviously good stuff from the obviously poor. Large lumps were broken up by hand using heavy hammers on a solid flag floor. Where a piece of galena adhered to a lump of otherwise barren rock a 'cobbing hammer' was used to separate them. The lumps of galena were then crushed using a 'bucker', a heavy iron plate on a short handle. All this very heavy work was done by women and boys. Then the material was stirred with water and allowed to settle, when the galena sank to the bottom first. This could then be scraped together for smelting and the rest of the material re-treated. Various developments of this basic method of separation were made as early as the end of the sixteenth century. They included wet-sieving, a hotching tub and buddles, the latter two being merely sophisticated versions of the wet sieve and the primitive slow flowing stream respectively.

By the eighteenth and early nineteenth century the power of the water-wheel was being applied to the ore dressing processes. Power driven stamps and crushers using heavy cast iron rollers were used for the crushing process, rotating inclined cylindrical sieves were used to separate the fragments into a series of different sizes which could then be separated more efficiently. A whole range of quite elaborate processes was used to separate the galena from the gangue in the wide range of different sized particles that were inevitably produced by the crushing process. That they were surprisingly efficient was shown by a war time assay of a number of old spoil heaps on Grassington Moor which gave only about 2 per cent lead!

Little or nothing is left of the various dressing floors on the moors today, only flagged floors and spoil heaps. Probably the best indication of the location of a dressing floor is a spoil heap of fine even-sized material, some like coarse sand, some bigger. The remains of storage bunkers for the floors can be seen low down in Gunnerside Gill and higher up at the Bunton Mine, where the wheel pit and leat bringing its water supply are also clearly visible. (Walk No. 11.4). The flag floor and wheel pit at Providence Mine above Kettlewell (Walk No. 3.3) are easily found, and its Cornish Rollers, used to crush the ore, are in the Earby Mining Museum. On Grassington Moor the main dressing plant stood on the site of the Dales Chemical Plant (Walk No. 2.6) now derelict. There are remains in Hebden and Bolton Gill. (Walk No. 2.7).

A good deal more seems to be known about the smelt mills of the Dales than about the dressing floors, thanks largely to the work of R.T.Clough, an architect who drew plans of many of them during and immediately after World War II, before so many had been wholly demolished. Lead smelting is not a simple reaction like iron smelting. Iron is mined as the oxide or carbonate and when heated with coke to a sufficiently high temperature is reduced to the metal. Galena behaves differently. When it is heated to just above red heat with free access of air it is converted mainly to oxide. This oxide is then reduced to the metal by heating at a much higher temperature with more galena. This two-stage process was mainly carried out in ore hearths. These were usually about 2 feet square, built of well-cut stone, lined with massive iron blocks and stood behind a wide arch, remains of which can be seen at a number of smelt mill ruins. They were fired by peat and the air blast needed to reach working temperature was produced by bellows worked by the water-wheel. Smelt mills usually had banks of four or more hearths worked by one wheel.

In the hearth the galena was roasted at just above red heat until it was converted to the whitish oxide. Then more galena was added and mixed in and the temperature raised with more peat and increased air blast. The metal oozed out of the mass of peat and dross and sank to the bottom of the furnace, eventually running out of a groove into an iron pot called a sumpter pot. From this it was ladled into moulds to make pig lead. The dross floated on top of the molten lead and was raked off from time to time and tipped on the banks of the nearest stream. Most smelt mills still have their tips, now well weathered and no longer obnoxious.

The ore hearth was suited to the production of a small mine and was often run intermittently. As production increased towards the end of the eighteenth century reverberatory furnaces came into common use. They were very much bigger and were heated indirectly by flames and hot gases from a coal or coke fire at one end of the rectangular furnace. The heat was reflected from the arched roof and they were designed for continuous running, needing large supplies of well-dressed ore. Essentially they were furnaces for big companies working rich veins and in the boom years they replaced ore hearths at Langthwaite Mill, Arkengarthdale, and the Cupola Mill, Grassington Moor. It is not possible for the untrained person to distinguish between the two types from the scant remains on the moors today.

Smelt mills are always provided with a characteristically long flue leading to a short chimney. The flue performed a number of functions: it dispersed the highly poisonous lead fumes which were liable to poison the vegetation and hence the livestock in a wide area. It increased the draught on the fires needing less use of the bellows, and hence ventilation and working conditions at the mill were improved. An economic benefit was the recovery of some of the lead fume that condensed in the cooler parts of the flue. It was scraped out and reworked to give a very pure lead in demand for chemical plants. Traces can be seen in many of the flues, where stonework is impregnated with a greyish white material which is lead sulphate. In other places the stonework is burnt red-brown: a sure indication of high temperatures. Smelting was recognised as a hazardous occupation, many men dying young from lead poisoning.

Recovery of lead from the flues increased in economic importance. Square stone towers filled with brushwood were built into the cooler parts of the flues and the fumes passed through them. Sometimes water was sprayed into the top of them to increase their efficiency. These towers were known as Stokoe Condensers and the remains of a few can be seen today, notably across the road from the Surrender Mill, Swaledale, and on the moor above the Cupola Mill, Grassington. Most Yorkshire galena contains 4-6 oz of silver per ton and in the last years of the Dales mining fields this was recovered. More important economically was the use of pre-roasted ore. It could then be fed in the correct proportions leaving less to the smelter's judgement. The remains of a roasting hearth with its own short chimney not connected to the main flue can be seen at the Old Gang Smelt Mill, Swaledale (Walk No. 11.6) and they can be identified in other mills. As the dross from the ore hearths usually contained around 20 per cent lead it was reworked as a low grade ore in a slag hearth which worked at higher temperatures and produced a molten glassy black slag instead of the sintered residue that can be found at every smelt mill ruin.

In these production-minded times the question of how much the old miners produced must inevitably be asked. Naturally, output was subject to big variations but in the peak years around 1850 Grassington Moor produced 1,000-1,500 tons of ore per annum. In Swaledale the Old Gang Mine alone produced over 2,000 tons each year between 1800 and 1810. After 1865 production diminished and was virtually finished by 1880. Imported Spanish lead was much cheaper than home produced where, because the best veins were worked out, production costs were high. In its heyday the industry employed more people than farming, influenced the growth of villages and played quite a part in determining the landscape of the Dales today.

Considering how much mining there was, there are deplorably few remains left today. Grassington Moor was an army shooting range during the war and much was demolished by the military. Some restoration and conservation was carried out by the Earby Mines Research Group and the Crosshills Natural History Society a number of years ago and more recently the Y.D.N.P.A.'s archaeologist started a programme of conservation work starting on Grinton, Surrender, and Old Gang smelt mills. Grinton has been reroofed and the adjacent peat store is due for attention, but although Grinton is the best preserved smelt mill in the Dales, it is not practicable to restore it fully, partly on grounds of cost but mainly because it is not clear what it was like in its last years of working. Owing to limited financial resources the rate of progress is slow, but Grassington High Moor mill and Blakethwaite mill will be conserved within the next couple of years or so. Ultimately information boards of a fairly general nature will be erected on the sites. Next in the queue for resources are some of the many dressing floors and mine buildings, particularly those in Gunnerside Gill, but they may have to wait five years for attention.

In the absence of restored remains it is necessary to turn to museums to try to get a more complete picture of the industry. There are a number of folk museums in the Dales. Reeth's has a particularly good display of hand tools and an exhibition showing the basics of the industry. It is open 10 am to 6 pm in summer. The Craven Museum, Skipton, is housed in the town hall and is open Monday, Wednesday & Friday, 2-5 pm, all the year round, all day Saturday, but never on Sunday. It has some large and impressive specimens of minerals and a good selection of hand tools, miners' caps and lamps. More importantly there is a pair of jack rollers and a number of diagrams and sketches reconstructing the mining scene. The Earby Mines Research Group's museum is housed in the Old Grammar School, School Lane (turn opposite the level crossing). Necessarily its opening hours are quite limited: at present Thursdays 6-9 pm Sundays 2-6pm. Most of its exhibits are from the Dales, a few from Cornwall. There is a wide selection of mineral specimens, hand tools, tubs and rails, a collection of photographs above and below ground, and most informative of all, a number of working models, notably a smelt mill with four ore hearths, each with its bellows operated by a water-wheel which perhaps understandably is electrically operated. All exhibits are fully labelled though there is no attempt to show any sequence of operations either in the mine or mill.

Footnote

It is easy to become fascinated by lead mining and you may wish to know of other areas where artifacts are common. The northern Pennines (Nenthead, Weardale etc.) and the Kings Field in Derbyshire are worth exploring. Three completely developed sites for tourists, however, are at Llynernog in Wales, Killhope in upper Weardale and Wanlockhead in Scotland.

At the Llynernog Historical Site, situated on the A44 some 15 miles from Aberystwyth, there is a miners' trail round the buildings, shaft and adit of this former silver-lead mine. It shows restored and working water-wheels, crushing and washing machinery and has a museum of reconstructed scenes from a mine that gives a véry good ideal of what it was like to work there. It is a most informative site, completely relevant to Dales lead mining practices. Open daily in summer, 10 am to 6 pm.

At the Killhope site, situated at a height of 1,500 feet by the side of the Stanhope-Alston road, A689, the principal attraction is the 34-foot diameter iron water-wheel, now fully restored. When the mine was working it powered the crushing rollers and hauled tubs or trams of bouse to the various stages of the dressing process. There was something of a boom in lead mining in the early 1860s and the Park Level mine was developed at that time using the latest techniques for ore dressing. Open 10-5 pm, Easter to the end of September.

In Scotland the Wanlockhead Mining Museum and Site give a more complete picture of lead mining and smelting than any other site. It is situated in the Leadhills area of the Southern Uplands on the B7040 which leaves the A74 south of Abington. Besides the usual hand tools and photographs the museum contains a reconstructed ore hearth and mine office. As an extension it offers a guided trip into one of the former workings. Its Miners' Trail is fairly extensive, but not as long as that at Grassington. Its most important feature is the beam engine that pumped water in early years of the nineteenth century, a unique example in the UK. The smelt mill has been excavated from a heap of rubble and shows the lay-out of the mill with reconstructed furnaces. This site is run by the Wanlockhead Museum Trust and is open Easter to the end of September. 11-4 pm the mine 1 3.30 pm daily.

CAVING AND POTHOLING IN THE YORKSHIRE DALES

There are many areas of limestone in the British Isles but none have the variety and complexity of caves found in the Yorkshire Dales. Four other interacting factors are needed to produce this and they only occur in the Dales. Faulting on a large scale must have shattered the limestone so that streams can penetrate and open it up. The bigger the stream the better for this purpose and big streams are only generated when the limestone is covered by an impervious layer such as glacial drift or gritstone on the fells above it and where there is a high rainfall. Glaciation plays a further part. The powerful melt water streams that developed as the ice retreated carved out large passages, now left as 'fossil' cave passages, lined or even blocked with boulder clay. Finally there must be a layer of impervious rock beneath the limestone but above the valley floor. The cave streams are then forced to the surface, sometimes as large springs, sometimes as streams issuing from cave mouths.

The exploration of the more obvious caves and potholes started between 1840 and 1850. John Birkbeck of Settle and William Metcalfe of Chapel-le-Dale were two of the leading pioneers. Amongst other explorations they descended Alum Pot by Lower Long Churn as far as the Bridge in 1848, and John Birkbeck was in Prof. Boyd Dawkins' party when they made the first direct descent of the shaft in 1870. Two years later Birkbeck made an attempt on Gaping Gill, known to be the deepest shaft in England, having first diverted the water of Fell Beck by digging a trench over 1,000 yards long. He reached the big ledge 190 feet (58m) down, now known as Birkbeck's Ledge. He still had a very long way to go as the shaft is 340 feet (103m) deep. No doubt it was this knowledge that, amongst other factors, decided him to turn back, for it was he who had determined its depth some time previously. Gaping Gill had to wait more than twenty years for its first descent.

The Yorkshire Ramblers' Club, which was founded in 1892, took a considerable interest in cave exploration and one of its members, Edward Calvert, had plans to make a descent of G.G. as it is often called, but was pipped to the post by the famous French caver, E.A.Martel. It is only fair to add that Martel was not aware of Calvert's

cave passage may simply continue as it has been doing or there may be sights undreamed of, for many caves and passages are decorated with stalactites and stalagmites. Decorated is far too simple a word to describe some of the formations, as the accretions of calcite are called. There may be icicle-like stalactites, sometimes so fine and long they are like straws, and like straws, hollow. Sometimes stalactites coalesce and form fringed curtains, sometimes they cling to the wall, sometimes they hang from the roof. They may be a translucent, pearly white, yellowish, even reddish in colour: they may occur in ones or twos or so profusely they draw a gasp of wonder and admiration from the caver. Stalagmites, the formations that grow up from the ground - a useful mnemonic that (stalactites grow down from the ceiling) - are not nearly so common or so variable as stalactites. They may be mere knobs or they may be quite impressive pillars, on rare occasions reaching the roof.

All these formations catch the light of the caver's lamp, sparkle and glint like jewels. There's nothing like a swift glimpse of them in the distance for urging a caver on, and a well decorated cavern is a sight to marvel at. Their sheer beauty makes one ponder, how are they formed, and how fast do they grow? In broad terms, water that passes through limestone rocks dissolves appreciable amounts and if that water, slowly oozing through a crack is evaporated by an air current, then the lime will crystallize out as calcite, taking a shape influenced by the rates of flow and evaporation, by the amounts of dissolved lime and the nature of the surface the water oozes from. It used to be said that they grow at the rate of an inch in a thousand years, but clusters of small stalactites hanging beneath the railway bridge at Horton-in-Ribblesdale and elsewhere give the lie to that. The factors mentioned above clearly influence rates of growth and they are not invariable. The scientific aspect of caving has a strong appeal to a limited number of cavers and there is a body known as the British Cave Research Association that collects and publishes the results of their work.

Plenty of walkers might want to see what it is like underground. It is tempting to have a go with a torch, but the number of caves that are safe, easy and worthwhile is very limited. Yordas Cave, Kingsdale is one of them and is marked on the 1:25,000 Outdoor Leisure 2 Yorkshire Dales Western Area Map. (See Walk No. 6.5.)

On a more sedate level are the show caves, offering guided tours. There are three, quite different, and all very well worth a visit. They are:

1. Ingleborough Cave, also known as Clapham Cave, reached from Clapham by a short walk. Park on the Y.D.N.P. car park and follow Walk No. 6.7 to find it. Allow about 30 minutes to get there. Tel: Clapham 242 for information.
2. White Scar Caves lies on the Ingleton to Hawes road a good mile beyond Ingleton. Car park and cafe on the site. Tel: Ingleton 41244 for information.
3. Stump Cross Cavern. Lies on the Grassington to Pately Bridge road about 4 miles above Grassington. Car park on site. Tel: Harrogate 711042 for information.

And of course, it may be possible to make a descent of Gaping Gill itself by the winch most summer bank holidays when one or other of the major potholing clubs are there.

1: LOWER WHARFEDALE
Bolton Bridge to Burnsall

Walks around Bolton Abbey

1.1	The Strid and other riverside walks. Category C	63
1.2	Sand Holme car park to Barden Bridge and back. Category C	64
1.3	An ascent of Simon's Seat. Category B	65
1.4	Beamsley Beacon via Kex Beck. Category B	68
1.5	Beamsley Beacon, Round Hill and Kex Gill Moor. Category B+	71

Walks on Barden Fell Barden Moor Access Areas

1.6	Halton Height and Barden Moor from Bolton Abbey Category B	74
1.7	Netherstone End and Lower Barden Reservoir from Burnsall. Category B	76
1.8	Rylstone Cross, Cracoe War Memorial and Upper Barden Reservoir. Category B	78
1.9	Embsay and Embsay Moor. Category B	81

ABOUT BOLTON ABBEY

Bolton Abbey is the name of the village that is often used when referring to this part of Wharfedale. 'We're going to Bolton Abbey today' is a common statement when the speaker really means that he/she is going to have a day by that part of the River Wharfe owned and managed by the Trustees of the Chatsworth Settlement, a trust set up by the Duke of Devonshire.

Management is necessarily along commercial lines. Three large car parks have been made, one at Bolton Abbey village close to the priory, one at Sand Holme close to the river, and another above the end of Strid Wood. All cost £2 for the day in 1990, and although the ticket for one car park is valid for the others for the rest of the day, it is cold consolation for the walker. It is worth knowing that there is limited free parking at Barden Bridge and close to the Strid Wood car park. All car parks have toilets and at the Sand Holme one refreshments are available in the Cavendish Pavilion. A great deal of footpath work has been done

LOWER WHARFEDALE

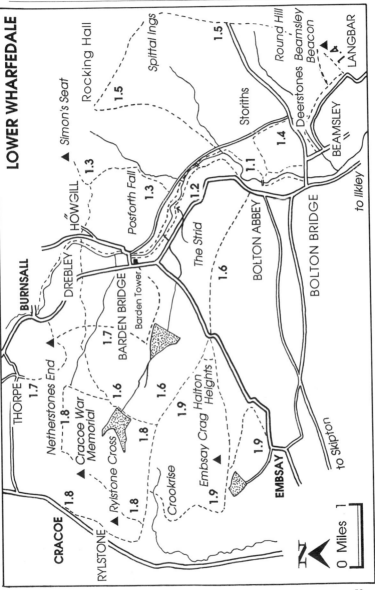

Rocking Hall

Spittal Ings

Round Hill

Beamsley Beacon

1.5

1.5

LANGBAR

Simon's Seat

Storiths

1.4

BEAMSLEY

Deerstones

▲ 1.3

Posforth Fall

1.3

1.1

HOWGILL

DREBLEY

1.2

The Strid

BOLTON ABBEY

BOLTON BRIDGE

to Ilkley

BURNSALL

BARDEN BRIDGE

Barden Tower

1.6

1.6

THORPE

Netherstones End

1.7

1.7

1.8

Cracoe War
Memorial

1.6

1.6

1.8

Halton
Heights

1.9

Embsay Crag

CRACOE

1.8

▲ Rylstone Cross

1.8

Crookrise

1.9

1.9

EMBSAY

RYLSTONE

to Skipton

N

0 Miles 1

and six nature trails have been laid out between the Sand Holme car park and the end of Strid Wood which is a Site of Special Scientific Interest. As its name suggests, the Strid car park gives the shortest route to the Strid but not the best walk, which is from the Sand Holme car park, indeed this is probably the most useful car park for the walker. The riverside walks are short, mere strolls, on good paths, and the routes are simple to follow. There are well maintained concessionary paths along both banks of the Wharfe from the footbridge at the priory to Barden Bridge and right of way paths from the priory to Bolton Bridge. From the very size and number of all these facilities it is clear that on a fine summer Sunday the River Wharfe must be a bit like Blackpool... The lover of the countryside should try to visit on a fine day late in October. Then the autumn colours are superb and the views undisturbed by crowds.

There are a number of interesting features between Bolton Abbey (the village) and Barden Bridge: the priory itself, the Friar's Stepping Stones, the Strid and the nature trails and Barden Tower.

The Priory

Bolton Abbey or Bolton Priory, to give it its correct name, was founded in 1154. This community of Augustinian canons had been established thirty years earlier at Embsay on land given to them by Cecil de Rumilly of Skipton, but they had found it rather bleak and inhospitable there. They were able to exchange these lands for this site by the Wharfe, a sheltered and beautiful spot today, but then it would have been very much wilder, a clearing in the primeval forest that still covered much of England. By about 1220 their first church and chapter house as well as some domestic buildings were reasonably complete. Today little is left of this early work except the part immediately east of the round-headed arches at the end of the nave, in particular the semicircular intersecting arches that formed the heads of the stalls used by the canons in their services. There's nothing left of the cloisters, chapter house or domestic buildings. Only the nave remains in good condition simply because it had always been used as the parish church and continued to be so used after the Dissolution of the Monasteries. It has a very fine though unfinished tower at its western end, unfinished because it was still being built when the priory was dismantled at the Dissolution. Because it is only a nave the parish church has no east window, the chancel arch being blocked up after Dissolution. This wall was decorated most beautifully in 1880, replacing in some measure the glory of an east window. The whole church, as one would expect, is rather grander than that found in most villages.

Augustinian canons, or Black Friars, so called because they wore a black habit, were fully ordained priests, qualified to take church services. They were ruled by a prior, hence the term priory for their establishment. Other orders such as the Benedictines were monks, were ruled by an abbot, and their buildings known as abbeys. Because the sole purpose in life of the canons was the worship of God with prayer and praises they employed all manner of craftsman on their building programmes and depended on a staff to run their establishment. During the heyday of the priory from 1286 to 1325 it had become big business. Accounts were kept in Latin and most fortunately have survived in the Duke of Devonshire's library. They tell us a great deal about the property the priory owned, how much was spent in its repair, the income from rents and tithes and trading. The priory owned land and property in Whafedale from Arncliffe to Harewood and in Airedale from Malham to Keighley. Some of these just paid rent to the priory, others were home farms and their produce went direct to the priory. Some grew corn, a group of farms round Appletreewick were stock farms, raising the oxen used for ploughing and sheep. Oats, not wheat, were grown and wheat for bread was either received as tithes or bought and stored in the Tithe Barn, still to be seen below the village. Oats were used for making porridge and for making beer because barley could not be grown well. The canons received a gallon a day, but don't forget, it was their only beverage. Wool was a very important cash crop from their farms, amounting to about half the total revenue. In addition they acted as middlemen for other wool producers. The staple diet was bread and vegetable soup with some cheese and a little meat, hunted in the forest. Fish from the river was insufficient, and salt herring was imported from the east coast. In all some 200 people were employed in the priory's activities, though it supported only some seventeen to twenty canons and a few lay brethren. It is only fair to add that they provided free shelter for travellers and alms for the needy on a large and generous scale.

In many ways the priory was isolated from the events of national life. It did, however, suffer such severe damage in raids by the Scots after Bannockburn (1314) that the canons were forced to take refuge in Lancashire and other places for a time and the priory did not function as such. Naturally it could not escape the Dissolution of the Monasteries brought about by Henry VIII in 1536, though its suppression was delayed until 1539. The Augustinian Order, in common with the other orders, had decayed. The canons were no longer serving their original purpose, they were out of date. The prior and the canons were pensioned off, some finding jobs as vicars of churches belonging to the priory. It has a very modern ring about it. The estates were broken up and sold off by the State. Lead was stripped from roofs and decay and ruin soon set in. It was the end of an era, far more traumatic in its effect on people and the countryside than some of the changes we are witnessing today.

Other noteworthy buildings around Bolton Abbey
It is hardly surprising that in an area so rich in historical associations there are a number of buildings of character and beauty. The priory and church, the gatehouse, and Beamsley Hospital are mentioned in the walks, but others do not lie so directly on the course of a walk. Some notes about these are now given.

Barden Tower, on the B6160 above Barden Bridge
Originally Barden Tower was a hunting lodge belonging to the Lords of Skipton, and was considerably enlarged in 1485 by the tenth Lord Clifford who made it his principal residence. After his death in 1523 the tower fell into disuse and decay, but Lady Anne Clifford, who finished Beamsley Hospital, restored it in 1659 and lived in it at times. There's a well-lettered inscription recording her work in the south wall. After her death the tower became ruinous again and remains so today. It isn't listed as an Ancient Monument nor given any special protection, but it is well worth a visit. As its name suggests it is close to Barden Bridge, a few minutes uphill walk from it. There's no car park but there is limited roadside parking.

The Old Rectory, Bolton Abbey
The picturesque Rectory House by the church, owes its origin very directly to a bequest of Robert Boyle , known to every schoolchild who studies chemistry as the man who expounded Boyle's Law. It was built on the site of some of the former monastic buildings, probably incorporating some of their stone and timber. There is a Latin inscription over the door that reads:

The Boyle School

'Robert Boyle bequeathed the cost of establishing and
a sum of money for founding and perpetuating it.
Charles, Earl of Burlington and Cork generously gave
the site, wood, stone and other things requisite for the
erection of the house....A.D. 1700.'

This new house incorporated the residence of the schoolmaster
who was also the curate, so it became school house and parsonage in
one. It's a fine building with clean lines, very different from the ornate
gatehouse. A new elementary school, the present Boyle and Petyt
School, was built in a more convenient place on the main road between
Beamsley and Bolton Bridge in 1874.

The Tithe Barn
This huge barn lies behind the row of cottages which contains the post
office. It is only single storey, quite different from the usual type of
Dales barn. Whilst not pretending that it is the original monastic tithe
barn, it is on the same site and its very size gives an indication of the
space needed to house the corn and other produce collected as tithes in
monastic days.

The Cavendish Memorial
This is the ornate fountain type of structure at the entrance to the drive
to the Sand Holme car park. It commemorates Lord Frederick Cavendish
who was assassinated in Ireland in 1882. Cavendish is the family name
of the Duke of Devonshire who owns most of the land around lower
Wharfedale.

WALKS AROUND BOLTON ABBEY
1.1 The Strid and other riverside walks
Every visitor to Bolton Abbey simply must visit the notorious Strid,
and it takes a little more than an hour from the Sand Holme car park,
less from the Strid Wood car park. The best approach is by following
the green nature trail from the Cavendish Pavilion. Much of it follows
a wide gravelled path through glorious woodland, at times close to the
river bank. First you come to High Strid and then to the Strid itself, an
awe-inspring sight when the river is high. Take heed of the warning
notices and keep well back. The rocks are extremely slippery when wet

with rain or spray. A little way beyond the Strid the green trail joins the blue and the yellow trails. The yellow trail goes up to the Strid Wood car park and the blue returns to the Cavendish Pavilion by a high level route through the woods giving fine bird's eye views of the river when there are few leaves on the trees and is highly recommended. Category C.

The Story

Legend has it that the Boy of Egremond, son of Alizia de Romilly, Lady of Skipton Castle, was drowned when he was held back by his dog when making the leap whilst out hunting. In her grief his mother gave the lands at Bolton to the Prior of Embsay so the priory could be moved there to better land. However, sceptics point out that the Boy of Egremond was a signatory to this charter...Well, it doesn't spoil the tale. Let it not be thought that these woods are the remains of the old deer forest. Though the ground has never been cultivated a good deal of planting has been done. The paths were made at the turn of the nineteenth century by the Rev Wm. Carr of the Priory Church. He appreciated natural beauty and began the tradition of public access to the woods. In those days people came by train to Bolton Abbey station and then by waggonette to the priory and the woods.

Today the woods are managed to maintain the delicate and complex ecological balance. A great many species may be seen in quiet times - dippers, flycatchers, tree creepers, woodpeckers, even the kingfisher beech, oak, ash and sycamore predominate, giving a field of gold in late autumn. In springtime there are carpets of wood anemones, celandine and bluebells, and because of the presence of a bank of limestone near the islands there is a wider range of species than is usual in this type of habitat.

A very popular stroll - it scarcely qualifies as a walk - is from the Sand Holme car park downstream to the abbey and return on the other bank. Another one is from the abbey itself down to Bolton Bridge.

1.2 Sand Holme car park to Barden Bridge and back

This must be the finest riverside walk in the Dales and can equally well be done from Barden Bridge, but be sure to do it this way round for the finest views. Most spectacular in winter when the river is high and there are no leaves on the trees to impede the very dramatic views. It will take about 2 hours. No map needed. Category C.

Geology: A sink-hole at Kirkby Gate, Whernside
Mining: The ruins of Surrender Smelt Mill, Swaledale

The stepping stones at Bolton Priory
Hebden Gill

From the car park cross the river and turn left along its bank. Follow the excellent path to a stout fence which you cross a little way up the hill and continue along the river bank to the road. Fifty yards beyond the bridge turn left onto the riverside path that goes through Strid Wood. In due course you will come to a fork: take the upper track, the lower one quickly becomes difficult and then disappears. The upper track climbs steadily to a fine ecologically constructed shelter with seats and stays roughly at this level with fine views of the river below, Strid and all. There are a number of other paths but always take the highest one. Eventually you emerge from the wood into pasture and the path continues to the road at Barden Bridge.

Cross the bridge and turn onto the path through the woods. It soon emerges into pasture and re-enters woodland at the Strid Wood where you have a choice: the Blue or the Yellow Nature Trail. The Yellow will give you a close up view of the Strid and the quickest return to the car park.

1.3 An ascent of Simon's Seat, 472metres (1,550 feet) on Barden Fell

This is a fine varied short day's walk taking 4½-5 hours and there is a choice of two quite different return routes, one by the banks of the River Wharfe, the other over Barden Fell direct to the car park. Category B. Simon's Seat is high enough for it to be cool up there in spring and autumn. There is very limited parking on the side of the road that runs on the east side of the Wharfe, close to the start of the walk near the Waterfall Cottage. Failing that, park at the Sand Holme car park, Bolton Abbey. Map: 1:25,000 Outdoor Leisure 10 Yorkshire Dales Southern Area.

Assuming you're out of luck and have to park at the Pavilion, cross the river by the wooden bridge and immediately turn left along the path on the river bank. Just before the first stile take the right-hand path up the road. Turn left and follow the road up the hill for about 200 yards to a house on the right. This is Waterfall Cottage. The footpath starts there and is signposted. It runs first through pastures and then goes towards the stream where it forks. The main path stays high on the right and crosses the beck above Posforth Fall by a narrow footbridge. If you want to see the fall, and it is well worth it in wet weather, take the left-hand branch down to it. You may boulder hop the beck below the fall and join the path at the bridge. Otherwise, retrace your steps to the path junction, go up to the steep slope on the right then almost at once drop down on the left to the footbridge. The path then traverses a lush vale known as the valley of desolation, ever since a storm 150 years ago which flattened the trees.

Some 400 yards above the waterfall the path forks. Take the left-hand branch that climbs up out of the stream to a gate.

At the gate you will join a broad cart track that runs through the wood to the open moor. At the next gate ignore the path to the left. You can see the one you want going straight ahead for a long way. It climbs steadily up the side of Great Agill onto the open moor. There are jumbles of great boulders in many places but Simon's Seat summit remains out of sight for a long time.

The track swings left at the top of the gill and continues to some shooting butts. After some time leave it for a well-defined path to the right. This will take you to the summit rocks and is cairned towards the top. The summit O.S. cairn is on the edge of the fell and has fine views both up Wharfedale and across to Barden Moor. On a poor day take care not to lose your sense of direction. The summit is a great heap of large boulders, full of tiny tracks and is quite a puzzling place. If you want to get off the high ground quickly because of the weather, go to the opposite end of the rocks from the trig point to find the track that leads steeply down to the end of Howgill Lane. There turn left and follow this pleasant unmetalled road to the notice board at the access point to the fell.

If the day is good you will want to keep your height to enjoy the views as long as possible. Locate the cairned path and keep to its right to find another rough track that runs along the edge of the moor and down to a wood. Follow the wall down to the gateway at the lowest point. Here a broad track leads down through the wood. At the bottom it opens into a triangular grassy space. Bear right and in a couple of hundred yards you will find yourself on Howgill Lane at the notice board mentioned above.

Go straight across this lane and down the lane opposite that leads to the river and the stepping stones to Drebley. Turn left at the river and follow the river bank path to the road just above Barden Bridge.

Now you have a choice of paths: which side of the Wharfe will you walk? If you are a bit short of time the path down the west side is better and quicker. This path starts on the other side of the bridge. The path on the near side stays high above the Wharfe almost the whole time but has good views of it especially when there are no leaves on the trees. Use this path if you are parked on the road and turn left when you have crossed the fence at the end of the woodland. Either route will take an hour, more or less, to get back to your car.

The return by Barden Fell

From the trig point take the boggy path to Lord's Seat, a chaos of rocks about ½ mile away, then turn right at the wall and follow the little track by the side of it for almost two miles straight across heather moor. Cross White Wham Beck where a shooting shelter may be useful, and having climbed up the other side of this shallow valley almost to the brow of the hill, take the second cart track to the right. It swings gently down the side of Hazlewood Moor and has wide and excellent views across Wharfedale. Shortly you join another track , keep right at the junction that follows and continue down until you reach Bolton Park Farm. Keep above the farm buildings until you come to a gate with a finger post where you turn left to enter the access road to the farm. Go straight across the road at the bottom of the hill, then cross the river and you are back in the car park. If you are parked on the road turn right to find your car.

Things of Interest

Barden Fell Access Area extends a considerable distance to the east beyond the boundary of the park and of the Yorkshire Dales Southern Area map.

If you are familiar with upper Wharfedale you will surely have noticed the big difference in scenery here and you may be wondering why the change from the flat-bottomed valley as at Kilnsey to a deep V cut as at the Strid, and why the heather moor instead of bog cotton and rushes? Towards the end of the last Ice Age some 8,000 years ago, upper Wharfedale was filled with a melting glacier that had scooped out the valley. As it retreated it dropped the load of rocks and gravel it was carrying just above Grassington and this caused a large lake to back up behind. Sediments deposited in the lake caused the flat valley floor.

The Craven Limestone that forms the base of upper Wharfedale ends just below Grassington. If you do Walk No. 2.7 you will see the change very clearly in the type of stone used to make the walls. Lower Wharfedale including Barden Moor and Fell are made of gritstone similar to that on the high tops of upper Wharfedale. Why then heather instead of bog cotton and rushes? The key is the lesser height of these moors. Great Whernside is over 2,300ft, Barden Fell is 1,550ft and Barden Moor is a shade more. This height difference means the climate is drier and a little less cold, and climate is the decisive factor where vegetation is concerned. Heather, and its associated plants - crowberry, heath rush and bracken will not grow in the extremely wet conditions of the highest ground even though they like the acid soils.

Barden Moor and Barden Fell are amongst the best grouse moors in Yorkshire. Grouse feed on young heather shoots and the moors are managed by selective burning in very early spring so as to produce a continuous supply of new heather shoots. Grouse make fine eating and command a high price in the market. The moor is managed so as to produce the maximum number of birds which are 'harvested' in the shooting season, starting August 12 and ending in December. A good grouse moor commands a high rent, an important factor in the economics of the countryside.

Just below Barden Bridge what looks like a bridge crosses the Wharfe. It is an aqueduct bringing water to Bradford from Nidderdale, and at present may not be crossed by the public.

1.4 Beamsley Beacon via Kex Beck from Bolton Bridge

Beamsley Beacon is the bold ridge that stands above the Wharfe when viewed from the river flats at Bolton Priory. Its ascent from Bolton Bridge by Kex Beck is much easier than it seems as well as being especially beautiful in late autumn. Beamsley Beacon is a fine viewpoint and the most southerly point over 1,000 feet (1,296 feet in fact,) in the Yorkshire Dales National Park. If you just want a quick dash up it there is room to park high on the Beamsley-Langbar road where the footpath leaves it at * in the text that follows.

If you can't find room to park in the layby at Bolton Bridge, use the village car park at Bolton Abbey, though that will cost you good money. The 1:25,000 Outdoor Leisure 10 Yorkshire Dales Southern Area map just - and only just - covers the walk. Time: about 4 hours, Category B.

From Bolton Bridge[1] walk up the A59 for a few minutes and turn off on the right to reach Beamsley village. Immediately past the first farmhouse on the left turn left into the lane there. About 50 yards up the lane on the right there is an unusual type of stile. Go over it and be prepared for a surprise. You'll find yourself on the edge of a disused water leat[2] which once supplied Beamsley Mill. Cross it by a little bridge and turn left, walking along its boundary wall to the next stile, and then cutting across the field to the point where the leat joins the stream. Turn left and follow the path up the stream. There are stiles all the way and it's well marked to Deerstones.[3] It's extremely beautiful in autumn. As soon as you are through the gate at Deerstones turn right, go down to the bridge across Kex Beck, and follow the path up to Ling Chapel Farm. (This path is not shown on the O.S. map but is sign posted by the Y.D.N.P.A.) Turn right on the access road and leave it after about 100 yards for a path on the left that cuts across the moor to the road. About 100 yards further up the road * a wide well-trodden path follows the wall at first then swings away to the left to reach the top of the Beacon.[4] There are wide views down lower Wharfedale. Ilkley Moor stands proud above Addingham and further round Fewston and Swinsty reservoirs can be seen. When you have had your fill continue along the ridge to the big cairn on the Old Pike: Round Hill lies ahead, but that is for another day.

Continue along the path a little further and drop off through the heather to the left aiming at an old wall. Just before you reach it you will pick up a wide deep-cut cart track. Turn left on this and follow it until you're directly above Ling Chapel Farm. Then cut straight down through the rough grass to it. You'll find a bit of a track towards the bottom. Cross the farm access road to a gate with a finger post pointing to Deerstones, and retrace your steps to it. Go straight ahead to the road and cross it with great care: traffic is fast moving. Just to the left is a gate and finger post to Storiths. There's not much path in most places, so look out for the stiles. After a bit where the path is walled there are two stiles side by side. Yours is the right-hand one. The next stile is straight ahead, though not easily seen, followed by a gate and a ladder stile by an oak tree. Now the way goes diagonally left towards two more stiles side by side. Again, yours is the right-hand one. Follow the wall round the field to the next stile, go the length of this field and through the gate to the right and out onto the road by a stile at a finger post at the hamlet of Storiths.[5] Go past the two farms straight ahead onto a very narrow road that becomes a narrow footpath. It goes straight down the hill to the bluff above the wooden bridge at the priory, and there you'll get a fine view of it. Don't go down to it unless you're parked there, but turn left, cross the stile and go through a gateway into a large field near the riverside. There are two more riverside fields with gates and then as the river swings to the right, climb up a little to a stile above the river. Then aim straight for the gateway between the farm buildings and almost at once you are on the road about 100 yards from Bolton Bridge.

A Variation to see Beamsley Hospital

If you are interested in old buildings you may prefer this variation. From Deerstones continue retracing your steps down Kex Beck to the point where the wall on the right makes a sharply angled point. A stile in the point followed by two fields lengths see you onto the road straight opposite the hospital. A few yards up the road is the lane that leads to New Hall Farm and from it the field path continues to Storiths joining the main route at a finger post.

The hospital is an almshouse built in 1593 by Lady Margaret Clifford, wife of the Third Earl of Cumberland whose grandfather had bought part of the priory estates at the Dissolution. The original part is a circular chapel with rooms around it for the accommodation of thirteen women, for this was built specifically for women.[6] Lady Margaret's daughter Lady Anne Clifford, completed the project by building two blocks of cottages on the roadside. Their linking archway has an inscription recording the foundation and the Clifford coat-of-arms. The buildings have recently been modernised internally by the Landmark Trust and are now let as holiday homes.

Things of Interest

1. There was a bridge across the Wharfe here as long ago as 1318, looked after by the canons of the priory. If you look underneath you may still see the arches of a much smaller, older bridge, though not necessarily the first one as it has been widened more than once.
2. The water leat brought water from a large reservoir a little higher up the valley and that in turn was kept topped up by a leat from a dam in the stream which, though heavily silted up, is still visible where you join it. The mill is now a private house.
3. Deerstones is a name from the days when the whole area was forested and part of the Langstrothdale Chase. Another of these names, Launds, means a clearing in a deer forest or park. You'll see this on the map just up the valley from Storiths.

4.   The Beacon, as its name suggests, was one of many hills in England where a warning fire was lighted in former times when there was a national emergency and dates from the time when people lived in fear of a Napoleonic invasion. It follows that it is a fine viewpoint particularly to the south and west, where Ilkley Moor forms the right-hand side of Wharfedale. You may notice the difference in vegetation on the north and south sides of the ridge. On the south it's all heather, on the north, the steep shady side, moorland grasses of various sorts cover the slopes. Heather needs the slightly better climate of the southern slopes.

5.   Storiths was owned by the priory but it was not a home farm simply being rented by the tenant. The narrow walled track is the ancient way to it.

6.   Lady Anne Clifford was born at Skipton Castle in the year 1590, and the celebrations of her 400th anniversary have brought the redoubtable lady into some prominence in the Dales. Though the only surviving child of the Third Earl of Cumberland she did not inherit the vast estates to which she was rightfully entitled and spent some forty-five years of her life in a determined effort to regain her birthright. Having done so, and having married in the meantime, becoming Countess of Pembroke, she spent the rest of her long life visiting and restoring her many properties scattered about the Dales and Westmorland. Skipton Castle had been partially demolished after the Civil War, and she restored it during the 1650s, dealing with the church soon after. Restoration of Brougham Castle followed in 1653; Barden Tower, originally a medieval hunting lodge may have been next on the list as she used it from 1657 onwards. Pendragon Castle probably followed as she spent Christmas 1663 there. Besides finishing the Beamsley Almshouses, she built St Annes Hospital, Appleby, another set of almshouses, for twelve widows. She spent the last few years of her life at Brougham Castle where she died in 1676, aged eighty-six, and is buried in Appleby church.

1.5 Beamsley Beacon, Round Hill and Kex Gill Moor

This walk is a very considerable extension of the previous walk, but except for one short section over Kex Gill Moor to Spittal Ings House, it is all on good tracks without route finding problems. From this house the walk follows a good track over the moor to Rocking Hall and then descends easily to Bolton Abbey. Category B+, time 6-7 hours.

    Pathfinder map SE15/15 is highly desirable and covers the entire

Beamsley Beacon

walk. The 1:25,000 Outdoor Leisure 10 Yorkshire Dales Southern Area map covers the western part of the walk and may usefully be supplemented with the 1:50,000 Landranger Map No. 104.

Follow the previous walk to the Old Pike, then continue dropping gently down the ridge towards Round Hill. At the fork in the path take the right-hand one: it snakes through the heather passing a number of old boundary stones bearing the letters B and LN on opposite sides, for this is a parish boundary as well as the boundary of the Y.D.N.P. Eventually you will reach a narrow gateway with substantial posts in the wall just below the true summit of Round Hill. Keep going straight ahead on a narrow grassy path cutting a very direct line through the heather. This track becomes very narrow then joins some old tractor marks but eventually almost gets lost in the bog that lies between the hillside and the road. Aim just to the right of the farm to find the gate onto the road, the A59.

Turn left on the road, and after about 100 yards cross into the access road to the farm. Bear left as you approach the house, and go through a gate on the left into the field. Follow the tractor marks into the next field and then to the barn in the trees ahead. Turn right here and continue up the short length of lane to the wall/fence corner on your right. At your feet is an excavated drainage ditch. (This is Old Intake Beck and the path is shown on the NEAR side of it on the O.S. map, not the far side. The channel seems to have rerouted the beck.) Cross it and continue up the field bearing right to a gateway, go through it and turn right to go through the next gate onto the open moor. Beyond the gate a faint path leads straight ahead but this, as the writer discovered the hard way, will not get you to Ramsgill Head where the next stile is located. Go along it for about 30 yards and then look for an even fainter path - imaginary if you like - going off on the left parallel to the wall. (It does not follow the line shown on the map.) If you hit upon it, fine, if not follow the wall slowly increasing your distance from it and swinging in a gently curve to the right. Shortly the ladder stile comes into view, a welcome sight. Simply make for it by the driest route you can. Its steps are enormous but once surmounted you are into the green intake fields above Spittal Ing House and all that remains is to follow the line of the fence to the farmhouse.

From Spittal Ings to Bolton Abbey

Turn left onto the access road and follow this good cart track that winds across the moor for almost a couple of miles to Rocking Hall, which you see on the skyline as you leave the farm. Turn left as you approach the hall and Rocking Stone in their surrounding wall and turn left again in about 100 yards, a corner-cutting operation not shown on the map. Now simply follow this good cart track all the way down to Bolton Park Farm taking the right fork after about 1 ½ miles. Keep above the farm buildings until you come to a gate with a finger post where you turn left to enter the access road to the farm. Go straight across the road at the bottom of the hill, turn left on the river bank before you cross the bridge (there are toilets and refreshments at the Cavendish Pavilion across the bridge) and follow the path downstream to the bridge at the abbey ruins. Cross it, turn left, and follow the river downstream to Bolton Bridge.

WALKS ON BARDEN FELL AND BARDEN MOOR ACCESS AREAS

Barden Fell and Barden Moor stand astride the lower Wharfe to east and west respectively. Both are heather-clad moorland as different from the soggy moorland heights of Great Whernside and Buckden Pike as the tree-clad, deep-cut valley of the Wharfe at the Strid is from the river flats in upper Wharfedale. The fell and the moor are private ground to which the public have access subject to certain very reasonable regulations, explained at length on the notice board at every point of entry. Most importantly, the owners retain the right to close these areas to the public on not more than thirty days a year for grouse shooting. These days occur between August and December but are never on Sundays. They are published on the notice boards at the access points well in advance. No less important to many people, dogs are not permitted in the access area even on a leash, in order to avoid disturbance to sheep, lambs and grouse. Great stress is laid on the danger of fire in this type of moorland and every care is requested of smokers.

Simon Moor offers a wealth of good walking to the moderate walker: The main paths are good and except for Walk 1.9 there are no route finding problems. Best time to go: August-September, when the heather is in flower, or later still in the year, for the autumn colourings are superb.

1.6 Halton Height and Barden Moor from Bolton Abbey

This long walk is full of variety - pasture, woodland, moorland and riverside scenery and has ever changing views, even though it does not rise up to the highest point on the moor. All is easy walking, with no steep hills, along good paths, though parts can be very muddy in wet weather. Time: About $5^{1}/_{2}$-6 hours; allow a full day. Category B. Map: 1:25,000 Outdoor Leisure 10 Yorkshire Dales Southern Area.

Park at the first car park on the left at Bolton Abbey and leave by the top exit. Turn left in the village by the P.O. and continue along the road until you're opposite the gatehouse.[1] Here the bridleway to Halton Height is signposted on the left. At the end of the first field there are three gates in a row. Go through the middle one.

The tractor marks swing to the right but keep straight on towards the fence surrounding a couple of artificial ponds. Go through the gate beyond them and at once turn right to go into the wood.

About 200 yards up the wide path, look for a small blue arrow on a post on the left directing you away from the main bridleway which is no longer a right of way. The blue arrow points you to another track climbing diagonally up the hill leftwards. It soon starts to curve back to the right and rejoins the bridleway close to the gate out of the wood.

At this gate follow a line of blue paint-dotted boulders across the large field to a distant stile. The guiding boulders continue, leading you to a stile and signpost in the top right-hand corner. Once over the stile the bridleway is fairly easy to follow. It runs close to the wall for a long way and then climbs over two minor humps on a little ridge up to your right. Ignore a tiny path that continues to follow the wall. Once over the ridge the line of the path becomes very clear right to the road at Halton Height.

Turn left on the road, cross the cattle grid and go along the track straight opposite. After about 200 yards another track comes in on the left. This is the old bridleway to Rylstone - you've taken a short cut. Follow this very good track as it winds its way over the moor above Lower Barden Reservoir.[2] Take the right-hand fork at both junctions and you will come in sight of the embankment of the Upper Barden Reservoir. It makes an inverted triangle amongst the darker moors. Now the track runs through rushes and deteriorates. At a sort of fork keep left, aiming at a finger post in the distance. This is on the near end of the dam and directs you across it for Burnsall and Drebley.

Turn right in front of the house on the other side and then immediately leave the tarmac road that leads to it for a green track. As this curves left round the hill look out for a large concrete manhole on the left. Opposite it a short cut leaves the main track. Don't hesitate to use it. It is well marked though a bit rougher than the rest and cuts off a huge loop. When you've crossed the stream you climb up a bit and rejoin the bridleway, at a cross roads. Go straight across and follow this track easily across the moor and down to the road. From here the best way is down the lane opposite to Drebley, across the stepping stones and down the riverside field path to Barden Bridge. If the river is high or the thought of stepping stones puts you off, there's nothing for it but a mile of road walking to the York Craft Centre. Immediately past the centre an unobvious stile takes you down the field to the road above the bridge cutting off a big loop of road.

Note: The stepping stones are rather widely spaced and are slippery if wet. Not recommended for other than the athletic!

Now join the previous walk with its alternative ways down the Wharfe. Turn to it and make your choice.

However, if you are interested in seeing a specimen of the now scarce cruck-built barns once in common use all over the north of England, it is worth going down the short lane to Drebley where there are two. The first one is on your right as you approach the hamlet, easily spotted by its very steeply sloping corrugated iron roof, but there is no access to it. The second one is on the continuation of the lane to the right and the barn is on the left. It has recently been rebuilt following a collapse after a storm. Ask at the farm you pass for permission to view its interior, whose massive curved oak timbers support the roof right from floor level. The barn may date from the end of the sixteenth century.

Things of Interest

1.   The gatehouse was once the entrance - the only entrance - into the priory. The central tower dates from the fourteenth century, the wings being added a couple of centuries later. At the dissolution of the priory in 1539 the gatehouse was saved from destruction and today remains as a fine piece of English domestic architecture, now known as Bolton Hall.

2.   From the path around here the views to Simon's Seat and up the Wharfe are particularly fine. The 'pattern' on the moor below is caused by different stages of growth of the heather after burning. Both reservoirs belong to Bradford Corporation Water Works.

1.7 Netherstone End and Lower Barden Reservoir from Burnsall

A prominent cairn marks this top of Barden Moor directly above Burnsall and it offers something of a challenge to the walker. It is, however, best out-flanked and climbed from Thorpe. The walk then continues to Lower Barden Reservoir and returns by Barden Bridge and the banks of the Wharfe. This will give a whole day's walking, 6-7 hours, full of variety.

Map: 1:25,000 Outdoor Leisure 10 Yorkshire Dales Southern Area. Category B.

Park at Burnsall and walk through the fields to Thorpe. (See Walk No. 2.3, the return, for details.) Turn left at the triangle of roads in Thorpe and keep left to find the old fell road that constitutes the access point to Barden Moor. Once through the wall follow the lowest one of four parallel, deep-cut grooves. It fades a little and other tempting tracks can be seen to the right, but keep left always to the top of the stream where you will join another quite well-marked cart track. Turn left on this, it needs care in following in places, and it will bring you on to the top of the fell between Thorpe Fell and Numberstones End. Here you will meet yet another cart track where you turn left again. If you look ahead you will see what looks strangely like a mill chimney - and that is just what it is. A closer look will take but a few minutes, and then retrace your steps. Let's not get confused about rights and lefts here. Turn your back on the old house you can see higher on the moor and follow this cart track until it starts to curve to the right. Look for a big stone with a heap of little ones on top and plough through the heather to it. There you should find a thready little track that makes the heather manageable and will lead you to a heap of stones. This is not the bold cairn you are making for, that's a bit further on. Continue to follow that little track and you will come to the cairn. There the bird's-eye view of Burnsall is stupendous.

Retrace your steps to the cart track and turn left on it. Follow it across the moor, descending gently as far as Lower Barden Reservoir, at first out of sight. You will have to deal with a number of junctions: keep left at the first one. A track then comes in from the right but ignore this junction. Go left at the second and right at the third junction to reach a corner of the wood. Continue to another track junction just above the reservoir, turn left and follow this rough road for about 1 ½ miles to the tarmac road a short distance from the B6160. There are two junctions on it: keep left at both of them. Turn left as soon as you reach tarmac and left again on the B6160, continuing steeply down the road to Barden Bridge, passing Barden Tower (see page 62 for a note about this historic pile) where refreshments were available in 1990. Just beyond the bridge turn left through the fields and follow the riverside path back to Burnsall. It is well marked all the way leaving the Wharfe briefly at Howgill to cross Blands Beck then rejoining it almost immediately. (Note that from Blands Beck this walk reverses part of Walk 2.2.)

The old colliery, Barden Moor

Things of Interest

Burnsall, judged by some of the ancient burial stones in the church, is one of the oldest villages in Wharfedale: Thorpe must be the most secluded, tucked away between Kail Hill and Elbolton Hill. So secluded is Thorpe that the Scots raiders who pillaged and plundered the length and breadth of Wharfedale as far south as Bolton Abbey in the years after the Battle of Bannockburn never found it.

The chimney high in the moor is just about all that is left of a former colliery. The round depression in the ground nearby was the shaft. These and other mines on the moor were worked in the seventeenth and eighteenth centuries and supplied coal to the Grassington lead smelting mills, for lime burning and for domestic use.

1.8 Rylstone Cross, Cracoe War Memorial, and Upper Barden Reservoir

The War Memorial is the obelisk on the skyline to the north of the cross, very well seen from the B6265 road to Grassington. The walk continues along the northern fringe of the moor and has exceptionally good views of Wharfedale, then returns by Upper Barden Reservoir and the bridleway across the moor. Category B. Map: 1:25,000 Outdoor Leisure 10 Yorkshire Dales Southern Area. Time 4½-5 hours.

Park in Rylstone in the large lay-by on the Grassington side of the B6265.

Cross the road and walk up the road to Rylstone Church. Just beyond it turn right into a short lane signposted to Barden Moor Access Area. At its end go over the stile on the left and follow the wall passing through a wood into a large open field. Cut across it to the right of the wood to find a couple of stiles that bring you into a roughish lane.[1] Continue up this lane to the top of the rise where you will find a signpost at a rickety gate - but no path. Keep going a little to the left and you will spot it on the hillock ahead, then follow it to the left of the group of trees to join the stony cart track. (The right of way bridleway [2,3] across the moor starts at the gate and goes past the trees on their right but all traces of path have gone. The stony cart track is a modern farm track and not a right of way, but the two unite higher up.) Follow the cart track to within sight of the wall that runs along the edge of the moor then go direct to any gap in it, turn left and pick up a little track that runs on the other side of the wall.

Rylstone Cross

This follows the wall right to the cross where a stile takes you to it. It is in a fine airy position. Look below at the curious Y-shaped bank and ditch in the rough ground immediately below: all that remains of the boundary of the deer park owned by the lord of the manor of Rylstone[4] in medieval times. Originally it would have had a palisade on top.

Now return to the path and follow it to the War Memorial, a fine obelisk deeply carved with initials and dates. Grassington is easily seen on the right with the fells of Wharfedale beyond. Opposite is that monstrosity, Swinden Quarry,[5] and behind you is Upper Barden Reservoir. Again return to the path. Continue to follow the wall until it starts to drop away to the valley then keep straight on along a rather vague cart track. A small cairn marks the correct spot to leave the wall. The track rapidly becomes well defined and winds its way around the northern flanks of the moor for a good mile whilst you enjoy first rate views of Grassington set out like toy town below you with the whole of Wharfedale beyond. In due course a house, yes, a house, will appear and as you approach it bear left to the shed on its left. Here is a splendid place for lunch - good grass to sit on instead of bog, fine views including Grimwith Reservoir and shelter should you need it. Continue along this gravel cart track for about $^1/_4$ mile to a junction just above a chimney[6]

Cracoe War Memorial

and take the right-hand one which passes close to the chimney. Continue to a tiny reservoir on the right, cross its dam and continue along a very pleasant green cart track to Upper Barden Reservoir, out of sight and around the corner to the right. As you round the corner the War Memorial/obelisk suddenly appears ahead and you may feel you are on the home straight, but that's not yet!

Cross the dam then continue up the stony cart track that winds its way up the hillside ahead. At the top of the brow you meet a good cart track; turn right on it and continue to a pair of shooting huts where there is shelter if needed. Here this cart track swings left over the moor and you must leave it at the lower of the two huts bearing right towards a pair of stone gate posts to pick up the boggy continuation of the cart track. Now simply follow it over the moor to a gateway in the wall marked by a blue dot and retrace your steps back to Rylstone.

Things of Interest

1. This lane is the old road between Skipton and Cracoe. The present road was built in 1853 as a turnpike road and Sandy Beck Bar is the old toll bar house at their junction.

2. This is the old road dating from medieval times that went to Bolton Abbey. Today it is only a bridle path across the moor waymarked by the Y.D.N.P. with blue-topped posts.

3. From the start of this track you will see a ruined tower on a hill top just ahead. This is Norton Tower built around 1500 as a summer residence by the Norton family who held the Manor of Rylstone at the time. They took part in the Rising of the North against Queen Elizabeth I in 1569 and consequently forfeited their lands and fortune.

4. Rylstone, or as it should be spelled, Rilston, is an ancient Anglo-Danish settlement but only traces of it are left.

5. Swinden Quarry is gradually eating away one of a row of limestone hillocks that fringe Barden Moor. This one is formed of particularly

80

pure limestone used in the chemical industry. The last of these reef knolls, as these green hillocks are called, is the smooth green hillock at your feet, Skelterton Hill, and the others are all to the right.

6. The chimney and the ruins beside it are all that is left of a colliery worked during the late eighteenth century to supply coal to the smelt mill on Grassington Moor. There is a large ring of spoil beside it where the shaft was. There were many small coal pits along the northern part of the moor: you have passed several shafts close to the track and there are a great many more.

Walk 1.9 Embsay and Embsay Moor

This walk goes over Embsay Crag, the rocky knoll behind the village, then over the moor - where there is some roughish going - to Waterfall Gill, and returns by the bridle track across the moor to Halton Gill.

Park in Embsay. The car park is on the upper one of the two roads through the village, almost opposite the village hall. Category B. Map: 1:25,000 Outdoor Leisure 10 Yorkshire Dales Southern Area. Time: The shorter one takes $3^{1}/_{2}$-4 hours, the longer one: 4-$4^{1}/_{2}$ hours.

Leave the car park by the stile and follow the well-trodden path to the road. Turn left, go round the corner and in 70 yards turn up a tarmac lane signposted 'Bridleway to Embsay Moor'. Follow this lane to the farm and go straight ahead up the fields to the access gate onto the bracken-covered moor. Turn left and follow the wall until a well-marked track swings away to the right and climbs quite steeply to the top of the crags, a fine viewpoint. Continue over the hill and descend to the footbridge. (A soft option simply follows the wall to the footbridge above the reservoir.) From the footbridge make for the gate in the fence but don't go through it. Turn right and follow the fence nearly to the wall where you will pick up a much better track that climbs steeply up the hill to the top of Crookrise. There are many tracks; it doesn't matter which you take near the wall. You will see a stile on your left, that is for climbers going to Crookrise, not for you.

Keep going on ever fainter tracks to the top of the moor and when the wall starts to drop away steeply to the left, make for a group of huge boulders. (There is good shelter under the furthest one should you need it.) Follow the track through the bracken to a heathery knoll above Waterfall Gill with Rylstone Cross and the Obelisk clearly seen on the edge of the moor. The track swings right and drops gently into the gill near a pair of shooting platforms. It is usually easy to cross the stream here and this you do. Go up the slope bearing to the left and follow such animal tracks as you can find until you reach the bridle track at a gate with a blue waymarker. Turn right on the bridle track, here a well-marked footpath having the occasional blue-topped post as waymark. It is very wet in places for the first mile or more, then takes to higher ground passing close to two shooting huts where you join a good cart track.

As this cart track tops the rise of the moor a signposted path leaves it on the right. This will return you direct to the access gate you used at the start of this walk, but it is a pity to leave this pleasant track just as the views into Wharfedale are opening up. Continue for another mile or so, and when the track has almost reached the dip in the moor, keep a look out for a small track on the right. It is directly opposite a cart track. Follow this track across a broken dam of some long disused mill pond to a couple of shooting huts, joining briefly another cart track. Continue along a hollow then along a low curved ridge until it disappears into the moor. The path effectively disappears too, but the way to the ladder stile is straight ahead and the distance short.

Bear right in the enclosure over the stile then follow the line of the gill down the hillside by a set of curious hollow ways to the road in Eastby. Turn right and after the last house turn left on a good path across the field to the church. Turn left on the road, cross it and just beyond the church go right onto the field path that takes you to the car park.

Things of Interest
Embsay is well known for its steam railway but it is an ancient village, the site of an Augustinian priory in AD 1130. Embsay is in a fairly exposed position on the hillside and the monks found life very hard there but were able to move to the site by the Wharfe in 1154 onto land given them by Cecily de Rumily of Skipton. This site became Bolton Priory. The bridleway across the moor was once a road that went to Bolton Abbey.

2: WHARFEDALE
From Burnsall to Grassington

Walks from Burnsall

2.1   The riverside path returning by Thorpe. Category C 85
2.2   Burnsall to Howgill by the Wharfe, returning by Trollers
       Gill. Category B 86

Walks from Grassington

2.3   To Burnsall by the riverside path. Category C 89
2.4   The riverside path to Grass Wood. Category C 92
2.5   Grassington to Kettlewell by the Dales Way. Category B 93

Walks around the old mine workings of Grassington Moor and Hebden Gill

2.6   The Miners' Trail on Grassington Moor. Category B 100
2.7   Hebden Gill, Yarnbury and Bare House. Category B 104

Other Walks

2.8   Around Grimwith Reservoir. Category C 107

ABOUT BURNSALL

Burnsall is a most attractive village with a car park, a pub, toilets, small shops, village green and picnic places next to the river bridge, the finishing point for one walk (which could be done just as well in reverse) and the starting point for two others. It is worth having a look

Burnsall

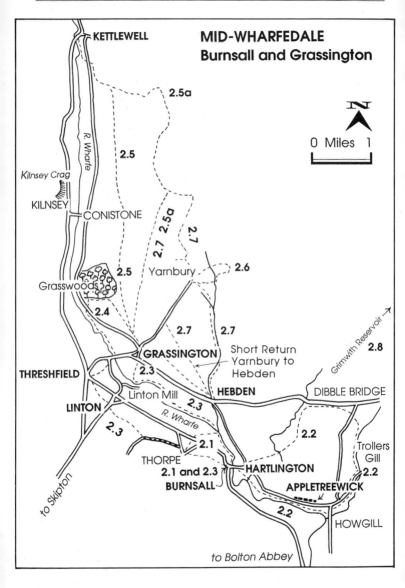

KETTLEWELL

**MID-WHARFEDALE
Burnsall and Grassington**

2.5a

R. Wharfe

2.5

N

0 Miles 1

Kilnsey Crag

KILNSEY

CONISTONE

2.7 2.5a

2.7

2.6

2.5

Yarnbury

Grasswoods

2.4

2.7

2.7

GRASSINGTON

2.3

Short Return
Yarnbury to
Hebden

Grimwith Reservoir

2.8

THRESHFIELD

Linton Mill

HEBDEN

DIBBLE BRIDGE

LINTON

2.3

2.3

R. Wharfe

2.3

2.1

2.2

Trollers
Gill

THORPE

2.1 and 2.3

HARTLINGTON

2.2

to Skipton

BURNSALL

APPLETREEWICK

2.2

HOWGILL

to Bolton Abbey

Burnsall School

at the church for the sake of the fragments of Anglo-Danish crosses and hogsback grave stones of Norse origin preserved in the east end. Burnsall was probably a Christian village well before AD 1000. The school is a little further up the road and was founded and endowed in 1602 by Sir Wm. Craven who also rebuilt the bridge. The school house is a very fine example of domestic architecture of the period, well-proportioned and elegant.

Walks from Burnsall
2.1 The riverside path returning by Thorpe

A short pleasant walk with a fair amount of variety. Category C. Time 1½ hours or a little more. The many stiles are time and energy consuming.

The riverside path starts between the side of the pub and the river. It stays close to the river bank except at Loup Scar and goes through the woods to the Suspension Bridge. Here you will find a finger post that points to Thorpe. There's not much of a path to be seen just here but strike up the hill in the right direction and the way becomes clear. On the road go up the lane opposite the stile to Thorpe. Just before you come to the first house look for a lane that goes left from a sharp corner. At the end of this there's a stile into the field. Turn right and follow the wall until you're opposite a gate, then turn smartly left and keep straight

85

down the field to a stile. Then cross the little stream and bear left a little making towards the wall. Go right here to a pair of stiles that take you across a narrow lane into the next field. The stile is by the trees, where you turn right. Now there are five or six narrow fields which you cut straight across by a line of stiles onto the road in the village. Turn right to get to the car park. Of course this walk can be extended to Grassington. Cross the suspension bridge and keep on that side of the river to Grassington. See Walk No. 2.3 for guidance.

Things of Interest
See the Grassington to Burnsall and return walk.

2.2 Burnsall to Howgill by the Wharfe, returning by Trollers Gill

A superb walk, despite two chunks of road. It takes in one of the best stretches of the Wharfe, Trollers Gill is a miniature Gordale and the return to Hartlington has some very fine views across Wharfedale.

Park by the river at Burnsall. In late summer there is an overflow car park which has a charge for parking on the Howgill side of the bridge. Alternatively the walk can be started at Appletreewick where in late summer there is parking (fee) at the campsite. Category B. Time: about 3 hours from Appletreewick, 4 from Burnsall. Map: 1:25,000 Outdoor Leisure 10 Yorkshire Dales Southern Area.

Cross the road bridge and almost at once you will see a stile and finger post in the wall on the right. Cut straight across to the river which makes a big loop here and keep on the path along the banks of the river all the way to the road at Howgill. There's a particularly fine stretch of river just before you reach the road. Turn left up the road, and in the corner on the right just beyond the chapel there is a stile. Go through it and turn left, but don't drop down to the stream. Keep your height on the edge of the steep ground above it and make for the caravan site. Stiles lead you onto its approach road, which you follow up to the tarmac road. Turn right here and follow the road to a T junction signposted for Parcevall Hall.

Turn left and follow the road to the entrance to Parcevall Hall Gardens. (If you are interested in gardens these are very well worth a visit in springtime as there are some unusual plants. Allow at least an hour. Entry charge.) Just before the entrance on the left there is a gate signed to Trollers Gill. A cart track starts here and goes very pleasantly up the gill to what looks like an old mine working, but turns out to be remains of a dam. Above this the character of the valley changes from a steep-sided, wooded gill to a broad, flat-bottomed grassy valley. The track continues up the left-hand side and, where the valley forks, swings away up the left-hand branch which it follows very easily to the rough road leading to Ghyll Head Mine. At the valley fork there is a highly recommended variation, quite sporting. Just keep straight on, passing the spring from which the whole of the water in this beck gushes forth in a quite amazing manner - unless you chose a dry spell. Above it the beck is dry. Go up the stream bed between overhanging limestone walls, most spectacular, a mini-Gordale. The going is very rough and apt to be slippery with no real path. As you emerge from the gorge you will see a pair of iron bars spanning the stream which has now reappeared. Cross the stream to the left-hand side before you reach these bars and climb steeply out of the gill on the left. You'll find a stile and in a few yards join the rough mine road which is the main route.

Follow this rough road to a corner where it swings sharply right, but here keep straight on across the moor past a pothole with a gurgling stream. Then as you come in sight of the wall, swing markedly left to find the stile onto the Appletreewick to Pateley Bridge road. Across the road in a corner another stile leads to a well marked green track that will bring you onto the Grassington to Pateley Bridge road. Turn left on the road and follow it down to Dibble's Bridge about $1/2$ mile away. Just free wheel and enjoy the views.

Just before the bridge there is a ladder stile and signpost to Appletreewick. Having crossed the stile climb steadily up the field through grass-grown quarry workings to the next ladder stile, continue to climb up to the gateway, and go past the end of a wall to find the next stile. This puts you onto a well-trodden path that leads across an enormous field to a stout post, the remains of a signpost, and allows you to enjoy your position high above the stream with fine views of Barden Moor. At the post go up to the gates in two parallel fences and having gone through both of them, turn right and continue to the far left-hand corner of this narrowing field to find a hidden stile. Turn right at the end of the wall and follow it for about $1/2$ mile passing through several fields until you reach a walled lane. If you are going to Burnsall turn right here (if going to Appletreewick keep straight ahead and turn to the paragraph below), pass in front of the barns and continue down the walled lane to the road. Go straight across it to Woodhouse Farm, turn right and retrace your steps to Burnsall.

Appletreewick finish
Follow the cart track to a barn and bear right into a walled lane. This brings you to the road by the Craven Arms where a right turn and 5 minutes walk sees you back at the campsite.

Things of Interest
The fine stretch of the River Wharfe in Haugh Wood is sometimes used by canoeists for races and competitions.
Note: The O.S. name is Trollers Gill, but local usage often spells it 'Ghyll'.

ABOUT GRASSINGTON
Grassington must be one of the best loved villages of the Dales. Perched on an open shelf above the Wharfe it has an air of business about its cobbled square, not to say a feeling of being a bit crowded. Though Grassington is as ancient a village as any in the Dales this crowded air comes from its prosperous days as the base for the Grassington Moor lead mining field in the early 1800s. Then mining was expanding and every available bit of land was needed for new miners' cottages. Before then the village was much as Linton is today. In those days they were part of the same parish and shared a common church with Threshfield and Hebden and the old church paths are part of our footpath network. Even today there is no church in Grassington, only a chapel, nor is there any ancient school and for the same reason - it was shared. Today there is a new school that serves the upper dale, for in effect Grassington is now its capital. It has suffered many ups and downs in its fortunes. After the decay of lead mining its population decreased a great deal but received an unexpected boost when the railway built a branch line from Skipton and had a connecting train to Bradford. Thus commuting played its part even in 1902. Now tourism is important. The village has a pub, cafes, shops to supply every daily need and a small folk museum open afternoons only in summer and at weekends in winter.

Partly because of its lead mining associations and partly because of the early development of farming by the Anglo-Saxons there is an incomparable wealth of footpaths around Grassington.

WALKS FROM GRASSINGTON

For all these walks it is best to park in the big car park on the road to Pateley Bridge. Here you will find the National Park Centre, toilets and a picnic area. The Grassington footpath map obtainable at the Park Centre is useful for these walks.

2.3 To Burnsall by the riverside path

This delightful, easy walk is part of the Dales Way. The walk back is not particularly satisfactory and you may prefer to spend some time in Burnsall and get the bus back (infrequent - check times). Best done when the trees have their autumn tints, or in summer when the horse chestnuts are in bloom. Time: 1$\frac{1}{2}$ hours, *plus* 2 hours to walk back. Category C but long if you do the return. Map: 1:25,000 Outdoor Leisure 10 Yorkshire Dales Southern Area.

The walk starts in the far left-hand corner of the car park where the signpost points to Linton Falls. Once through the swing gate turn right in the narrow walled lane that leads to the river. Immediately before the bridge there's a stile into the field on your left and Linton Falls[1] are on the right. Go through the stile onto the riverside path all the way onto a rough lane. From these fields you have a good view of Linton Church across the river.[2] Turn right in the lane and follow it past a house with a beautiful garden into the field. Here signs saying 'keep to the path' are misleading. The only good path is the cart track going to the N.W.W.A's plant and you don't want that. Nor do you want the path to the Hebden road that goes left here. Just strike across the field aiming for a wooden bridge which is just visible: it's quite a distance away. Soon after this the path becomes very well marked, impossible to lose.[3]

Cross the river at the suspension bridge[4] and turn left through the woods. The path keeps close to the river except for a short distance at Loup Scar where the river goes through a little gorge and reaches Burnsall at the bridge, pub and village green, a most pleasant spot.

The Return

If you decide to walk back a bit of careful route finding is needed in places and it is only after Thorpe that it is not so interesting. Time: 2 hours

Go up the village street to a converted barn called 'The Gallery'.

Linton Falls and Linton Mill

The path starts here and is signposted 'Footpath to Thorpe'. It looks as if it points into somebody's back garden, it certainly goes very close, but the path it is. Now go straight across half a dozen narrow fields, all with good stiles, and then, quite out of character, the next stile can't be seen. Make for the trees just on the right of a wall that runs down to a point. The stile is on a level with the trees and almost at once the path swings left to find the stile into a lane which you cross and continue to a tiny stream. Then go up towards the obvious field gate but bear right before you reach it and use another small gate to leave the field. Enter the lane ahead, turn left and continue into Thorpe.[5] Bear right at the triangle of roads and climb up the hill past the houses until you see a lane going off on the left labelled 'Unsuitable for Motorists'. Turn along this and after about 10 minutes you will come to an old barn. The stile you want is just before it. Don't go down the narrow walled lane you pass first. Turn left towards the trees, from where you will see the next stile, and if you look left, a good view along the foot of Barden Fell. The way to Linton is now clear.[6]

Turn right as soon as you reach the road, and it will bring you past the Fontaine Hospital Chapel and the village green. Find time to have a look round, and then continue by the road you were on. Turn right just past the youth hostel and follow the road across the main Threshfield

Fountaine Alms Houses, Linton

to Burnsall road down towards the river. In a corner a branch goes off to the right. Take this, turn left just before the first building and right as soon as you're past it to get back to the Tin Bridge which you cross and climb up the little lane to the car park.

Things of Interest

1. Linton Falls are on the line of the North Craven Fault, seen more dramatically at Malham Cove. The new houses across the bridge have been built on the site of a former cotton spinning mill that finished work in 1950. In earlier times it had spun woollen worsted and was powered by a waterwheel. In medieval times there was a water-powered corn mill on this site.

2. The stepping stones enabled the people of Hebden to attend their parish church at Linton.

3. The horse chestnuts which make this part of the walk memorable in spring or autumn are not native to this country and have almost certainly been planted there. The grass is so well cropped by sheep that you'll see few flowers except in the wet places. There, besides marsh marigold and meadow sweet you will find brooklime, common scurvey grass, crosswort, water avens and sweet cicely: all flower in June.

4. Notice that although the walls are built of limestone, the stile is built of gritstone, which is easily cut and split to give shapes that fit together and are not slippery in the wet.

5. Thorpe is a delightfully secluded village tucked away between Kail Hill and Elbolton Hill, two of the reef knolls that fringe Barden Moor. See the chapter on the geology of the Dales for an explanation of the

91

term. There is a particularly fine Georgian house on the right at the beginning of the village.

6. As you walk down the next field past the trees you may notice you are going down a set of terraces. These are Anglo-Saxon ploughing terraces called lynchets, of which there are many in Wharfedale, but particularly well seen here.

2.4 The riverside path to Grass Wood

This is a superb walk of varied riverside scenery and woodland. Grass Wood is famous for its flowers and is owned and managed by the Yorkshire Wildlife Trust. A whole network of paths criss-cross it, many of them made in order to give easy access to members of the Trust as they go about the work of maintaining the woodland and conserving the rarer plants found there. The public can hardly feel free to use these but there is one right of way path through the wood used by this walk. Please, please do not pick the flowers, however plentiful they may seem to be; it's all too easy to deplete plant stocks to vanishing point. Category C. Time: 2½ hours. Map: 1:25,000 Outdoor Leisure 10 Yorkshire Dales Southern Area.

Leave the car park by the narrow walled lane that starts in the lower left-hand corner, and follow it down to the footbridge. Leave it here, turn right and follow the path to the road by the bridge over the Wharfe. Go straight across into a lane on the right where there is a stile leading to the riverside footpath. It is quite well marked with good stiles and passes Ghaistrylls Strid. Shortly after the path enters woodland it climbs the little bank on the right. At its top the path forks: take the left-hand one that runs along the edge of the steeper ground; it has fine views of the river and leads round in a wide curve to the end of the wood and the correct stile onto the road.

Across the road is another stile into Grass Wood and from it a little path leads quite steeply upwards to join a much wider path, a cart track almost, in a couple of minutes. Turn left on this wide track and follow it for perhaps ½ mile to its junction with the right of way path. When you reach this turn right and follow it gently uphill. Quite soon you will come to a junction where you take the right-hand track and follow it up the hill, quite steeply at times. As you approach the top of the hill you will be on a length of path reinforced with thin logs. Just beyond this the path forks: take the left-hand branch. At the top of the hill there is

Splendid riverside scenery at Ghaistrylls Strid

a 'cross roads' with a reassuring signpost. Keep straight on and follow this well-trodden track for about a mile to the stile into the fields above Grassington.

Once in the field go to the right of the barn and take the right-hand one of the gates that are side by side. Then you are in the lane leading to Grassington. This is much used by cows and becomes very muddy, not to say filthy, so it is better to leave it where it makes a sharp bend right. Ahead in the corner is a stile that takes you up the field to a track through the farm onto the road back into the top of the village. The farmyard may be muddy, but there's less of it.

A Note about Grass Wood

This piece of woodland is so rich in flowers and shrubs it is worth being slightly technical to try to understand a little of the reasons and its importance to botanists. Some is quite low down the hillside not far from the river and the rest is on a steep rocky hillside. The lower part has a richer moister soil and deeper shade than the upper part. Here you will find most of the bigger trees, ash, oak and beech, together with shrubs such as buckthorn, bird cherry, white beam, the burnet rose and

93

dogwood, all characteristic of limestone woodland. Higher up it is mainly hazel with some ash, sycamore and whitebeam, but a good deal of planting has taken place and it's not really natural woodland at all.

In the lower woodland there's a lot of dog's mercury, stone bramble, woodsage, the early purple orchid and some rarities such as herb paris, lily of the valley and Solomon's seal, but here and there leaf mould has accumulated and produced an acid soil where bluebells and bracken grow. Higher up you will find cranesbill, herb robert, rockrose, violets, ladies bedstraw, harebells, field scabious, wood sanicle, marjoram, golden rod and many others that prefer lighter shade and will tolerate poorer soils. About 400 species of plants are found in the wood.

2.5 Grassington to Kettlewell by the Dales Way

This superb walk over upland limestone should be on every moderate walker's list. There's nothing else quite as good in the whole of the Dales on a good day, and it must be done this way round. Plan your day to get a morning or early afternoon bus from Kettlewell (not Sundays) and walk back. Category B. Map: 1:25,000 Outdoor Leisure 10 Yorkshire Dales Southern Area.

Note: The walk is very exposed to wind and rain from the west or north beyond Dib Scar. Time: allow 3½ hours including a short rest. There is no riverside path between Grassington and Kettlewell, and no satisfactory return. Use the bus.

The true start to the Dales Way is by the riverside path to Grass Wood, but there are so many paths there that it is difficult to find the way. It is better to start by going up Main Street. Bear left into Chapel Lane and where this lane turns sharp left at the de-restriction sign, go into the farmyard turning left behind the barn. In the first field ignore the stile on the left which leads to Grass Wood and go through the left-hand of the two gates into a large field. At the far end is a fat man's agony of a stile. The path runs around the hollow in front of you and the stile is at the end of the wall. From it you enter the vast field called Lea Green.[1] Tractor marks lead the way. Bear right when they fork. Eventually they run out and a path continues parallel to and some 50 yards from a wall on your right. It passes an ancient dew pond, and 100 yards beyond this, not seen until you're close to it, is the stile. This dew pond is marked on the map with a tiny blue dot, so you can pin-point

*The Scandinavian-style church at Scargill House
lies amidst beautiful woods*

your position and progress. Now go to the right of a rocky knoll with
trees on it. A gate there leads you into a field with bracken in it and you
can see the next stile. From it a pyramid-shaped hill of limestone is well
seen, go round its left-hand side. There you will find an old limekiln,
useful if you need shelter. Keep straight on up the brow of the hill, from
where you will see ladder stile, and from that, the next one. You can
now see the lane coming up from Conistone to Mossdale.[2] Make
slightly uphill to the point where it disappears from view and you will
find a good track. Use this to cross the bed of the gill onto a cobbled
lane, called Bycliffe Road, cross that and go along the grassy terrace at
the foot of a little limestone outcrop. There is no path here, but keep just
below the rocks to find the stiles. A very good landmark hereabouts is
a curious knob of limestone shaped a bit like a round box with a knob
on its lid. It's called High Hill Castle, and the stile is on its right. Now
both Littondale and Wharfedale come clearly into view and the views
up these two valleys are one of the great things about this walk done this
way round.

Continue to walk this high limestone terrace above Swineber Scar
always holding your height until close to the wood. Then drop down a

little to the wall and follow this to a gate into the lane in the wood. Turn left and follow the lane down past Scargill House[3] to the road. The best is now over but it isn't all road to Kettlewell.

After about ¹/₄ mile look out on the right for a finger post to Kettlewell at a gate into a field below a barn. Turn left at the gate ahead then follow the wall to a green lane at the back of Kettlewell. The route - there's barely a path - weaves about from one side of the wall to the other. The key to it all is to go through the gate on the left in the third field, then simply keep your eyes open for the stiles. Turn left in the green lane, right at its T junction and it will bring you to the road just above the church. Turn left again to find the village and car park by the river bridge.

Things of Interest

1.   Lea Green contains any number of traces of early settlements, most of them only visible to the trained eye. Quite easily seen are the remains of a number of lozenge-shaped hut bases about 100 yards left of the dew pond. They are on a limestone pavement and are slightly masked by it, but can be traced as can the wall that enclosed them. Despite this enclosing wall it is not thought that this was a defended position - there are far better ones close by - but a Romano-British settlement rearing cattle rather than ploughing the land, and that its water supply was the dew pond.

Cattle are reared there today. You'll often see a great herd of them complete with bull. Don't be afraid. Just keep your distance and move quietly and you should have no trouble at all.

A vein of lead bearing rock runs right through this field and was worked many centuries ago. The grass-grown holes and trenches can be seen close to the prehistoric settlement, and perhaps even better, soon after you've come into Lea Green, on the left of the tractor way.

2.   This lane, Bycliffe Lane, is a very ancient track. Where it leaves Conistone and climbs the valley side it is deeply cut, always a sign of age, and the stone walls built around the turn of the eighteenth century are not a part of the original lane. It became part of the packhorse marked road between Settle and Kirkby Malzeard in Nidderdale.

3.   The modern Scandinavian-style church and nearby house of Scargill are a Church of England conference centre.

Walkers clambering up the tufa deposit at the waterfall, Gordale

Halton Gill with Fountains Fell in the distance
Clints on Knowe Fell, with Malham Tarn beyond

2.5(a) An Alternative Finish, returning to Grassington

If you are not inclined to bother with buses and are prepared to tackle a much longer walk (5 hours), you may prefer this return to Grassington. Follow the Dales Way path as just given until you are approaching a large plantation of conifers (not shown on the 1:25,000 map) about 1½ miles from Kettlewell. The Dales Way path enters this plantation to join a cart track which runs up to the moor above. You turn right on this cart track. In 1989 the best place to find the track was marked by an animal drinking trough. Look right at this point and you should see the cart track. Follow it through the gate and all the way up to the gate in the wall[1] separating the moor from the fields. Turn right here and follow thready paths to Capplestone Gate, a gate with a ladder stile on its left. Ignore this invitation to turn right: it is better to follow the wallside all the way to the good cart track which is Bycliffe Road.[2] There is a steadily improving track all the way, though it is not a right of way. Turn right on Bycliffe Road and look out for a faint track on the left that cuts the corner across to a broken wall. Continue in the same general direction to the next broken wall and keep going in this direction, for there is no path just here, until you can see a ladder stile well ahead and make for this.[3] To the right of the large spoil heap here there are two gates close together. Go through the left-hand one into a lane.

A few minutes after you have passed through it you will come to the ruins of High Barn. Turn right through the gate and continue down to Bare House, another ruined building. Go through the gate here (the signpost is to Conistone, but that is in the opposite direction), and follow a wide well-marked track on springy green turf through a collection of enormous fields. After about 1½ miles of this marvellously easy going which leaves you free to enjoy the most excellent views down Wharfedale flanked by Barden Moor on the right with the Cracoe War Memorial a prominent feature, and Barden Fell on the left, you enter a short lane on the outskirts of Grassington, hiding coyly round the corner almost out of sight whilst Threshfield across the river stands brash and bold for all to see. This short lane brings you into the top of Main Street almost opposite Low Lane. Turn right into the village where you may find an ice cream or visit a tea shop en route to the car park.

Things of Interest

1.   As the cart track climbs to the moor it crosses the junction of the limestone and the gritstone. The lower walls are built of limestone, the moor wall of gritstone.

2.   Bycliffe Road is a very ancient track from Conistone to Nidderdale. As you drop down the hill a little, Mossdale Scar can be seen away to the left, looking like an old quarry. It is the site of the notoriously dangerous Mossdale Caverns where four cavers were caught in flood water and drowned some years ago.

3.   Old lead mine workings abound here, and not all the ground is safe. Avoid any hollows.

WALKS AROUND THE OLD MINE WORKINGS
OF GRASSINGTON MOOR AND HEBDEN GILL

Lead mining became the principal occupation of Grassington and Hebden during the eighteenth and nineteenth centuries and the moors behind them were highly industrialised in the style of the times. Lead mining ended there about 100 years ago and time has mellowed the devastation caused to the landscape. The old spoil heaps and shafts are weathered and grass-grown, but sufficient remains of the old structures to fascinate those who are interested in industrial archaeology. In 1981 a part of the moor was declared a conservation area and a miners trail for visitors was devised. There is a notice board giving some information at the start of Walk 2.6, but it is out of sight behind some spoil heaps on the left and was vandalised in the summer of 1990. There is another at the Cupola Smelt Mill. Note that not all the moor tracks are rights of way.

Lead was discovered at Yarnbury as long ago as 1603 and in the early years was worked by small partnerships. Later in that century local capitalists put money into developing the field, deepening shafts and installing horse whims for winding, but despite this it was not very successful until around the end of the century when the Cavendish Estate developed the area. Yarnbury then became the headquarters of the Grassington mining field. Here were the mine manager's house, the offices, workshops and the starting point of the transport system that served the mines. From it new roads were built to the mines and smelt mill, a tiny railway track crossed the road to the workings there, and there was an incline up which the ore was brought by pony haulage. The

Grassington Moor mining field was remarkable for the extensive and intensive use made of water power at the height of its prosperity. The lead veins are high on the moor and the terrain does not lend itself either to the technique of 'hushing' so commonly used in Swaledale, nor to the driving of levels from the moor. The mines were worked almost entirely by shafts of increasing depth and size as the years passed. These shafts, up to 400 feet deep, met increasing problems with water and pumps worked by waterwheels were developed to get rid of it. This became ineffective because of the very depth of the mines, and a level known as the Duke's Level was driven from low down in Hebden Gill in order to drain them. Any shaft that went deeper than the Duke's Level was drained by pumping up to the level. This level forked, one branch coming towards the Yarnbury shafts, the other towards the Cupola Mill shafts. Winding of the ore was also done by waterwheel: wire ropes could travel long distances over the moor by a system of pulleys supported on stone pillars.

It was essential for this important work to have a reliable water supply. To ensure this dams were built high on the moor and in particular three in Blea Beck to conserve water for use in dry spells. In normal weather the stream was brought across the moor by a very accurately levelled and constructed ditch, some sections of which can still be traced though today much overgrown with rushes. This was known as the Duke's High Water Course. It eventually came into Coalgrove Beck and from there another water leat, the Duke's Low Level Water Course, served even more installations. It can be most easily seen where it runs round the dry valley above the embankment crossing Hebden Gill.

Power was also needed to work the ore crushing and purifying plants. Ore was roughly picked over at the shaft and then sent to the specialised dressing plants which needed plenty of water to wash and separate the ore from the gangue minerals and rock. The new reverberatory furnaces needed ore prepared to high standards to function satisfactorily and a new one was built on the site occupied by the derelict Dales Chemical Plant. Nothing is left of it today.

Smelting had long been carried out at the Cupola Smelt Mill using the 'ore hearth' type of furnace, but with increasing production from the mines the Cupola Mill had a new reverberatory furnace installed in 1778, and these are the ruins that are left today, with their long flues reaching over the moor to the chimney.

The mines closed in 1881, worked out, having produced some 57,000 tons of lead between 1765 and that date.

Finally a botanical note. If you do these walks in late June or early July you will see that many of the old spoil heaps are covered with a low growing starry white flower. Called spring sandwort it is a rather specialised plant that only grows on disturbed ground such as mine spoil heaps. Indeed, it is often the only plant to grow there because it will tolerate the lead present in the soil in these heaps which other plants will not. Another quite rare plant peculiar to lead mining areas, the alpine penny cress, can be found high on the moor.

WARNING: It can be quite dangerous to wander round old working areas because of the possibility of collapse of the ground. Keep to the hard roads or well-trodden areas. (For more information see the chapter 'The Lead Mines and Smelt Mills of the Dales'.)

Two walks are given across the mining areas, the first one is rather more comprehensive than the miners' trail, for which a leaflet was never issued. The second one covers Hebden Gill and the area north of Yarnbury.

Both are Category B and need the 1:25,000 Outdoor Leisure 10 Yorkshire Dales Southern Area map.

2.6 The Miners' Trail on Grassington Moor

Best done on an afternoon of good visibility as the early part of this walk gives a wide view across the moor. Drive up to Yarnbury and park at the end of the tarmac road. Time: about 3 hours. Category B.

Before you start, take a look at Yarnbury. The houses were the mine manager's house and the offices, but the small ruined building right up to the road was the Count House. Here the pigs of lead produced at the mill were counted as they left the moor. Behind it is another small ruined building, the powder house.

Turn right across the cattle grid where the notice says, 'No unauthorised vehicles'. The area below you is being reworked for barytes and just beyond it you will see one of the old dams used to conserve water. When you are opposite the dam, cut across going immediately below it to a stile over the wall. Climb the stile and walk along the bank of the leat to the shaft ahead. This is the top of the Union Shaft, restored by the Earby Mines Research Group which has done

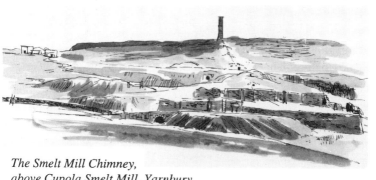

The Smelt Mill Chimney,
above Cupola Smelt Mill, Yarnbury

much good work on the moor. It was almost 400 feet deep and worked a vein that went deeper than the Duke's Level. If you now go down the banking you will find a channel and short tunnel built into the side of it. This guided the wooden rods that worked the pump lifting water to the Duke's Level where it could drain away. These rods were operated by the crank of a waterwheel situated roughly where the new spoil heaps are. If you let your eyes get accustomed to the gloom you can see some of the mechanism that converted a horizontal push-pull movement into a vertical one. Just to the left of the tunnel as you face it are the remains of two bouse teams, one in quite good condition. Originally it had an iron grid in the bottom. It was used to store and wash the bouse before crushing and dressing for the furnace. You walked in along the leat or water channel that supplied it with water.

Now let's go back on route, which is the track just above the capped shaft. The route winds through the spoil heaps and through a gate. There's a ladder stile just up on the left and from it and the field beyond a wide view of the moor and Hebden Gill. To the left, high on the moor is the cupola chimney with the long flues below starting at the smelt mill ruins. To the left of the chimney is a large concrete structure, the derelict Dales Chemical Mill, designed to recover fluorite. Beyond it are all manner of spoil heaps and old workings. Well to the right of this is Bolton Gill dropping steeply down into Hebden Gill. It has a number of spoil heaps and what looks like a railway tunnel entrance. This is the entrance to the shaft and winding gear. The crushing and washing floors in Hebden Gill are out of sight.

Now back to the ladder stile. Go diagonally right across the field aiming to the right of a spoil heap. There's not much of a path, but the slit stile is easily seen. From it go slightly right to a gate in the wall; there immediately turn left and you will find yourself in a walled lane that brings you down into Hebden Gill at the foot of Bolton Gill.

Go through the gate on the left and follow the stream at first then climb over a big spoil heap. Just beyond is an old limekiln in quite a good state of preservation, probably built to produce quick lime for the lead mining buildings. Follow the cart track up the hillside to a gate then turn right through this gate. As you pass below the spoil heaps of Union Mine (visited on the outward leg of this walk) note the little stone hut below them. It was the power house for the mine. Keep straight on at the first junction then turn right at the second one. (If you want to return to Yarnbury quickly turn left at this junction and 10 minutes will see you there.)

Now keep straight on crossing the embankment of Hebden Gill then cut across on a grassy track to the lower gate of the Cupola Smelt Mill. As you cross the stile the end of the old slag heap is on your right, poised above the stream. What a foul, polluted place this must have been when the furnaces were in full production.

Here you will see a Yorkshire Dales National Park notice board explaining the features of the conservation area, and, much more importantly, the areas where it is dangerous to wander because of the risk of the ground collapsing into old workings under your weight. Then go through the gate: you are in the yard where pigs of lead were stored after smelting. The first of the two big reverberatory furnaces was installed in 1778 and was opposite. A second one was added later. Only parts of the chutes down which the ore was fed can be seen and there were six of them. At the bottom left-hand corner of the yard you will just make out the waterwheel pit that worked the bellows. The small furnace at the left-hand end was for reworking the slag to recover lead residue. At the right-hand end is a small vaulted room that was the store. In order to see the complex system of flues leading to the chimney go out at the left-hand side (by the wheel pit) and onto the grass above. You will see how each reverberatory furnace had its own flue all joining together a little higher up then running like a great mole run for 600 yards up the moor to the chimney. Follow the flue by walking besides, not on it - there's too much risk of it collapsing. Where it has collapsed you can see it had a flagged floor and arched roof.

A little way up on the left is the remains of a small building, a Stokoe condenser that trapped some of the lead fumes from the furnace gases.

There are various junctions and branches and a huge loop to cool the gases to recover more lead from them. Higher up there is a big flagstone built into the flue, clearly some sort of damper or control, for just above it the flue splits and takes a diamond-shaped course to the chimney as well as a direct one. The chimney was restored by the Earby Mines Research Group in 1971 and has a big inspection slot in the back which enables you to see some little way into the flue on a bright day. It's a very impressive tunnel about the height of a man.

From the chimney continue past the spoil heaps to the dam. Turn left on the lower bank and just beyond you will see the wheel pit of the big 45-foot wheel that powered the High Winding House and sent power by wire rope to other installations on the moor. From here the water went to the dressing plant across the road where the now derelict Dales Chemical Plant stands. There was another giant 50-foot diameter 6-foot wide wheel at the Brake House a little lower down and this too supplied power by wire rope to other shafts. From the wheel pit of the High Winding House turn left and make for the point where four roads meet in a sort of Y with an extra leg in the middle. You take the top left-hand leg of the Y. Just to the right here there used to be an upright stone about 3 feet wide with the initials D.D. carved on it, not easy to find. It's one of the old boundary or meer stones that marked out a length of vein worked by someone whose initials were D.D. though we don't know who he was. There are many such stones on the moor, mostly dating from the early eighteenth century. This old mining road wanders around the old spoil heaps and shafts and continues down the hillside. When you are nearly down to the dry valley you will cross a little ditch, or so it seems, but it is much more than that. Look along it to the right and you will see it contouring the hillsides for a long way before it disappears from sight. It runs right round the dry valley and you can see it across on the other side as a green level running to a mine working. This is the lower part of the Duke's Water Course, the system of channels that brought water to the many waterwheels on the moor. The cart track now runs between walls back to Yarnbury. If you don't fancy the pull up the hill, and I assure you it's far less than it looks, there is a stile on the first bend on the left which enables you to gain a hard track that goes back to Yarnbury without the climb. If you do this you miss the last item of interest on this walk. As you are climbing the hill there's a solitary ash tree on the right. Look over the wall there and you will again see the water channel on its way to Yarnbury.

When you are almost there look on the left for a low wall with rounded capstones. Below it is the mouth of Barratt's Incline, its portal bearing the date 1828, when it was built to link all the shafts at the 120-foot level. A few paces lower down is a blocked up gateway in the wall. On both sides of it you can see stone railway sleepers, identified by the round holes to which the rail chairs were bolted. A light railway ran across the road here, designed for pony haulage not steam engines. Over the wall is the empty dam into which the Duke's Lower Water Course discharged its water for use on this part of the moor.

2.7 Hebden Gill, Yarnbury and Bare House

There is limited parking and toilets at Hebden on the Burnsall road. The short version of the walk will take about 2¹/₂ hours, the return via Bare House and Grassington 3¹/₂ to 4 hours. Category B.

Go straight across the Pateley Bridge road by the stream and you will see a bridge leading to a group of cottages. Cross the bridge, turn left and follow the footpath to the left along the beckside. Over the stile climb steadily up the hill to the next stile, not the gate next to it, then go up towards the buildings and immediately turn left through the gate. Here turn right and follow the wall steeply up the grassy hillside. You'll see a white arrow high on the rocks above. Keep in this direction but as soon as you're through a gate (which is out of sight until you're upon it), turn left and follow the wall to pick up the cart track in the gill just above the bridge. The last part is pretty rough here and there and is best given a miss in high summer because of giant bracken above the top wall. Then it is better to stay on the road up the gill as far as Hole Bottom where you go through the right-hand gate to join the route through the fields at the bridge.

The cart track runs close to the beck and the scene is quite impressive with dark rocks and crags towering over the track for a time. Just past the second gate look left and you will see a tunnel mouth now built up with stone. This is Duke's Level built to drain the whole of the Grassington Moor mine field in 1790. A little higher up there are a number of ruined buildings and on the right of the track, not very obvious, is the pit of the waterwheels that powered the ore crushing machinery here. Just beyond it is Bolton Gill, not far up which are extensive spoil heaps and what looks like a railway tunnel. In fact it is the shaft of the Bolton Gill mine, built about 1856 and now filled in but worth climbing up to have a look at. Then retrace your steps.

At this point the good cart track ends and you must cross the stream, no problem even in wet weather, to continue by a smaller path. Go through the gate on the right and follow the stream at first then climb over a big spoil heap. Just beyond is an old limekiln in quite a good state of preservation, probably built to produce quick lime for the lead mining buildings. Follow the cart track up the hillside to a gate then turn right through it. You pass below the spoil heaps of Union Mine and will see the little stone hut below them. It was the power house for the mine. Keep straight on at the first junction then turn left at the second. Ten minutes will see you at Yarnbury.

The Short Return

From Yarnbury go a short mile down the road to a lane on the left signposted to Hebden. Follow this until it leaves its containing walls at a gate. Follow the wall for about 50 yards when you will see another stile, climb this then right through a little gate just before a house on the left. Strike diagonally left across the field through a gateway, hopefully reaching a stile you can't see in the wall below. The next stile is visible, then make for the gate at the bottom of the field. Go through the sheep fold, turn right and in a few yards you're on the road in Hebden.

The Main Route, continued

At Yarnbury turn right and walk up the lane to the first gateway on the left above the houses. As you walk up the lane to the gate look to the right for a blocked up gateway in the opposite wall. This is where the light railway built in 1836 crossed the road from the workings there to the Yarnbury headquarters. If you look in the grass close to it you will see some of the old stone sleepers with round holes for the bolts that held the chairs to the sleepers. It was not a steam engined railway, ponies provided the traction. Just a few yards further on is the portal to the incline used to bring the ore from the workings on that side. It has the date 1828 carved on it. Look over the wall and you will see a dam that received water from the Duke's Low Water Course and passed it onto another dam lower down.

From the gateway a pleasant cart track follows the wall into a walled lane. Almost everywhere on the left are the remains of the old mine workings now grassed over and evidently far older than many of the remains on High Moor which are hardly grassed over at all. The characteristic rings made by the bell pits are quite common. Where the path leaves the walled lane for open pasture follow the grassy track round the wall to a gate leading into a narrow strip of field. At the other end of this is another field with some interesting remains. Just to the left is a prominent bell pit ring and in its centre a shaft with its walling still reasonably intact. Look left and you will see a row of grassed-over shallow pits in a straight line. These are even older workings, mere scratchings in the surface of the vein. Beyond there is a rough ring of stone, the remains of a building with another well-preserved shaft. Neither of these seem particularly deep, but they may well have fallen in lower down.

Retrace your steps through the narrow strip of field and along the wall to the ruins of High Barn. Turn right through the gate and continue down to Bare House, another ruined building. Go through the gate here (the signpost is to Conistone, but that is in the opposite direction), and follow a wide well-marked track on springy green turf through a collection of enormous fields. After about 1 ½ miles of this marvellously easy going which leaves you free to enjoy the most excellent views down Wharfedale flanked by Barden Moor on the right with the Cracoe War Memorial a prominent feature, and Barden Fell on the left, you enter a short lane on the outskirts of Grassington, hiding coyly round the corner almost out of sight whilst Threshfield across the river stands brash and bold for all to see. This short lane brings you into the top of Main Street almost opposite Low Lane. (Turn right into the village if you wish to sample an ice cream or a tea shop.)

About 50 yards along Low Lane there is a walled Lane marked 'footpath to Hebden'. Follow this, which is apt to be muddy in places, until it enters an open field. Now there are fine views across to Barden · Moor and Simon's Seat which stand either side of the River Wharfe. At the start of the field a finger post directs you to leave the stony cart track and cut across the field to a gate. Here you will pick up another cart track that ends abruptly in a little square with a gate on each side. The stile is on the left just before you get to this, but if the field is fenced off for hay, go through the left-hand gate and look for the next stile on the right almost at once. Two more fields follow and then you find yourself rather puzzlingly on the road in the hospital grounds. Turn right and once past the buildings, look for a path to the left leading to a pine wood. Now a line of stiles leads clearly through the fields to a short lane down to the road to Hebden. There's a fine view of the gill from these fields as well as down the Wharfe. Turn left on the road to the bridge, where you join the main walk from Hebden.

Things of Interest
It is worth noting that Low Lane is the old road to Hebden before the present one was built. Shortly after leaving it you may notice that the walls are no longer limestone but a sandy gritstone, a sure indication that the ground below is the same. The stone walls of the Dales were built of stone lying about the fields, not brought in from a distance. The hospital was once a T.B. sanitorium but now is used for geriatric patients.

OTHER WALKS
2.8 Around Grimwith Reservoir
Grimwith Reservoir lies just north of the Grassington-Pateley Bridge road about 4 miles from Grassington. In 1984, following an increase in the size of the reservoir, the Yorkshire Water Authority created three new paths that enable a walk round the reservoir to be made. There is a car park (fee) with toilets close to the banks, and it is reached from Dibble Bridge. Though the walk around the eastern arm is not especially attractive it may be enlivened by wind surfers' activities, good fun to watch on a windy day. The north-western arm, however, gives very attractive walking, so the circuit is best done this way round. Category C. Time: 2-2$^{1}/_{2}$ hours, Map: 1:25,000 Outdoor Leisure 10 Yorkshire Dales Southern Area, but hardly needed for the walk.

Leave the car park at the opposite end from the toilet block and simply walk round the reservoir following the signposts. Take care to leave the cart track on the far side in order to cross the dam and return to the car park.

3: UPPER WHARFEDALE

Walks from Kettlewell
3.1   Great and Little Whernside. Category A 111
3.2   The traverse of Great Whernside, Tor Mere Top and
        Buckden Pike. Category A. 113
3.3   A walk up Dowber Gill to Providence Pot. Category B .. 113
3.4   A walk into Littondale. Category B 115

Walks around Buckden
3.5   Buckden Pike and Tor Mere Top from Buckden.
        Category B+ 117
3.6   Two walks round Hubberholme, Cray and Yockenthwaite.
        Category B 118

Walks from Arncliffe
3.7   Arncliffe to Malham Tarn. Category B+ 121
3.8   The traverse of Fountains Fell. Category A 122

ABOUT KILNSEY, KETTLEWELL AND BUCKDEN

Kilnsey

Kilnsey Crag is the most striking feature in Wharfedale, yet not a single walk goes by it, for Kilnsey lost its riverside right of way paths years ago. The nearest is Mastiles Lane which ends in the hamlet but fails to give sight of the crag. The best views are from the road. Mastiles Lane is an essential part of Kilnsey. In monastic days it was a packhorse way linking Kilnsey, the base of Fountains Abbey's commercial operations in Wharfedale, with its properties in Malham. Today it is partly metalled and hard cored and is in danger of being converted to a motor road. There are traces of the monastic days to be seen even now in some of the old buildings at the back of the village - door and window heads with a look of church architecture about them. There remains too, the old manor house with the date 1648 over the door. Nothing of its former splendours remain, for it is used as a barn and is now crumbling away.

Kilnsey's place in present day Wharfedale life is assured by its pub, its trout farm, open to visitors, and in the summer, pony trekking.

Kilnsey Crag

Climbing on the crag would surely bring trade, but it is forbidden at weekends because of the traffic congestion it has caused in the past. The big overhang was first climbed in 1957. It is worth noting that the crag was formed partly by glacier action and partly by the cutting action of the river at the end of the last Ice Age.

Kettlewell

In many ways Kettlewell is the most picturesque village in the Dales. It lies in a deep cleft on the flank of the dale and has many fine old houses nestling close to the beck side. Yet its church and school, often noteworthy buildings, are Victorian and uninteresting. By contrast, it has a surprisingly large number of old pubs for so small a place, a reminder of the days when Kettlewell was a market town on the coaching road from Keighley to Richmond. It was involved in lead mining but never to such an extent as Grassington.

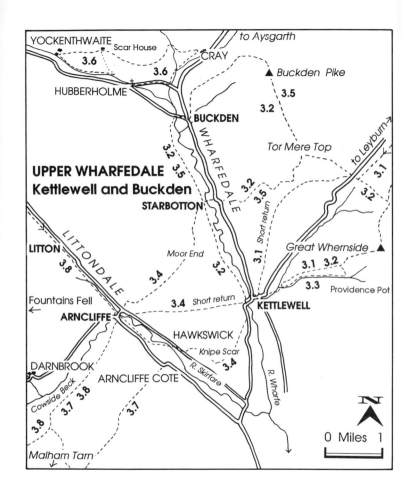

Buckden

Buckden is the highest village in the valley, though there are higher houses and farms. In the days following the Norman Conquest this part of Wharfedale was hunting forest belonging to the Percys of Northumberland and Buckden was one of their hunting lodges. Today the village inn is still called the Buck. More importantly for today's walkers the village has a car park with toilets and picnic areas and can be used as a starting point for some of these walks if other more convenient parking areas are full.

WALKS FROM KETTLEWELL

For these walks park in the car park just over the New Bridge as you come into the village from Threshfield. It's a pleasant spot by the river and there are toilets in the village on the right.

3.1 Great (704m) and Little (607m) Whernside

Great Whernside alone is rather too short to give a good day's walking but the addition of Little Whernside converts it into an excellent day of about 6 hours duration. Little Whernside is a 2,000-foot top by the skin of its teeth and the traverse to it gives fine views into upper Nidderdale, but the return to the top of the Park Rash road can be extremely wet.

NOTE: THE PATH FROM HAG DIKE TO THE TOP OF GREAT WHERNSIDE IS NOT A RIGHT OF WAY AND THE LANDOWNER IS ATTEMPTING TO STOP WALKERS USING IT. IN DUE COURSE IT WILL GO TO A PUBLIC ENQUIRY, MEANWHILE YOU TAKE A CHANCE.

Category A. Map: 1:25,000 Outdoor Leisure 2 Yorkshire Dales Western Area. Park in the Y.D.N.P. car park by the bridge.

From the car park turn left and take the road that goes past the public conveniences. In 200 yards turn left along the road to Leyburn, then go straight across the little cross roads at the King's Arms. This road becomes a rough lane and 100 yards further on it crosses a bridge. Immediately turn right and go into the field at the gate.

Go up the field to a stile in the wall, then follow tractor tracks until they suddenly pull to the right. Here you go straight on to find the stile. Just beyond the second steep bit the main tractor route goes into a field, but you keep to the right of the wall and follow the very pleasant grassy track up to Hag Dike[1]. The path goes through its gate to the stile to the left of the house. Now turn left but bear away from the wall towards the collection of cairns on the top of the stony escarpment. From them a well marked track leads across the moor and more steeply up to the rocky summit. On a fine day the views are very wide. Unless the

Kettlewell and Great Whernside

weather is clear the next stage can be a bit tricky. The long top of Great Whernside, though it's the boundary of the Park, has neither wall nor fence to guide you.

A vague path runs along it passing a large hollow cairn (useful for lunch on a poor day) and continues, here and there, to a wall corner* on the grassy ridge that veers right towards Little Whernside. Keep on this grassy ridge following a pleasant path beside the wall to the col below Little Whernside. On the way down you will pass a little gate; note it carefully, for you return to this point for the descent, remaking quite a bit of height. Soon after it the main track veers to the right to descend to Nidderdale. Look out for a branch to the left that follows the wall and continues to the top of Little Whernside which is crowned with a mass of incipient peat hags - very hard going. The summit is marked by a little heap of stones topped with a defiant fence post. Return to the gate mentioned above and descend by a well marked track, very wet. towards the end, to the road by the cattle grid.

Note: If the weather deteriorates or you think going out to Little Whernside will take too long (it's a good 2 hours from the wall corner marked * and back to the road by the cattle grid), it can be omitted by descending to the road direct from the wall corner marked *.

Things of Interest

1. Hag Dike was given to the 1st. Ben Rhydding Scout Group in 1947.
2. Tor Dyke as marked on the map is said to be an Iron Age fortification but there's little to be seen by the untutored eye.
3. The lane by which you descend to Kettlewell is part of a packhorse

road associated with the days when lead was mined and smelted in Kettlewell. It continued over into Nidderdale.

3.2 The Traverse of Great Whernside, Tor Mere Top and Buckden Pike

Without doubt the finest fell walk in Wharfedale. Much of it is hard going and it can be exceedingly wet. SEE THE NOTE AT THE START OF THE PREVIOUS WALK. It is best done starting in Kettlewell and returns there by riverside paths, taking about 8 hours including a stop of 30-40 minutes. Both maps 1:25,000 Outdoor Leisure 10 Yorkshire Dales Southern Area and 1:25,000 Outdoor Leisure 30 Yorkshire Dales Northern and Central Areas are needed. Category A.

Follow Walk 3.1 as far as the wall corner* then turn left down the side of the wall and follow the path down to the Leyburn road close to the cattle grid.

Here there are two alternatives; the first is shorter but very wet. Go across the road onto a green track some 50 yards right of the grid and keep left at the fork ahead. (At the moment it bears a bold notice: Private Land No Access.) Continue over the boggy moor to a stile in the wire fence. The rough, very wet path continues to follow the fence to Tor Mere Top from where it follows the wall to the top of Buckden Pike.

Alternatively, continue to follow Walk 3.1 to the signpost at the junction of the Kettlewell and Starbotton tracks and there go steeply up the hillside for about 100 yards to a ladder stile. Now simply follow the wall to Buckden Pike, reversing Walk 3.5, and crossing the ladder stile to reach the trig point and descend to Buckden. The path is well marked all the way but does not leave the summit as shown on the map. It arrives in the car park (toilets) and on leaving it (village shop opposite, The Buck a little further on), cross the grass to the Hubberholme road and follow this down to the river bridge. Just beyond it a stile puts you onto the riverside path that takes you back to Kettlewell. It is a justly popular route, well trodden, and all changes of direction are signposted.

3.3 A walk up Dowber Gill to Providence Pot

This walk may take a bit longer than you think because it's climbing all the way once you've left the lane and some of it is rather rough. Allow 2½ hours at least. Category B. Map: 1.25,000 Outdoor Leisure 30

Upper Wharfedale with Buckden Pike on the right

Yorkshire Dales Northern and Central Areas.

Start exactly as Walk 3.1 and follow it up to the point where you go into the field. Now you turn sharp right in the field and follow the path up the beck all the way.

The notorious Providence Pot stands like a square man hole in the bed of the stream just below a Y-shaped junction of two streams. It is indeed a square concrete man hole with an iron lid through which you can peep into the dark shaft below. Originally it was just a slit in the bed of the stream into which flood water and stones could pour, a big hazard to any potholers below.

Just above the pot on the right bank of the stream is Providence Mine, the old lead mine from which the pot takes its name. The spoil heaps are very obvious, but if you want to see the remains of the old crushing floor and the pit that housed the waterwheel that powered the crushing machinery, you must scramble up the steep hillside. The crushing machinery has been restored by the Earby Mine Research Group and can be seen in its museum in the Old Grammar School, Earby. (See Lead Mining chapter.)

To return, either retrace your steps, or, better, if you have any puff left, climb the steep track that starts by the man hole. It soon eases and becomes faint at a sort of ridge running up the hillside. Follow this ridge up to Hag Dike where you pick up the access path and follow it easily down the hill to Kettlewell. There are stiles all the way. The openness and fine views across Wharfedale are a great contrast to the feeling of being shut in you may have experienced in the deep-cut gill.

114

Note: The bit of path from the pot hole to the Hag Dike path is not a right of way.

3.4 A walk into Littondale

Littondale is divided from Wharfedale by Old Cotes Moor, a long rib of moor that has five ways across it. This walk uses two of them. The others are much longer and perhaps not so worth while. The valley has an excellent path from Hawkswick to Foxup. There is limited parking at Arncliffe which is a good place to explore from on a 'there and back' type of walk. Otherwise this walk uses the path from Hawkswick to Arncliffe and can be started from there equally well or it can be done the other way round just as pleasurably. Category B. Time: About 5½ hours; shortened by over an hour by the direct return to Kettlewell from Arncliffe. Map: 1:25,000 Outdoor Leisure 10 Yorkshire Dales Southern Areas and 1:25,000 Outdoor Leisure 30 Yorkshire Dales Northern and Central Areas.

Turn right on leaving Kettlewell car park, cross the Wharfe by the New Bridge and go about ¼ of a mile along the road to a gate on the right. Ignore the level grassy track ahead and at once climb up diagonally right and you will find a good, if stony, track. This climbs quite steeply through the wood up to some ruined buildings. Go between them to a stile that is out of sight at the top of the wood. Turn left here, and in general keep going left and up. The path is well marked at first but becomes less so as the ground levels out. Look out for the ladder stile on the right and don't go downhill until you've crossed it. Beyond it the way to Hawkswick is clear.

Turn right on the road and continue to the footbridge. Cross it and the riverside path starts on the other side. It is waymarked and generally the next stile can be seen except when quite near Arncliffe. Then drop down to the river and you will find it. The path comes out, rather surprisingly, in the vicarage yard, a fine house which you have been able to see for some time. Turn right on the road and pause on the river bridge. Here you have an option. If you now prefer to return direct to Kettlewell instead of going to Starbotton, you may easily do so. (See Note A below.)

If you're going on to Starbotton, cross the bridge, and straight opposite there's a stile and a path that leads very steeply up the hill to join the main track that starts a bit further left along the road. Follow this cart track right up the fell to the wall that runs down the full length of Old Cotes Moor. It is waymarked in blue. As you go over the stile here the view appears with breath-taking suddenness: Buckden Pike and Tor Mere Top are opposite, Great Whernside a little to the right. Go straight down the fell - the path becomes faint on the limestones pastures - and you will find a ladder stile. Cross this and the track suddenly becomes very well marked and runs quite steeply down through the wood to the footbridge over to Starbotton. Turn right here and follow the waymarked field path back to Kettlewell. It's easy to find but if you want any guidance turn to the last few lines of walk 3.2.

Note A

Cross the river bridge and take the field path immediately to the right. This usefully cuts the corner and brings you onto the road with the stile of the Kettlewell path straight opposite which slants steeply up the hill through Byre Bank Wood and is steep and rocky towards the top. The path is waymarked in orange and is reasonably clear through the heather right up to the long wall that runs the length of the moor. From here the views are excellent. Keep heading the same way, cross a stile and follow the path down to the top of the crag below. The descent through the Slit is easy if very steep, and the way back to Kettlewell is now obvious.

Points to watch if you go the other way round

Having crossed the Wharfe take the second gate on the right. You will see a track climbing very steeply up to a crag above you on the left. It looks impracticable but is really easy. From the top of this aim for a point in the skyline half-way along a limestone scar. Then it's clear enough down to Arncliffe. The path through the vicarage yard is signposted, so is the start of the bridleway at Hawkswick. It is well marked to the top of the fell, but over the ladder stile fainter. Keep diagonally left until you find the well marked path.

Things of Interest

This is a good naturalists' walk and has fine views down Wharfedale from Knipe Scar, the first high point reached. Hawkswick is of Scandinavian origin and is mentioned in Domesday Book. The stretch of river between it and Arncliffe is rich in bird life. If you move quietly you may see the grey and pied wagtails, dipper, sandpiper, sandmartins, even the kingfisher and stately heron. Byre Bank Wood is a piece of ancient woodland. The ground is too steep for sheep to graze intensively and the trees have been able to regenerate themselves. In springtime it is rich in flowers.

WALKS AROUND BUCKDEN

3.5 Buckden Pike (702m) and Tor Mere Top from Buckden

Not quite so fine a walk as either walks 3.1 or 3.2 but it is less demanding. There are fine views down Wharfedale during the long descent of the ridge to Tor Mere Top. This walk has the option of a fairly direct descent to Starbotton should the weather deteriorate, or an extension to Kettlewell. All the variants then return to Buckden by the banks of the River Wharfe, but, should your timing be right, a return to Buckden by bus may be possible. Like Walk 3.2 it has very wet sections but no route finding problems. For that reason it is Category B+, though the extension to Kettlewell is rated A because of its length. Map: 1:25,000 Outdoor Leisure 30 Yorkshire Dales Northern and Central Areas. Times: for the route as described, 4½ hours; for the short return, 4 hours; for the extension to Kettlewell, 6 hours.

Leave the car park (toilets) by the gate at the northern end and climb steadily up the wide track to Cray as far as the second gate, a short mile. Bear right just after the gate onto a wide green track and follow this easily over the moor towards the limestone escarpment. There's just one place to watch: after passing through a pair of stout stone gate posts in a broken-down wall go more steeply uphill to keep on the correct track. Now simply follow the well used track all the way to the summit cairn and trig point. (Note that this track does not follow the right of way track shown on the map. Its route has been changed since the map was published.)

Having enjoyed wide views and possibly puzzled over the identity of Pen-y-ghent and Ingleborough, cross the stile, turn right and continue to follow the wall the length of the moor to Tor Mere Top, about an hour away with many boggy patches. You will pass a memorial cross to five Polish airmen who were killed in a crash nearby in January 1942. The sole survivor followed the tracks of a fox in the snow to the valley and found help, which is why a bronze fox's head is built into the base of the cross. At the corner of the wall beyond it there is a little gate. If you want the shorter descent to Starbotton go through it and turn to Note A, below.

Otherwise continue to follow the wall on your right as it swings about the moor continuing right over the Top, an undistinguished hump not possessing a cairn, down to a good ladder stile in a wall corner just above the Starbotton Road. If you are extending the walk to Kettlewell go down to the Starbotton Road to the fingerpost and follow the Kettlewell track from there. See Note B, below. The track takes you into the Leyburn road at the second corner where you turn right to reach the village. Otherwise bear right to pick up the Starbotton Road rather more conveniently. Now simply follow this wide track, open and grassy at first, then stony between walls right down to the hamlet of Starbotton. There are fine views of the end of the ridge of Buckden Pike which looks quite impressive across the great hollow of Cam Gill Beck. In Starbotton itself continue down to the main road: turn right to find the Fox and Hounds if you need refreshments, left to find the gate for the riverside path. This starts on the right at the very end of the houses and a lane takes you down to the river bridge. From here a wide, well used track takes you up to the river bridge on the road between Buckden and Hubberholme, overshooting Buckden by about ¼ mile to do so. All changes of direction on the path are well signposted.

Note A
A well trodden path leads from the gate to a ruined building on the edge of a steeper section of path. Carry on here, and where the path levels somewhat and is joined by one from the left, continue to the right, traversing round the head of Cam Gill Beck on a good track that leads right down to Starbotton.

Note B
Having reached Kettlewell where there are toilets and plenty of places for refreshment, continue to the bridge over the River Wharfe, cross it and go through the stile on the right. Turn right and follow the well marked riverside path to Starbotton where you simply continue to Buckden.

3.6 Two walks around Hubberholme, Cray and Yockenthwaite
This is really one long walk that can be divided neatly into two roughly equal halves by the rough road that goes up to Scar House from the

right-hand side of the church. If you haven't time for the whole, which will take 2-2½ hours, the first half as it is given here is the finer unless you've a passion for riverside paths. Category B. Can be done either way round equally well. Park as best you can by the river at Hubberholme. Map: 1:25,000 Outdoor Leisure 30 Yorkshire Dales Northern and Central Areas

Before you start, spare a few minutes for a look at the church. Many Dales churches have lost their original character in the 'restorations' of the last century, but St Michael and All Angels at Hubberholme has not. It is still small, squat and rugged. It was built some time in the twelfth century as a chapel in the forest of Langstrothdale Chase, and the rough arches and piers of the northern aisle date back from that period. The rest of the church dates from the sixteenth century when the tower was added and a good deal of it rebuilt. Its main claim to fame is its rood loft. Rood lofts are exceedingly rare in England, never mind in Yorkshire. They are the galleries where the musicians sat before the day of the church organ and most of them were destroyed in Puritan times. This one is neither large nor elaborate; one wouldn't expect it in a small church like this. On a sunny morning, it is best seen from the chancel side, when you will see quite how finely carved it is and painted a dull yellow, red and black. It was constructed in 1588.

But to start our walk...Go along the road to Cray for a good ¼ mile

Path by Cray Gill

until a sizeable beck, Cray Gill, comes in on the left. There's a gate into the field here, and this is where the path starts, though rather faint at first. Keep close to the gill, a delightful stream with cascades, waterslides and falls and little gorges, all overhung by trees. Soon after you've crossed a little packhorse bridge[1] you will see a line of telegraph poles. Leave the beck and follow the poles climbing steeply up the hill to a gate in the wall corner below the farm. There's hardly any track and you're likely to pant a bit. Once at the farm you'll be pleased to know you've done all the climbing for the day.

Turn sharply left behind the house and go through the middle gate of three. In the second field make to the right of an isolated bit of wall and towards the barn. Pass behind it into the head of a stream, cross a stout little bridge and start walking a wonderful open terrace of level turf with fine views down Wharfedale.[2] Follow this all the way to Scar House, tucked away in a sheltered hollow. If you want the short walk, turn left past the farm and 10-15 minutes will see you back to your car.

Otherwise keep on through the gate with the orange waymarker disc. The route is now waymarked all the way, but down to Yockenthwaite it is not as clear as it might be. From the end of the terrace the path goes through a plantation of sycamores, across a narrow bridge and at once drops steeply down the field to a slightly lower terrace. When you're above Raisgill Farm which is now on the road opposite, keep a look-out for an arrow that points down the hill towards Yockenthwaite. Soon after the path turns right along a wall, even climbs up a bit until it is directly above Yockenthwaite[3] and takes the old fell road down to the hamlet. A signpost beneath a pair of mighty sycamores directs you to the path back to Hubberholme by the river. It is well trodden and waymarked all the way back to the Scar Head road just behind the church.

Things of Interest

1.   The bridge is thought to have been on an old packhorse route that went from Askrigg to Settle in the days before carts where used to carry goods. The path is too steep for a horse and cart to manage.

2.   On the left lies Buckden Pike, 2,300 feet, and on the right the flank of the moor is called Birks Fell. The word 'birks' appears in several place names round there and has its origin in the Danish word 'birk' and the Norwegian word 'bjork', both meaning birch tree. This is a pointer to the common tree in those days of the tenth century when Scandinavian

Yockenthwaite

peoples migrated into northern England. Place names are a good indication of the origins of the people who founded a settlement. Cray, for example, is of Celtic origin, over a thousand years old. There are not many birch trees on the fell today but there's a good deal of planted pine. The flatness of the valley bottom is well seen from here. During the melting at the end of the last Ice Age a large lake formed here and the silt deposited in it made this level floor.

3.   Yockenthwaite is a fine example of a Georgian farmhouse, probably built around the middle of the eighteenth century. It is unlikely that it was the first house here. The word ending -thwaite indicates the place was colonised by the Danes, and there are remains of ancient walls and enclosures on the fell above. Not far from Yockenthwaite there is a Bronze Age burial mound but it is not visited on this walk.

WALKS FROM ARNCLIFFE

3.7 Arncliffe to Malham Tarn

This walk uses the so called Monk's road from Arncliffe to the tarn and then returns by Gordale Beck and Cote Gill to Hawkswick Cote. It then uses field paths to return to Arncliffe.[1] Category B+, time about 6½ hours. Maps: Outdoor Leisure 10 Yorkshire Dales Southern Area. Park in Arncliffe as best you can. There is a little space over the bridge on the Malham Road.

Turn up the lane by the side of the pub and after a few minutes leave it at a finger post on the right signed to Malham. The track climbs steeply up the hillside at first then traverses the limestone areas above Cowside Beck reaching Dew Bottoms[2] after about an hour. It continues over the limestone pastures, is fairly well trodden and supplied with ladder stiles at almost every wall until it reaches Middle House Farm, recently restored. After you have crossed the stile on the skyline you look down onto the wide open spaces of Great Close and descend towards the fence at the bottom of the hill. Keep straight on at the sharp corner of the cart track and continue first to a stile beside the gate then to the dip in the skyline just to the right of Great Close Hill. Here you will have a surprise view of the tarn[3], much bigger and nearer than you ever expected.

Bear left to the road and leave it for the cart track that runs left beneath the crag. Cut the corner to the right behind the wood to regain Middle House Farm's road. (If you are short of time you can stay on this road, but you won't see the tarn and the road is a bit dreary.) Now follow the road to where it makes a sharp bend to the right and here go through the gate on the left, Street Gate. Immediately follow the broad green cart track that goes diagonally left. It crosses Gordale Beck - a bit splashy and then climbs steadily and unmistakably upwards. There's a sudden view of Buckden Pike and Great Whernside as you breast the hill, then go steadily down leftwards into the head of Cote Gill. It soon swings to the right and is clear right the way to the road at Arncliffe Cote.

Here turn right and follow the road for about $\frac{1}{4}$ mile to the path and the footbridge to Hawkswick; here take the footpath back to Arncliffe. See Walk 3.4.

3.8 The traverse of Fountains Fell

This walk reaches the foot of Fountains Fell by the so-called Monk's Road, traverses it to the head of the Stainforth - Halton Gill road then takes the green lane down to Litton and returns by riverside paths. It is long but most of it is easy going and there are few route finding problems. It has a great deal of variety and the best time to go is late May. Category A. Time: about $6\frac{1}{2}$-7 hours. Maps: Outdoor Leisure 10 Yorkshire Dales Southern Area, and Outdoor Leisure 30 Yorkshire

Dales Northern and Central Areas. Park in Arncliffe as best you can. There is a little space over the bridge on the Malham road.

Start as the previous walk and follow it to a dip in the skyline just to the right of Great Close hill above Malham Tarn, then bear right a little to join the approach road to the field studies centre[4] just as it enters a wood. Turn right and follow the track past the house and outbuildings, continuing until to the first stile on the right, marked with the Pennine Way acorn symbol*. The footpath follows the wall keeping it always on your left and crosses just one stile. At the second stile turn left and climb up to the Arncliffe-Malham road.

Turn right on the road and after only 100 yards take the gravel track on the left that goes to Tennant Gill farm. The Way leaves the farm track just as it goes into the farmyard and climbs up to a gate. Beyond the gate turn left and shortly you will come to a broken-down wall. Turn right and follow the greensward by the wall to its very end. At this point a well defined tractor route continues up the fell but the correct route turns sharp right here. The spot is marked by a small cairn but many have been deceived.

The path continues, wet and peaty but well defined, all the way to the stile in the cross-wall on Fountains Fell. The true summit, marked by a large cairn, is about 5 minutes away on your left, and you will notice many small depressions[5] in the ground as you go. Return to the stile, cross it, and follow the well-made track that deteriorates to a badly eroded ramp that was the road to the nineteenth century coal pits on the summit plateau. It takes you unmistakably to the wall which you then follow to the road. Turn right and in less than 10 minutes bear right onto the grassy bridleway that goes down to Litton. There's no need to go into Litton unless you wish to - there's a pub if the time of day is right - but some 300 yards from the village bear right through a gate at a finger post signed to Arncliffe. About 100 yards after splashing across a ford turn right into the field at a finger post to Arncliffe. This puts you on the start of the field path, at first on the river banks,[6] later cutting directly across a big loop of river to join a stony lane that brings you to the Malham-Arncliffe road by the river bridge. A couple of minutes straight ahead returns you to the village.

Things of Interest on these two walks
1.   Arncliffe is a village of character built round a spacious village green. It is believed to date back to very early times and to have been

built around the green so that the cattle could be brought safely into it at night. Clearly it has been rebuilt since then. The pub has only a six-day licence, though you may find ice-cream etc. on sale. As you start to climb up to Dew Bottoms, the wettish pastures have some of the finest Dales' flowers. In May you'll find that choice little flower, bird's-eye primrose, rather like a tiny pink polyanthus. There's the early purple orchid, unmistakably brilliant, and higher up, the yellow mountain pansy speckles the ground, turning its face to the sun. As the path climbs the scar there are good views into Yew Cogar Beck which runs on the usually porous limestone only because most of its course is lined with boulder clay.

2.   After about an hour's walking you come to a fairly large piece of limestone pavement on the right. This is Dew Bottoms. It is worth going over for a better look if you have time, for it contains traces of old enclosures and huts that are thought to date back to the Iron Age. There are other ancient fields just past Middle House Farm. Look over the wall by the solitary sycamore tree and you'll see a jumble of stone walls enclosing a number of microscopically small fields. By way of contrast, very shortly afterwards you drop down into Great Close, which as its name suggests, is the biggest field or close in the dale. In the eighteenth century when cattle were driven from Scotland through the Dales to the English towns and markets they were rested and fattened here before the final trip to market. It has a great boggy patch on the left. In the times soon after the last Ice Age when all the countryside was wooded, this bog hole never grew any trees and so has retained some of the arctic-alpine flora that grew just after the last Ice Age. These are very rare plants indeed and not particularly attractive.

3.   For a note on Malham Tarn see the geological notes to the Malham walks. Lapwings and curlews nest in the rough ground around the Tarn, and ducks of various sorts can often be seen swimming on it.

4.   Malham Tarn House, which you see across the tarn, was presented with its estate to the National Trust and is run as a field study centre. Besides doing scientific work, it runs courses on various aspects of natural history in the Dales. These are not too technical for the ordinary person to enjoy and will give increased appreciation of the countryside. The house itself is an eighteenth-century farmhouse which had been used as a shooting lodge and was bought in 1885 by a wealthy industrialist, James Morrison. He had many intellectual friends and study groups were in fashion even then. The limestone cutting you go

through just after passing the house was made by him to make the passage of heavily laden farm carts easier.

5.   Fountains Fell takes its name from Fountains Abbey which owned this and other vast acreages of land in the Dales. The start of the path is on the well drained ground of the Carboniferous and Yoredale limestones. Higher up you come onto the Millstone Grit layers. Here the plant life changes. Peaty ground with cotton grass, a little heather and bilberry is found. On the first of the two tops the coal of the Yoredales is close to the surface, no more than 60 to 100 feet down and was mined from bell pits from 1790 to 1860. A bell pit, as the name suggests, is just a shaft that opens out at the bottom like a bell. It is the simplest possible manner of mining, requiring no props or draught. When the bell becomes dangerously large, another pit is started. That's why there are so many of the rocky depressions that were the shafts on the summit plateau. Two of these old shafts remain reasonably intact and are fenced around. This coal was used for calcining the ore produced from Pikedaw Calamine Mine, for lime burning and for local domestic use.

6.   The walk down Littondale is far from the road, quiet and pastoral. Near the stream which may disappear in dry weather, you will find primroses, water avens, violets, celandine and wild strawberry in spring, and a much rarer plant, common scurvy grass. It isn't a grass at all; in fact its leaf is shaped like the ace of spades, and the flowers are a little head of white four-petalled florets. There are many ash trees, especially in the wood on the hillsides, which are best spotted in late May when they are still leafless and all the other trees are in leaf. Ash is a very common tree of the limestone dales.

4: AIREDALE

Walks around Malham Cove, Gordale Scar and the Tarn

4.1   A short visit to the Cove. Category C 130
4.2   The Cove and Gordale Scar returning by Janet's Foss.
        Category B 130
4.3   The Cove, Gordale Scar, Weets Top and Hanlith.
        Category B 131
4.4   The Cove, Gordale Scar, Weets Top and Calton
        Category B 132
4.5   A visit to Janet's Foss and Gordale Scar. Category C 132
4.6   Continuation to the Water Sink, returning by the
        Dry Valley and the Cove. Category B 133
4.7   A walk to Malham Tarn. Category B 134

Other Walks

4.8   Pikedaw, Nappa Cross and Langscar Gate. Category B .. 138
4.9   Fountains Fell. Category B 141
4.10   Mastiles Lane and Bordley. Category B 141

ABOUT SKIPTON AND MALHAM

Skipton 'belongs' to Airedale in much the same way as Richmond 'belongs' to Swaledale and neither of them is in the Yorkshire Dales National Park. For most Lancastrians it is the gateway to Wharfedale and is worth an afternoon of anybody's time especially if the weather is unkind. There's more than one large car park.

Skipton is a very ancient place of Anglo-Danish origin. The name means 'sheeptown' and even today a town centre street is called Sheep Street. The Liverpool and Leeds Canal passes through the town and has contributed to the town's economy in past times, carrying coal, lime, limestone, agricultural products and textiles. Today the town still has a small textile industry but it is predominantly an agricultural centre. You will find a variety of shops and cafes as well as the ubiquitous supermarkets. There are elegant shops selling clothes and antiques, workaday shops supplying farmers' needs, others specialising in books and maps with a local flavour, others in equipment for outdoor pursuits.

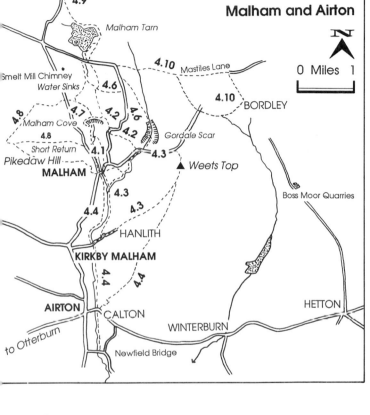

to Fountains Fell

4.9

AIREDALE
Malham and Airton

N

0 Miles 1

Malham Tarn

4.10 Mastiles Lane

Smelt Mill Chimney
Water Sinks

4.6

4.10 BORDLEY

4.8

4.7 4.2 4.6

Malham Cove

4.2

Gordale Scar

4.8

Short Return

Pikedaw Hill

4.1

4.3

▲ Weets Top

MALHAM

4.3

Boss Moor Quarries

4.4

4.3

HANLITH

KIRKBY MALHAM

4.4 4.4

AIRTON CALTON

HETTON

to Otterburn

WINTERBURN

Newfield Bridge

However, it has a great deal more to offer the visitor than shops. First, there's the castle at the head of High Street. It probably dates from 1150, but was enlarged and strengthened by Robert Clifford in 1307 when he added the round towers which were then the latest thing in defensive structures; an idea that came back with the Crusaders who had observed how effective they were. The castle was the seat of the Clifford family who were Lords of the Manor of Skipton for centuries. It was partly demolished on Cromwell's orders after the Civil War and

127

restored by the redoubtable Lady Anne Clifford who also restored Barden Tower. The entry fee to the castle includes an admirable broadsheet which in effect gives you a personal guided tour. Next to the castle, not at the other end of the street as in the usual case, is the church. It is large and much restored but still very well worth a visit, if only to see the elaborate tombs of the Clifford family. The church backs onto the canal and across it is the George Leate's Corn Mill, now an industrial and folk museum. There has been a water-powered corn mill on this site since the early days of the castle; today you can see wheat ground as it used to be, but only on Sunday afternoons as a rule.

Quite different is the Craven Museum, housed in the Town Hall, High Street. It is open on Mondays, Wednesdays, and Fridays from 2 - 5pm all the year round, all day Saturday (except lunch hours) but never on Sundays. A large section is devoted to archaeology, a well organised display including a considerable amount of material from the Dales. In addition there is a display of former lead mining machinery and tools, such as heavy chisels and hammers, rollers and crushers as well as such human items as the leather caps with long tails to keep dripping water from running down a man's back. Much of this is put into perspective by a local watercolour painting showing how Grassington Moor must have looked in the early years of the nineteenth century, when lead mining was at its height. It is based on Arthur Raistrick's work and interpretations of what remains on the moor, and should be high on the list of anyone who is interested in early mining and intends to do the walks in this book. There are some extremely good specimens of minerals associated with lead mining.

This does not exhaust the supply of worthwhile exhibits in the museum. If you've ever wondered why so many pubs in the Dales are called 'The Craven Heifer', you will see a painting of this prize beast which was raised at Bolton Abbey at the time when there was a great interest in improving breeds of cattle. There are also many relics of bygone Skipton, as you would expect.

Across the road, the public library has a fine section on local history which can be looked at on request. It contains some quite rare books about the Craven dales.

Malham is the most popular village in the south-west of the Park, and with good cause. It really nestles in its green fields with the Cove as a backdrop, not too far, just enough to draw you on. It has very good facilities for visitors and a wealth of first class walks start from the village. No wonder there are pressures on the environment and footpath erosion has become a problem. A great deal of effort has gone into remaking the popular paths. The prime example is the new path to the foot of the Cove and the flight of steps leading to the top. There is no easier way, so people keep to the path, unsightly erosion scars have been eliminated and the pasture is preserved intact for sheep.

There is a large car park at the entrance to the village on the road from Airton which is often full. There is additional parking (fee) at Town Head Farm, the last farm on the right on the road to Settle. Otherwise you will have to do the best you can on the grass verges. The Y.D.N.P. Information Centre is next to the car park and is well worth a visit. It has some superb life-size photos - no not quite! - of the Cove, and shows something of the problems caused by too many visitors to the wonders of the Cove and Gordale Scar. It has displays demonstrating something of the features that make up the local landscape and should enhance anyone's enjoyment of it. Besides that, there is a little notice board that tells you what's on elsewhere in the Dales.

The village itself is of very ancient origin. The lands of the valley were occupied sometime around the seventh century by the Anglo-Saxons, as shown by the -ham and -ton endings of most of the village names. But not Kirkby Malham. This is of Scandinavian origin, possibly as late as the ninth or tenth century. The Scandinavians were sheep farmers and occupied the land of Malham Moor, founding the isolated farms there. Most of Malham's houses date from the late seventeenth or early eighteenth century, built by the prosperous yeomen farmers of the time. The best examples are probably Town Head Farm and Beck Hall, with its clapper bridge. Lead, copper and zinc were mined but the industry never had the effect on the village that it had on Grassington.

WALKS AROUND MALHAM COVE, GOREDALE SCAR AND THE TARN

Quite a number of walks go by one or the other of these two spectacular limestone cliffs which are the essence of Malham's scenery. Each of the first four is a logical extension of the previous one, and they are amongst the best short walks in the whole of the Y.D.N.P. spectacular scenery, fine pasture and riverside paths. The second one could be called Malham's classic short walk.

The first and fifth are in Category C. the rest in B. The first two and the fifth hardly need a map, they are so well waymarked. The others need the 1:25,000 Outdoor Leisure 10 Yorkshire Dales Southern Area map.

Some of the things of interest are common to more than one walk and so are lumped together at the end of this group of walks.

4.1 A short visit to the Cove
Time: about 1 hour. Category C. This is an easy walk suitable for those who haven't enough puff to climb the great flight of steps that takes you to the top of the Cove.

Turn left on leaving the car park and follow the Settle road for 100 yards past the Town Head Farm to a swing gate on the right. From it a well-made path leads almost to the foot of the Cove, though you may have to splash about a bit to see the water flowing[1] from a dark opening at the bottom of the beetling cliff. Retrace your steps to the first swing gate and a good 100 yards beyond it cross the stream by a little flag bridge. Bear right up the hillside to find a gravel path that takes you to a lane that emerges in the village by the Listers Arms. Turn right and 5 minutes walk sees you back to your car.

4.2 The Cove and Gordale Scar returning by Janet's Foss
Time: about 2½ hours. Category B.

This walk extends the previous one from the start of the steps on the left-hand side of the Cove. Go up these steps, a solidly built stone staircase some 270-280 feet high that take you onto the limestone pavement running across the top of the Cove. Take care when it's wet; it can be very slippery. Cross the pavement to the right to a stile,[2] then keep straight up the hillside for about 50 yards until you see a yellow-topped waymarker post. Follow these posts to a wall corner when the track you join becomes plain and takes you down to the road. It is important to keep to the rights of way here.

The next stile is across the road and the green track you join is not so easy to see. First look over the road side wall at the fields to the left (east) of the Cove. These are Malham's prehistoric fields.[3] Now keep going down to the wall and follow it until you come to a stile on the right. Cross it and keep left down the field to Gordale Bridge. Turn left

Malham Cove

along the road, and the stile leading to the Scar is on the left, just before the farm. Follow the well-made path as far as the waterfall where you are well within those towering, almost overwhelming portals. Then retrace your steps to the road, turn right and in less than 200 yards you will find the start of the path to Janet's Foss[4] and the village. The way through the wood, a deep cleft called Little Gordale, is obvious. When you have passed the second barn turn sharp right and follow a line of waymarking posts across the field to the footbridge onto the road 20 or 30 yards from the car park.

4.3 The Cove, Gordale Scar, Weets Top and Hanlith
Time: about 3½ hours. Category B.

This picks up the previous walk at Gordale Farm. Alternatively you can start direct from Malham. See Walk 4.5 and deduct ¾ of an hour. Continue up the road to the walled track on the right almost at the top of the hill. Ten minutes along it will bring you to Weets Top,[5] a fine viewpoint. Now follow the path signposted 'Windy Pike'. After a few minutes at a fork in the path take the right-hand one that leads to a gate. Go down the field to the bottom right-hand corner where you will enter a walled lane which takes you down to Hanlith. There are fine views of the Cove and Gordale. Soon after you come onto the tarmac road it makes a couple of S bends. Right in the corner of the second is the signpost for the Pennine Way which you follow back to Malham. It is signposted and stiled all the way back.

4.4 The Cove, Gordale Scar, Weets Top and Calton
Time: about 5½ hours. Category B.

This one is really a much longer finish to the previous walk using a longer length of the Pennine Way by the river. It picks up the previous one at the fork in the path after Weets Top and takes the left-hand one. This path swings away from the wall and is never well marked; it is exposed to the wind and weather too. As you approach the first wall which will take you almost 30 minutes, keep high on the left of the stream to find a gate. Now the path is better marked for a time. It swings to the right when Airton comes into sight and then goes left again down to a gate onto a lane. Ford the stream (easy) and follow the lane through Calton to the tarmac road and so to the river by Airton Mill.[6] Here you will find the Pennine Way crossing the road. Turn right to get to Malham. It's perfectly plain with yellow dots of paint to guide you. Look out for a footbridge on the left across a minor stream soon after leaving Airton but do not cross the River Aire as well.

At Hanlith Bridge[7] the Pennine Way makes a diversion up the hill, but you cross the bridge and take the pleasant cart track on the other side and follow it all the way to the former mill, now holiday flats. Here the path continues to the left alongside it and then follows the former water leat in a most pleasant way through the fields to Malham. Just beyond the leat you will pass above a large spring. This is Aire Head, the source of the River Aire.

4.5 A visit to Janet's Foss and Gordale Scar
This must be second only to a visit to the Cove in popularity, and as far as the waterfall is Category C and will take a couple of hours there and back.

On leaving the car park turn left on the road for just 20 or 30 yards to a little footbridge that is not very obvious. Across it, turn right and follow a line of poles and stiles through the fields to the right of a barn. Turn left here and from the barn the way is obvious along a made path most of the way right to the road. Janet's Foss, a beautiful and unusual waterfall, is almost at the end of the wood. On the road turn right and

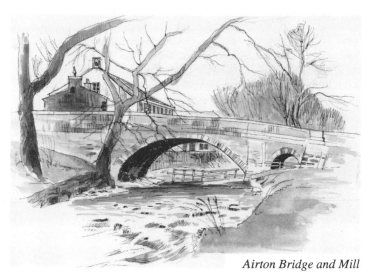

Airton Bridge and Mill

the stile to Gordale is on the left just before the farm. Again a well-made path leads into the amphitheatre below the waterfall. Retrace your steps when you are ready or continue as below.

4.6 Continuation to the Water Sink, returning by the Dry Valley and the Cove

The total time for this walk will be around $3\frac{1}{2}$ hours and it is Category B.

It involves a scramble up the waterfall which is not difficult but is certainly not walking. There's some rough going beyond the waterfall and on the return from the Water Sink. Not recommended in wet weather or if it's frosty.

Cross the stream and climb the waterfall on its left-hand side as you face it. The ground is very steep and rough for some distance beyond the top of it. Take great care not to dislodge stones onto anyone below. There is a second waterfall coming from a hole in a barrier across the gorge and soon after this point the path climbs left out of the gorge and this is your way. It leads onto some fine greensward between limestone pavements and continues for at least $\frac{1}{2}$ mile before reaching the road by a stile a couple of hundred yards beyond a solitary tree. Turn left on the road, and just across the cattle grid there is a snicket gate on the right. There is no right of way track to start with, and tracks are faint and confusing. It is best to follow the wall right to the Water Sinks, passing the Pennine Way stile on the way. Cross the stile by the Sinks, then turn left and follow the greensward by the wall that leads you to a path cut in the side of a little gorge and brings you to the head of the Dry Valley. Turn sharp left to find the stile and follow the Dry Valley right down to the limestone pavement at the top of the Cove. Turn right here and cross the limestone pavement at the top of the Cove to the stiles at the start of the long flight of steps down the side of the Cove. Then simply follow the path back to the road and your car.

4.7 A walk to Malham Tarn

There are four footpaths to the Tarn, so you are spoiled with choice. My recommendation is to go by the Cove and the Dry Valley and return by the Pennine Way. The Tarn has plenty of open space and footpaths to the Field Centre and there is a nature trail. It is not worth walking round the Tarn, there's too much road. Time: 2½ hours plus whatever is spent at the Tarn. Category B.

Follow Walk 4.1 then 4.2 to the top of the Cove. Cross the pavement taking great care if it is wet and muddy. Turn left when you reach the wall and stile and follow the Dry Valley until it ends at a stile. Turn sharp right here and follow a path cut into the hillside that goes into a little gorge, (actually the upper part of the Dry Valley), then follow the wall to the Water Sinks. Bear left here to find the gate onto the road. The Tarn is just beyond.

To return, turn right and walk along the road a little way to the Pennine Way signpost, turn right and keep straight up the slope to a stile. Now go past a couple of tiny pools and keep straight on a grassy track until you see the edge of the Cove. Here you have a choice of ways: cut down to the Cove and retrace your steps, or keep on this path to the road and go down the road. Strangely, this is the recommended option for its good southward views.

Alternative start

If you prefer a 'real' path, that is to say one that disappears from time to time but is far from the crowds that visit the Cove, then continue up the road past the start of the Cove path for about ½ mile to a slit stile on the right signed Dean Moor. Simply go up the fields to find the first

Malham Tarn

stile and continue in this direction all the way to the stile at the head of the Dry Valley where you join the main route. A wide but faint path develops and there are yellow waymarks from time to time to guide you.

Things of Interest

1. *The geology of the Cove, the Scar and their streams*

Both Malham Cove and Gordale Scar were formed by the thrusting actions of the Mid-Craven Fault, though not in the form they have today. The line of the fault escarpment has been cut back by weathering, particularly by the melt waters of the glaciers of the last Ice Age. Then all the crevices which drain ground water today were still frozen and the river from Malham Tarn came down the Dry Valley and poured over the edge of the Cove as a stupendous waterfall almost 300 feet (90 metres) high. The waterfall has been recorded as appearing in times of heavy flood right up to about 1850, but has never been observed within living memory. The glacial drift in the Dry Valley has by now been eroded away more thoroughly and the river from the Tarn now disappears partly by the road and more of it below the road, depending on how much rain there's been. Surprisingly the water that sinks here is not the water that reappears at the foot of the Cove. This comes from a stream that sinks into the ground near the smelt mill chimney on the moor and the Tarn water reappears at Aire Head Springs[8] just below the village. The courses of these underground streams have been traced using powerful dyestuffs.

If you have read the chapter 'The contribution of geology to the scenery of the Dales' you may be wondering how there came to be a Tarn in the middle of an expanse of limestone. Perhaps you will remember that the North Craven Fault runs just south of the Tarn, in

135

fact almost along the line of the road. North of it is an upthrust of Silurian slates, impervious to water, and for good measure covered with boulder clay. The terminal moraine of the glacier that scooped out the hollow of the Tarn holds up the water in the hollow. The Tarn is unique in the British Isles. It is the only one at so high an altitude (1,226 feet) with water alkaline from the dissolved lime. Altitude has a marked effect on climate and the combination produces a particularly interesting flora, especially in the boggy area, but there is no public access to this part.

In some ways Gordale Scar is even more impressive than the Cove, partly because of the sense of enclosure its overhanging walls produce. They are only about 30 feet (9 metres) apart at the waterfall and are 150 feet (27 metres) high. Clearly erosion had been more severe here than at the Cove. At one time it was thought that the gorge was formed by the collapse of a cavern, but that is now discounted and the effect of glacial melt water is favoured. The interesting question is, why does Gordale have a stream and the Cove not? It's not simply that the underground drainage system is still sealed by the glacial drift, but the waters of the stream, rising on Great Close Mire, are already saturated with lime when they arrive at the valley, and having thus lost their erosive powers, stay on the surface. They deposit some of their dissolved lime on the rocks of the waterfall making a soft deposit called tufa. There's more of it at Janet's Foss for the same reason.

The Cove faces south, dries quickly, and has become a favourite place for today's expert climbers - there's nothing here for beginners. The top of the Cove makes an excellent vantage point for watching climbers at work on the Right Wing where some very hard, good routes are located. Incredible as it may seem, the Main Overhang of the Cove has now been climbed without any aid from inserted bolts, though they are used for protection. The guide book recommends levitation as a means of progress. This and other climbs on the lower central section of the Cove can be observed from the footpath that leads to its foot.

Gordale, too has some extremely good modern hard climbs. As you come in sight of the lower waterfall the overhanging edge just to its left is climbed by a route called The Rebel, one of the first to be done here, using bolts and pegs for aid, in the style of the 1960s. It was climbed without aid in the 1980s. Cave Route, which you pass under as you enter the little amphitheatre of bulging rock, was first climbed with aid in 1956 and soon became a test piece for aspiring alpinists dreaming of the big wall routes of the Dolomites. It was first climbed without aid in 1982 by one of the mastermen of Yorkshire climbing, Pete Livesey - on his honeymoon to boot! New supermen have appeared on the scene and the Malham area is now internationally famous as a climbing ground as testing as any in Europe.

2. This long wall at the far side of the Cove that runs right up the Dry Valley dates back to monastic times. It divided the lands of Fountains Abbey from those of Bolton Priory. Those on the east of the wall belonged to Bolton Priory, those on the west to Fountains Abbey.

3. If you are wondering just what to look for, the illustration should make it clear. What you are seeing are the remains of the low boundary walls or banks of some ancient fields. Do you see that you walked right through them on the way to the Cove? You were too near to make out their shapes. There are more just over the road wall, but again, you can't see them from around here. These fields are thought to have been made sometime between 500 B.C. and A.D. 500 and are very similar to those at Grassington. The walls that make up today's fields were built between 1750 and 1800, but those on the moor not until 1850.

As you bear left in about 200 yards you come into sight of the tarmac road going past Gordale Farm to Bordley. On its left is a whole series of small fields each very markedly terraced. These terraces were made by the Anglo-Saxon farmers and are known as lynchets. See the chapter 'Man's contribution to scenery of The Dales' for more instruction.

The old field patterns
on the path to Malham Cove

137

Harking back to the geological side, you are walking behind Cawden Hill at this point, one of the most westerly of the reef knolls.
4.   Janet's Foss is an unusual and beautiful waterfall. The waters of Gordale Beck contain a great deal of dissolved limestone and here some of it is deposited to build up the shape of the rock cone over which the water flows. Foss is a word of Norwegian origin and Janet is said to be queen of the local fairies and to live in the cave behind the waterfall.
5.   Weets Hill is a gritstone hillock and a wet one at that, yet Gordale, barely a mile away is of limestone. The Mid Craven Fault lies between and is the cause of the marked differences in scenery.

The old cross, now restored, marked the boundaries of a number of the townships that made up the parish of Kirkby Malhamdale in medieval times. They all meet at this point which was therefore a very important boundary.
6.   Airton Mill has a well-kept air about it for it has been converted into flats. It was originally a cotton spinning mill, worked by a waterwheel that was housed in a pit at the far end of the building. The leat bringing water from the river to work it is still in good order and can be followed along its length. Cotton was brought from Liverpool along the Leeds and Liverpool canal which reached Gargrave in 1818, and from there it was only a short journey by horse and cart to Airton. The second mill you pass has an almost identical history.
7.   As you approach Hanlith Bridge you will see a fine house straight ahead. This is Hanlith Hall and it dates back to 1668 though the front is quite a modern addition.
8.   Aire Head Spring is the true source of the Aire and the water from Malham Tarn that sinks just below the road reappears here.

4.8 Pikedaw, Nappa Cross, and Langscar Gate
This walk starts by climbing quite steeply to a height not far short of 1,700 feet (518 metres), the highest point around Malham, with wide views over Wharfedale. It's open, windswept country, with easy walking underfoot. Category B. Time: about 3 hours, or 2 hours by the short return. Map: 1:25,000 Outdoor Leisure 10 Yorkshire Dales Southern Area.

Leave the car park by the lane at its entrance. Take the right fork after 50 yards and the left-hand branch after about ¼ mile. Follow this lane and take its left-hand branch which goes to several barns. Opposite the fourth one there is a ladder stile, but once you're in the field, very little path to follow. Make somewhat left, cross the stream - there's a plank by the wall - and make for the barn.[1] Then go right up the long field more or less following the course of the stream until you come to a stile on the right. From it go straight up towards the steep ground ahead and turn left following the wall at the foot of it. Here you'll pick up a useful little path - don't lose it! It winds its way round all manner of humps and hollows before reaching a ladder stile onto the open fell. Once on the open fell the path continues ahead for a while and then pulls right. Look out for a yellow dot. Keep straight ahead until you come to a finger post on a broad green track. Turn left and continue up to the gate in the wall, the last shelter for a rest or a bite to eat for a long time.[2]

The views towards Malham Tarn are particularly good. On its right the conical hill with the crag is Great Close Hill. Behind it, fairly distant, is a long horizontal ridge. This is Horse Head Moor. Behind that is the ridge of Buckden Pike and Tor Mere Top. Great Whernside is away to the right. The smelt chimney is just on view to the left and lower down than the Tarn. (If you now want to take the short return see Note A.)

Otherwise go through the gate and immediately turn right. After a couple of hundred yards you come to an obelisk in the wall, Nappa Cross,[3] and from here the path cuts across to the gate. Then the track becomes broad and green, and probably well used by agricultural vehicles. Follow it down to the road. Opposite, a green track leads down to the Dry Valley where you have a choice of route. Cross the first stile, bear right and up the hill a little and you join walk 4.7 to the Tarn. Alternatively, having crossed the first stile, if you then turn right you start to go down the Dry Valley to the top of the Cove.

A better finish, is to stay in the fields above the Valley. To find the start, turn right at the stile before you drop down to the Dry Valley. After 50 yards or so you'll see a yellow-topped post and the stile ahead. There's not much path, but keep a level course through this long field and the next two shorter ones, then bear left across the corner of a field to a ladder stile. Follow the faint path down the hill, look for more posts that will lead you to the stiles and the road. Then 15 minutes will see you back to Malham and the car park.

Note A

Retrace your steps to the finger post and follow the bridleway right down to the road. Then either follow it into the village or if you prefer, turn right into the fields at the first sharp left-hand bend. At the end of the field there is the lane you started out on. Just follow it back to the car park.

Things of Interest

1. If you look back here you will see the distinctive terraces of lynchets made by the ploughing of the medieval farmers, just the same as those in Gordale.

2. A few yards before you get to the wall is the shaft of Pikedaw calamine mine, now sealed with concrete and fitted with an iron trap door to allow potholers access. In 1788 copper miners searching for deposits of copper ore broke into some caverns containing a unique deposit of smithsonite, zinc carbonate, also known as calamine. It was mined and calcined at Malham, then taken to Cheadle where it was smelted with copper ore to make brass. The coal needed for the calcining process was one of the reasons for mining coal on Fountains Fell.

3. Nappa Cross was one of the old crosses marking the parish boundary in monastic times. Only the base is the original stone, the little obelisk being a modern replacement.

Pikedaw Hill, - old field patterns on the right

4.9 Fountains Fell

Fountains Fell looks well from Malham Tarn and may tempt you for a quick ascent. This is most easily done from a little car park in an old quarry not far from the Tarn on the road from Stainforth to Arncliffe. Time: about $3^{1}/_{2}$ hours return. Category B, but note that the going is often extremely wet and boggy. Map: 1:25,000 Outdoor Leisure 10 Yorkshire Dales Southern Area.

Go through the gate almost opposite the quarry onto a permissive path that takes you onto the track that leads from this road to the Malham Tarn Study Centre. Turn right when you reach it and left after a few minutes at a stile with the acorn symbol of the Pennine Way. Here you join Walk 3.8 at *. Follow it to the top then retrace your steps.

Things of Interest
For a note about Fountains Fell, see *Things of Interest* to Walk 3.8.

4.10   Mastiles Lane and Bordley

Mastiles Lane is an ancient track that linked Fountains Abbey with its property in Malham and in modern times links Malham Youth Hostel with the Kettlewell one. Its eastern part is now either hard core or tarmac and not at all attractive, but this walk uses the western part, a pleasant green track, to approach Bordley, a tiny hamlet tucked away in the rolling green uplands. Category B. Time: $5^{1}/_{2}$-$6^{1}/_{2}$ hours depending on the finish used. Map: 1:25,000 Outdoor Leisure 10 Yorkshire Dales Southern Area.

Use Walk 4.7 to reach Malham Tarn then turn right on the road and follow it to Street Gate where Mastiles Lane starts. Go through the gate and follow the track by the wall down to Gordale Beck which you cross by a neat slab bridge.

After a while you will come to a walled section of lane which starts to drop gently and after about $^{1}/_{2}$ mile you will come to a gate. Immediately beyond it go through a gateway on the right and follow a wide green track that bears left to reach another wall. Continue left along this wall, enjoying fine views towards Rylstone Cross, all the way to Bordley, half-hidden in its sheltered hollow. Turn right at the gate into the hamlet and go straight ahead to the gate on the right of a barn. It has an unusual doorway, a reminder of the days when Bordley

From Weets Top looking across the entrance to Gordale to the wooded hills behind Malham Tarn. Fountains Fell in the background

was a monastic grange or farm belonging to Fountains Abbey. Go through another gate then follow the wall on the left through two big fields to a stile in the corner of the field. Go diagonally left to the next one, only 50 yards away, turn right, go through the gate and follow the wall. A track develops as the wall drops away to the stream; follow it to the stream and cross it easily. Make steeply up to a little gate-cum-stile and then follow the wall up to the end of the field where a hidden gate brings you to New House. Now follow its access road to Lee Gate and continue past the suburban-type bungalow to the end of the tarmac road. Follow the road for a good ¹/₂ mile to a rough lane on the left at the top of the hill. This leads to Weets Top where you join Walk 4.3 and return to Malham by that walk, or if you prefer it, by its longer variant, Walk 4.4.

5: RIBBLESDALE

Walks around Settle and Stainforth
5.1 Settle to Stainforth via Victoria Cave. Category B. 145
5.2 A visit to Victoria Cave. Category C. 147

Walks from Stainforth
5.3 Walk to Catrigg Force. Category C. 149
5.4 To Langcliffe, returning by the river. Category C. 151
5.5 To Fcizor and Austwick. Category B. 152
5.6 Fountains Fell. Category B. 154
5.7 Pen-y-ghent, Plover Hill and Pcn-y-ghent Gill.
  Category A. 154

Walks around Horton-in-Ribblesdale
5.8 Pen-y-ghent a) and Plover Hill by the Pennine Way path
        Category B. 158
        b) via Brackenbottom returning by the
        Pennine Way path. Category B. 159
5.9 Pen-y-ghent from Helwith Bridge. Category B. 161
5.10 The Three Peaks Walk. Category A+ 162
5.11 To High Birkwith, returning via Selside. Category B. 164
5.12 Horton Station to Settle via Pen-y-ghent. Category B+ ...166

Walks around Ribblehead
5.13 A visit to Alum Pot..167
5.14 The caves and gills of Upper Ribblesdale. Category B. ...169
5.15 Blea Moor and the Dales Way. Category B. 172

ABOUT SETTLE AND HORTON

Ribblesdale is the most easily accessible dale for many Lancastrians and Settle is the gateway to it. A small market town, it has regained much of its character lost in the rush of traffic since the opening of the by-pass. In Chapel Street (the road to Airton) is the Museum of North Craven Life, run by volunteers and open only April to October in the afternoons. Noteworthy is a display of old photographs, part of an account of the building of the Settle-Carlisle railway, and some

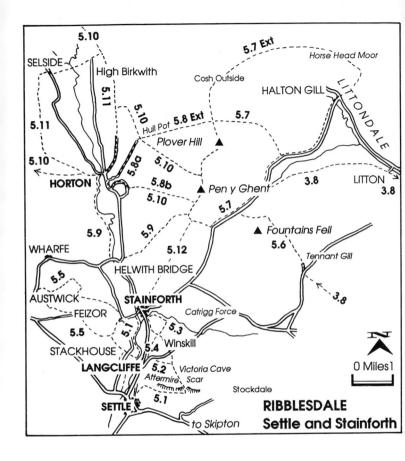

RIBBLESDALE
Settle and Stainforth

material from Victoria Cave. There are two car parks, one near the station, the other on the A65 near the railway bridge, and both charge daily fees. There are toilets, super loos that cost (fee) on the A65 car park, and cafes, shops, and pubs abound. Horton is the best centre for the walker, having a car park with toilets, the well-known Pen-y-ghent cafe which caters especially for walkers and, of course, a pub. The village church is a particularly fine one, having been sensitively restored in Victorian times. A fair amount of Norman work survives, including a large font. The old character of the village has vanished in Victorian villas for lime workers, railway cottages and modern bed and breakfast bungalows. Stainforth is a good base for a great deal of the easier walking and it too, has plenty of facilities.

WALKS AROUND SETTLE AND STAINFORTH

There is a network of good paths on the limestone uplands linking these two places as well as a riverside path. They allow a number of excellent walks to be done, suitable for the short days of winter or poor weather when the high ground is unattractive. As all of them have such good views it would be a pity not to do them on clear days. The 1:25,000 Outdoor Leisure 10 Yorkshire Dales Southern Area map covers all these walks.

5.1 Settle to Stainforth via Victoria Cave

This walk can be done equally well from Stainforth, but whichever starting point you choose be sure to do it in the direction described for the sake of the fine north- and westward views. Time required: about 4 hours or $2^{1}/_{2}$-3 hours using the shorter finish. Category B.

If you can, park in the main car park on the A65 in Settle, though there are others if that one is full.

From this car park turn right along the main road for about 100 yards to the Market Square, turn left into this and keep left up Constitution Hill. After about $^{1}/_{4}$ mile take the walled cart track on the right. Follow it into the open field and at the first wall turn right where the finger post points to Malham. The path is scarcely visible at this point but soon becomes a well marked green track climbing steeply up the hill. As soon as you come over the brow of the hill a limestone escarpment comes into view to the left in the distance. At the far end is a dark vertical slot: this is Attermire Cave.

The path now follows the walls dropping down into a shallow valley at the foot of the limestone escarpment. Having crossed a ladder stile, go through the next gateway and then turn left into a valley that divides the escarpment. The path is well marked and leads directly to the enclosure where Victoria Cave is situated well up on the right. Its entrance is large but it is not well seen as you approach. After a look at the cave,[1] a good spot for lunch if the weather is unkind, return to the

145

footpath by the wall and follow it over a stile to a rough lane. Here you can take a short way back, not visiting Stainforth at all. (See Note A.)

Assuming you continue, go up the lane for about 100 yards and cross the stile on the left. Drop down to the well marked track just below it, turn right, cross the next wall near a huge stone trough and continue along a well marked green track to the Langcliffe-Malham road. The views from here on a good day are very fine. On the far left are the rounded hills of the Bowlands. Then if you're lucky, you may see the Lakeland hills far away. Near at hand, just across the valley the conical hill is Smearsett Scar, to its right is the flat top of Ingleborough and further right still is Whernside. Pen-y-ghent is not seen from here but it was visible just as you left Victoria Cave.

Turn right on the road and in less than 100 yards take the road off to the left to Winskill. Though surfaced it's a pleasant enough unfenced road through the pastures. Look out for a big black boulder on the right. [2] The road ends at Winskill at a sort of cross roads. Take the left-hand lane down to Lower Winskill. It's got a pointer 'Footpath to Langcliffe' on the wall, though you don't want this path on this walk. You keep on to the end of the cart track to Lower Winskill. Go through the gate at the end and bear right behind the barn where you will see the stile. Over this, keep diagonally right to find the next stile, and keep on the same line into the wood. Here a set of well-made limestone steps leads gently down to Stainforth. Turn left when you arrive in the little lane, then right, then first left onto the old road in the village. There's a shop, cafe, and pub in the village to the left, but you go to the right, past the car park

Victoria Cave

onto the by-pass road. Follow this past the school to the old lane that crosses the railway and the River Ribble.

As soon as you've crossed the river bridge[3] go through the stile on the left and start the riverside footpath. There's a fine deep pool or two here for a dip on a hot day, if you are a good swimmer. The footpath stays close to the river all the way, climbing up a little to avoid the steep bank just beyond the Stainforth camp and caravan site. Nowhere is it well marked, always it gives delightful riverside walking on good green turf and all the stiles are in good order. Soon you come to the footbridge at the weir[4] at Langcliffe, and regretfully, the right of way path does not continue. Take the lane on the right to Stackhouse, a tiny secluded hamlet, and turn left on the road. After about ½ mile you will see the signpost 'to Giggleswick' on the left leading back to the river. The path is now very clear back to the A65 road at the river bridge, where a left turn and 5 minutes walk sees you at your car.

Note A

Turn left through the gate and follow the wall to the Langcliffe-Malham road which it joins on a sharp bend. On the left you will see a pointer through a gate, 'Bridleway to Settle'. Follow this keeping close to the wall beneath the wood, then strike across to a little gate in the long narrow wood. The next stile leads you into a rather open field: just contour round the hollow and you will find the stile at about the same height on the other side. Once over just follow this wall side until it leads you into the walled lane at the top of Constitution Hill, Settle, where you started.

5.2 A visit to Victoria Cave

If you just want to visit the cave the best way is to use the short finish up the Langlcliffe-Malham road for just over a mile to the cattle grid where the road is nearly level. It is possible to park on the grass just before the cattle grid and the broad grass track you want starts here on the right. When you've crossed the first wall, look up left to find the stile; this takes you to the cart track and cuts off a big corner. Turn right and you will soon see a wall corner with a stile on the left. Go over this and another five minutes will see you just below the cave. Allow about ¾ hour walking time for the return trip. Category C.

Things of Interest

1. Victoria Cave. It seems strange in view of its large opening to

*The old packhorse bridge
above Stainforth Force*

realise that Victoria Cave was not discovered until 1838, the year of Queen Victoria's Coronation, and the cave was named in honour of the occasion. Then the entrance was quite small, similar to a fox hole, and high up, under the roof of the cave's present entrance. This entrance was enlarged to its present size to facilitate the excavations carried out between 1870 and 1875. These were done mainly because of the interest aroused in the cave by one Joseph Jackson, a Settle man, who visited it many times seeking 'antiquities'. He built up a fine collection of Roman coins, brooches, bronze implements and the like that aroused interest in high places and the British Association organised the careful excavations that made Victoria Cave famous, for they offered conclusive evidence of Man's early occupation of the Pennine uplands. Romano-British objects were found in the surface layers of the cave floor - coins, beads of amber and glass, brooches, coarse pottery and weapons of iron. It seems likely that the cave was used as a refuge in times of trouble during the first three centuries after Christ. Intertribal wars, raiding Picts and Scots were commonplace in the troublesome times when the Roman Legions were being withdrawn from the North of England. Below this layer were 6 feet of cave earth devoid of objects of archaeological interest. This indicates a long period of disuse. Below this were remains of Neolithic man - flints and a stone axe, and lower still, in a bed older than the last Ice Age, remains of rhinoceros and hippopotamus. Some of these finds are in the Settle Museum.

2. The big black boulder perched on the limestone pavement is a glacial erratic, dropped here by the retreating glaciers at the end of the

148

last Ice Age some 8,000 years ago. The stone is of Silurian grit and is a smaller edition of the famous Norber Boulders. (See Walk 6.8.)

3. The ancient packhorse bridge across the Ribble belongs to the National Trust and is part of the old packhorse way that ran from York to Lancaster in the Middle Ages. No doubt it replaced an earlier ford as indicated by the 'forth' part of the village's name. Stainforth Force below the bridge is really a series of steps in the hard limestone that makes a number of small waterfalls when the river is high.

4. The weir was constructed to provide a reservoir of water - seen on the other side of the houses - to drive a water-mill. In 1785 this was a corn-mill and was converted to cotton in the early years of the nineteenth century, at the start of the Industrial Revolution. The mill is now used for storage. Note the fish ladder to give salmon and trout access to their spawning grounds in the shallow waters in the uppermost part of the river.

WALKS FROM STAINFORTH

There is a large Y.D.N.P. car park with toilets at Stainforth (daily fee) and there is a shop, cafe, and pub in the village. Parking is also allowed by the river in summer at Little Stainforth and this is a better starting point for Walk 5.5. If you intend using this it is far better to approach Little Stainforth from Settle, not Stainforth, and pay your dues at the farm in passing. This also avoids the need to cross the extremely narrow and delicate packhorse bridge.

5.3 Walk to Catrigg Force

The shortest way is just to go up Goat Scar Lane, but it's a steep dull plod. The way to do it is *up* via Winskill and *down* this lane which has glorious views up Ribblesdale, or extend it to Langcliffe. See the next walk. Time: 1½-2 hours. Category C. Map 1:25,000 Outdoor Leisure 2 Yorkshire Dales Western Area.

Leave the Stainforth car park for the village and take first left after you've crossed the river. Bear right at the corner ahead into a short lane with a signpost to Winskill at its end. Go through the upper gate in the first field and after passing the barn keep well up the hillside just below the wood. A little path leads you to a gate into the wood, not very obvious. From it a flight of rough stone steps takes you up through the wood, then you climb up a little in a large field to find the next stile.

Catrigg Force

From it Lower Winskill is a sight, keep to the right to find the stile into the farmyard between the buildings.

Go up the lane to a sort of cross roads and there keep straight ahead into open field. Usually there are plenty of tractor marks to follow. Go through the gateway and down the next field[1] to a gate on the left. Ignore the stile straight ahead. Go through the gate and over the stile immediately on the right.

Below you are two stiles. The left-hand one takes you to a newly made path and a good viewpoint for the fall. This path goes pleasantly on down the little wooded valley, but it does not go back onto the road at a lower point. Come back to the stile by which you entered the wood using whatever little track you fancy. When you've looked around go back to the lane, turn right and follow it down to Stainforth. If you are extending it to Langcliffe retrace your steps to the ladder stile on the left just before Lower Winskill. On a good day you look right up the upper

Ribble Valley to Pen-y-ghent, Ingleborough and Whernside. (See cover photograph.) When you come to the village green, go ahead on the right-hand side of it to the river, Stainforth Beck. A good set of stepping-stones takes you across to the Arncliffe road and a left turn back to the car park.

Things of Interest
In the Middle Ages Stainforth village belonged to the monks of Sawley Abbey, a less-well known foundation than either Fountains or Furness Abbeys, and situated lower down the Ribble not far from Clitheroe. Little Stainforth on the other side of the Ribble did not belong to them. The village has a number of old houses but is not picturesque as, say, Kettlewell. The word force or foss is of Norwegian origin and illustrates the penetration of the Vikings into the North-West, where it is a common word for a waterfall. This fall leaps 60 feet in two steps into a deep pool.
1.   This field has any number of dark boulders scattered over it. They are glacial erratics of Silurian grit, like the ones at Norber.

5.4 To Langcliffe, returning by the river
This walk starts in exactly the same way as the previous one, if you like it can be used to extend a visit to Catrigg Force. Time: about 3 hours. Category C. Map: 1:25,000 Outdoor Leisure 2 Yorkshire Dales Western Area.

When you get to Lower Winskill farm go up the lane until you see ladder stile on the right. Cross this, keep diagonally left and you'll soon see the next stile. Once over this turn sharp right and drop steeply straight down the hill to a little gate in the wall. There's no path in the right place here and many misleading ones, but once you're through the little gate the path to the green lane that takes you to Langcliffe is clear. You reach the village at its cross roads with the war memorial fountain, ancient sycamore tree, and on a more mundane level, village shop. Now turn right to get onto the main road. Here turn right and stay on the road until you've crossed the railway bridge and then immediately turn left down a narrow lane marked with a 'no through road' sign that leads to the hamlet of Locks and a footbridge across the Ribble. Once you've crossed the bridge the stile is on the right and the path follows the banks of the Ribble closely all the way to Stainforth. At the packhorse bridge follow the lane steeply up the hill to the main road.

Turn right and in a moment you will see the Stainforth car park.

Things of Interest
Langcliffe is a particularly pleasant village away from the traffic roar of the main road. Like so many Dales villages it has a large green, a relic of the days when the village's cattle were corralled within it at night, safe from marauders at any rate for most of the time! In 1315 the village was razed to the ground by Scottish raiders. After the Battle of Bannockburn in 1314 Scottish raids were common in the north of England. Bolton Priory suffered badly at the same time. Today there are a number of attractive houses in the village. See the notes with the other walks in the district for more background information.

5.5 To Feizor and Austwick
This walk makes a circuit of the limestone knolls and scars on the opposite side of the Ribble from Stainforth and has fine views. There are no route finding problems so it is very suitable for walkers who are using the train to and from Settle. Time from Stainforth: 4-4½ hours. Add on a good hour if starting from Settle station. Category B. Map: 1:25,000 Outdoor Leisure 2 Yorkshire Dales Western Area.

From the car park get onto the main road, turn right and after a few minutes turn left down a minor road to Little Stainforth. As soon as you have crossed the delicately arched packhorse bridge turn left onto the riverside path and follow it to its end at the footbridge below Langcliffe.

Turn right here and left on the road at the hamlet of Stackhouse. After 7 or 8 minutes, at the end of the wood, there is a fine set of stone steps* over the wall and the start of the path to Feizor. Follow it besides the wall that runs round the back of the hamlet until you reach a finger post directing you up the brutally steep field. It soon eases and you come in sight of the stile. Here you will find a tractor track that curls up the hillside between the limestone outcrops and will take you all the way over to Feizor. After the first gate there are branches on the left in many places into the pastures: just ignore them. On meeting the third wall the track turns right through a gate and continues on the other side, clear all the way to Feizor. As you reach the road there is a slit stile and signpost to Austwick directly opposite. A line of ladder stiles leads you very pleasantly across pastures and hayfields[1] to a walled lane which you cross and shortly reach another lane where you turn left for

Austwick Bridge. Turn right here and you are in the village in a moment or two.

Turn right at the cross and wander through the old village,[2] passing the new houses and the lane to the sports field. Then turn right down a lane by a barn. It brings you in a few moments to Austwick Beck again which you cross by an ancient clapper bridge. On the left there is a stile and a footpath that cuts the corner of the lane but if you're there in midsummer and you like flowers you'll stay in the lane.[3] In that case turn left at the 'cross roads'. A little further on the lane forks: take the right-hand one which ends almost at once in a field. Now follow the wall all the way to the access road to Jop Ridding and continue along until it swings sharp left. Straight ahead a ladder stile takes you into a field on the right. There's not much path, just follow the side of the wood until you reach the gate level with the farm. Now turn left and follow the wall to the farm. Here turn right on a good cart-track that goes over the Feizor and follow it almost to the top of the hill where you will see a finger post to Hargreaves Barn. Now follow the cart-track with excellent views of Pen-y-ghent, an unfamiliar shape from here. It bears right behind a hillock and as it drops into Ribblesdale it goes right again a little, then straight down to Hargreaves Barn, the only one surrounded by trees, and the road. Turn right and 5 minutes walk sees you back in Little Stainforth.

Settle start

When you reach the road from the railway station turn right and follow it to the main road through Settle, the A65. Turn left on it and follow it through the heart of Settle to the river bridge. Cross this and take the well used path through the playing fields on your right. It brings you to the road a little short of the stone steps* at Stackhouse.

Settle finish

When you reach the packhorse bridge follow the Stainforth start to the walk as far as the steps over the wall at Stackhouse, then retrace your outward route. Alternatively, for a change, cross the footbridge and continue to the main road where you turn right. Go past Langcliffe (the quite attractive village lies hidden away from the main road) and in the dip beyond take the lane on the left. It brings you into old Settle, quite picturesque, where you simply bear right to reach the A65.

Things of Interest

1. The higher parts of these fields below the wood are not mown and are rich in late summer flowers - knap weed, clover and betony, the latter a rich magenta colour.

2. Austwick is an ancient village of Norse origin. See page 198 for more information.

3. This lane is a delight in late July. It has great banks of rosebay willow herb, meadow sweet, meadow cranesbill, clumps of harebell and yellow bedstraw with the occasional great bell flower.

5.6 Fountains Fell, 670m (2,200 feet)

Though Fountains Fell can be climbed quite easily from Malham Tarn (Walk 4.9) the shortest and easiest way is from the top of the Stainforth-Halton Gill road. This is too short for anything but a stroll (!) and in any case you must return as you came. The energetic can complete the day with an ascent of Pen-y-ghent (Walk 5.7). Time: 4½-5 hours, Category B. Map: 1:25,000 Outdoor Leisure 2 Yorkshire Dales Western Area. Park on the grass just beyond the cattle grid at the top of the hill.

Walk along the road towards Halton Gill for about 15 minutes until you come to the first wall. (A stile on the right after about 100 yards leads to the Pennine Way path. This disappears on rough ground after the next stile and is more trouble than it is worth.) At the wall turn right and follow it until you come to a ladder stile where you meet the P.W. stile on the path mentioned above. Cross it and follow the well marked path[1] all the way to the top of the fell. If you want to visit the highest point turn right and follow the wall for about 10 minutes.

Things of Interest

1. The well-made track slanting up the shoulder of Fountains Fell was constructed to bring coal to the valley from the many pits on the summit plateau. See the note on page 125 for more information. It is worth a look down the two pits nearest the path by the wall. Both are extremely narrow and are lined with stone. In good light what looks like a band of shaley coal can be made out about 30 feet down one of them.

5.7 Pen-y-ghent, Plover Hill and Pen-y-ghent Gill

This walk starts at the top of the Stainforth-Halton Gill road and gives

Halton Gill

the quickest ascent of Pen-y-ghent - less than an hour - and the return over Plover Hill gives a short but satisfying day utilising two new paths negotiated by the park authorities. Strong walkers may make a full day of it by extending it over Cosh Inside and Horsehead Moor to Halton Gill, and it may be quite well done starting at Horton-in-Ribblesdale.

All routes are Category A. Time: 5 hours for the route given, $6\frac{1}{2}$ for the Horton Start. Add another 2 hours if you do the extension. Map(s): Outdoor Leisure 2 Yorkshire Dales Western Area, and Outdoor Leisure 30 Yorkshire Dales Northern and Central Areas if you do the extension.

Turn back to cross the cattle grid and take the lane on the right. It becomes a cart track just past Dale Head house and where it swings sharply left, half a mile past the house, your path branches off right. The 'sharp end' of Pen-y-ghent lies ahead. Though a stiff pull it doesn't last long. It needs care and is not recommended in the wet or in winter conditions.[1] The view from the top is good, if not as good as from the other two of the Three Peaks.

The Horton start
Use either route 5.8a or 5.8b to the top of Pen-y-ghent.

Have a breather and then continue to Plover Hill following the rough track along the wall to the stile on top of Plover Hill. Cross the stile and follow the broad track, rather faint but marked by poles, over the moor to the steep rocky escarpment where a well-trodden, neat little path takes you easily down to the Foxup track. Turn right on this wide grassy track which traverses the hillside on a band of limestone and gives easy going. After a short mile the track suddenly turns down the hillside and makes for a distant gate identified by a blue-topped pole. You continue to descend but immediately after the next gate you join a rather faint track which starts in Foxup and climbs gently up the hillside to the road at Hesleden Bergh. It has a signpost so there is no doubt as to the direction to be taken. Turn right on the road and continue for about ¹/₂ mile. Soon after you have passed the Nether Hesleden sign, you come to a cattle grid and the new footpath (which is clearly signposted) starts* there. It is vague at first, but more or less follow the wall down the field to a small gate in the wall below then turn right as directed by the sign and you will pick up a narrow but well-trodden track that has excellent views into the depths of Pen-y-ghent Gill. It is easy to follow and there are a number of reassuring signposts. As you pass below Pen-y-ghent House keep up to the wall to find the stile then continue through the fields aiming for the distant building which is at the side of the unfenced road.

Here, if time is short, you many prefer to follow this unfenced road with good grass verges back to your car, for the field route that is signed from the cattle grid is little walked and not easy to follow. If you opt for it follow the wall until you come to a wide corner then swing first to the left then to the right to reach the gate. Now cross two hay fields making well to the left of the gateway by the barn to locate the stile. Then turn left to reach the road by a little gate in the wall. Here you will find a spring of cool water even in a dry spell and a fine place for afternoon tea if you are continuing to Horton. Turn right on the road and 15 minutes walk sees you back at your car.

Horton finish

Continue to the cattle grid at the top of the hill and turn right along the lane to Dale Head. Pass the house on the right and continue along the lane. It loses its guiding walls and a good cart track continues, turning sharp left as it approaches the ridge ahead. A little more height must be made then as you top the ridge a fine view of Ribblesdale opens in front of you. (There are fine sunset views in winter from this length of lane.) After the next gate the descent steepens appreciably and a cart track leaves it cutting back towards Dub Cote farm. Continue straight down by a line of stiles to the farm and turn right on the road. Turn right again when you reach the next road, and when you have just passed the school, cross the footbridge and turn right to enter a lane on your left. Follow this to the next lane where you turn left, then turn right on the main road to find the car park.

The extension over Cosh Outside and Horse Head Moor

When you reach the Foxup track turn left and continue a little way beyond the next gate before going across to Cosh Outside, aiming for the O.S. cairn on its green top. Rough, hard going, undulating ground.

Once on top, go through the wall - there are many gaps in it and walk on the north side where the views are better and you will automatically cut the bend in the wall. The views down Littondale are very fine. Continue along whichever side of the wall you please until you start the long rise up to Horse Head Moor when you will find yourself forced onto the north side by the availability of the gaps in the walls. There's a bit of a path, but not much. The top, 1,985 feet, is marked by an O.S. cairn.

A few minutes after leaving it go through the gate on the right and follow the cart track (not a right of way) down to Halton Gill.

Now there is an unfortunate drag up the road to Stainforth for about 1½ miles to the start* of the footpath used on the main walk. Those with time and energy in hand could go up to Foxup by the riverside path and pick up the track used on the main walk there, it would add about ½ hour.

Things of Interest

The views and the changing scene are the chief interest of this walk. The steep end of Pen-y-ghent is composed of Yoredale limestones topped by a gritstone cap. You start first up the limestone ledges and as you come to the boulder field, you change to the gritstone which stays all the way to Plover Hill. You drop down onto limestone and stay on it more or less to Cosh Outside, except for the peat deposits in the bottom of the drop. As you climb up from Cosh you go back onto the gritstone and stay on it until you reach the shooting hut, where you drop onto the limestone and stay on it all the way back.

WALKS AROUND HORTON-IN-RIBBLESDALE

Excepting Ingleborough, Pen-y-ghent must be the most popular Dales peak and like Ingleborough, has a number of routes up it. It is most quickly but not most easily climbed from the top of the road between Stainforth and Halton Gill (Walk 5.7) and most commonly from Horton-in-Ribblesdale. Even when combined with Plover Hill it scarcely gives a full day's walk.

5.8a   Pen-y-ghent and Plover Hill by the Pennine Way path

The Pennine Way path must surely be the most popular way up Pen-y-ghent, though it is not the most interesting, which is via Brackenbottom. This walk can be done just as well going via Brackenbottom. Time: 5½ hours or 2½ hours for Pen-y-ghent alone. Category B or B+ if you continue to Plover Hill as the ground between the two can be hard going. Map: 1:25,000 Outdoor Leisure 2 Yorkshire Dales Western Area. Park in the car park (toilets) at Horton-in-Ribblesdale.

Turn right on leaving the car park and continue along the road for about ¼ mile to a rough, walled lane on the left signposted Pennine Way. (To avoid confusion remember that the lane by the Crown is also the Pennine Way but goes to Hawes.) This lane climbs steadily to reach the open moor at a gate in about 1½ miles. Turn right here on a remade path that takes you past the repulsive slit of Hunt Pot to the wall at the start of the moor. Here a newly restored path of limestone chippings takes you easily up to the escarpment where you turn right and follow a cart track to the last rise where a badly eroded length of 'path' takes you to the top. (Hopefully, by the time this book appears, it will have been restored.)

Having visited the summit cairn over the wall and enjoyed the view - quite different on that side of the wall - return to the Horton side and either retrace your steps, or continue to Plover Hill following the rough track along the wall to the stile on top of Plover Hill. Cross the stile and follow the broad track, rather faint but marked by poles, over the moor to the steep rocky escarpment where a well-trodden neat little path takes you down to the Foxup track quite easily. Turn left on this wide grassy track and climb gently to the low col that separates Littondale and Ribblesdale. The track now becomes very boggy in parts especially where it meets the wall. When you come to the end of the wall in about

Pen-y-ghent from above Horton-in-Ribblesdale

½ mile the track is vague. Take care to keep straight on or you will find yourself going back up Pen-y-ghent! The track quickly becomes well marked and drops down to the great chasm of Hull Pot[1] where, having had a good look into its awesome depths, you turn left to reach the walled lane you used for the ascent at the gate. Then simply follow it back to Horton.

5.8b Pen-y-ghent via Brackenbottom returning by the Pennine Way path

This used to be quite the best way up Pen-y-ghent but erosion became so bad that the Park authorities have put a long length of duck boarding complete with a flight of steps on the upper part of the moor. Though utterly foreign to the environment it gives good, easy going. The steep upper part of Pen-y-ghent gives a rocky scramble and for that reason this route is not recommended in wintry conditions. Nor may everybody care to come down it! Time: 3 hours. Category B. Map: 1:25,000 Outdoor Leisure Map 2 Yorkshire Dales Western Area. Park in the car park (toilets) at Horton-in-Ribblesdale.

Turn right on leaving the car park and continue along the road for about ¼ mile to a rough, walled lane on the left signposted Pennine Way. (To avoid confusion remember that the lane by the Crown is also the Pennine Way but it goes to Hawes.) Follow this for about 200 yards then turn right into another lane which will bring you out by the stream

almost opposite the school. Cross the bridge and turn left, then follow
the lane to Brackenbottom, a tiny hamlet tucked under the steepening
flank of Pen y ghent. On the way you pass the resurgence of Douk
Ghyll,[2] the stream you crossed to reach the school. The path to Pen-y-
ghent starts on the left just before you reach the houses and is
signposted. Simply follow it unmistakably to the stile* below the steep
end of Pen-y-ghent. When you've crossed the stile onto the long
moorland ridge turn left and continue to the steep stony end. It gives a
pleasant scramble along rock ledges[3] and over boulders to the domed
top of the hill where more remade path takes you to the top.

Returning, cross the wall and go straight ahead down the badly
eroded slope to meet a sort of cart track that runs at an easy angle down
the escarpment. It brings you to the start of the limestone chipping path
that leads you easily over the moor, past Hunt Pot and to the gate where
you turn left and follow the lane down to Horton. Turn right on the road
to find the car park.

Things of Interest
1. Both Hull and Hunt pots have been formed by faulting aided by
water action. The stream only runs over the top of Hull Pot in times of
flood, but after melting snow it is a quite spectacular, 60-foot force.
Hunt Pot always engulfs a stream and is a black repulsive slit on the left

Pen-y-ghent from the south

of the track just after the crossing of the wall on the descent. Its total depth is 200 feet and it was first descended in 1898 by the Yorkshire Ramblers', Club.

2. Douk Ghyll and Brants Gill, the stream opposite the car park in Horton are two of the biggest resurgences in the Dales, both issuing from large cave mouths. There is no access to them; a pity, for they take all of the underground drainage from the pot holes on Pen-y-ghent.

3. Notice that the first set of ledges on the steep end are of limestone. Higher up, at the boulder field, they change to gritstone, for Pen-y-ghent's upper part is composed of the Yoredale limestones capped by gritstone.

5.9 Pen-y-ghent from Helwith Bridge

This approach to the start of the upper part of Pen-y-ghent is long and easy and the return has the considerable merit of being along the banks of the River Ribble and can be extended to include Plover Hill (Walk 5.8a). A walled cart track leaves the Helwith Bridge-Horton road at the first corner beyond Helwith Bridge, which is best identified by the pub sign. There is a good lay-by on the Horton side of the corner. Category B. Time: 4-4½ hours, 6 if you include Plover Hill. Map: 1:25,000 Outdoor Leisure 2 Yorkshire Dales Western Area.

Turn up the cart track and follow it until it forks, then take the left-hand lane, Long Lane, and continue along this pleasant gently climbing cart track until it meets the route from the top of the Halton Gill-Stainforth Road (Walk 5.7).

Follow this route to the top of Pen-y-ghent, cross the wall and continue to Horton; the path is wide and unmistakable. Turn right on the road and cut across the end of the car park to cross a footbridge where there is a stile on the left. The footpath is obvious most of the way to Cragghill Farm, for it is part of the Ribble Way and well used. It follows the river bank closely and is a first rate stretch of riverside walking. As you approach the farm keep to its left on the very brink of the river and continue to follow the bank until you reach a finger post that directs you across the field to a gate where you enter a walled lane, often deep in water in wet weather. The lane leads you under the railway onto a tarmac road leading to those huge quarries that destroy a whole hillside. Turn left and follow the road to a T-junction close to the pub at Helwith Bridge. Turn left on this road and at the junction ahead turn left to find your car.

5.10 The Three Peaks Walk - The Circuit of Whernside, Ingleborough and Pen-y-ghent

This is the great classic walk of the Dales: for the not-so-experienced a challenge, for the harrier a gruelling test, for the good fell walker just an average day. It was, I believe, 'invented' by the Gritstone Club and in the days when few people had cars it was commonly done from Dent, which could be reached by train, to Horton-in-Ribblesdale where the 7pm bus took you to Settle and another to Hellifield and the train home on a Sunday night. In fact, the first couple of times I did the walk I used that route myself. Today times have changed and it is usually done as a circuit from either the Hill Inn or Horton-in-Ribblesdale.

Route finding is scarcely a problem except, possibly, on leaving the top of Ingleborough in thick mist. Most of the paths have been remade by the Three Peaks Footpath Project and the rest are well trodden. Shorter times than those that follow will be commonplace as the going is now very much easier than it was in the days when broad boggy swathes passed as 'paths'. 8-8½ hours for the circuit used to be a good time, my own was 10 hours and there's nothing to be ashamed of if it takes you 12 hours even today. Preferably make an early start from the car park at Horton-in-Ribblesdale and do Pen-y-ghent first. The psychological crux of this walk is the long drag between Pen-y-ghent and Whernside, when you can see Whernside all the time and it never gets any nearer. Best tackled whilst you're fresh! Besides, the Pen-y-ghent Cafe at Horton (Tel. 333), runs a badge/control service, gives weather forecasts and does simple cooked meals, and drinks hot and cold. Open Sundays. Category: A+. Map: 1:25,000 Outdoor Leisure 2 Yorkshire Dales Western Area.

Turn right on leaving the car park and continue along the road for about ¼ mile to a rough, walled lane on the left signed Pennine Way. The lane climbs steadily to reach the open moor at a gate in about 1½ miles. Turn right here on a remade path that takes you to the wall and stile at the start of the steep stretch up the moor. Here a path of limestone chippings takes you easily up to the escarpment where you turn right and follow an old miners' track to the last rise where a badly eroded length of 'path' takes you to the top. (Hopefully by the time this book appears, it will have been restored.)

Retrace your steps below the escarpment where the signpost directs you either to Horton or the Three Peaks. The Three Peaks 'path' is still

162

extraordinarily boggy and badly eroded all the way down Pen-y-ghent and across the rest of the moor. It is better to go about 150 yards down the path to Horton and take the well marked but less boggy track across the moor that goes to the left of Hull Pot. It is particularly advantageous in wet weather as you do not have to cross the stream flowing into Hull Pot. Note that this route is not shown on the O.S. map though the harriers' route is, but it is shown on Arthur Gemmel's inexpensive *Three Peaks Map* published by Stile Publications of Otley, and available in the Pen-y-ghent cafe.

Pass Hull Pot on the south side taking a moment to look into its gaping chasm with rumbling waters, an awesome place, then continue on a narrow track up the hillside beyond to the broken wall on Black Dub Moss. The track is now very well marked and continues to its junction with the Harriers' route. The erosion caused by the increase in traffic is now all too apparent. Go straight across the Pennine Way cart track, and over the next hillock when you are on the limestone pastures above Birkwith Cave, beautiful green turf, a most welcome change from the bog. Here you join a farm cart track which you follow to a gate on the track to Old Ing farm. Cut the corner to the track from High Birkwith to God's Bridge, a natural limestone arch over Brown Gill. Now the track bears left a little and goes down to Nether Lodge.

From Nether Lodge there is a choice of route. By far the easiest but having no other merit is to follow the stony farm road to the Ribblehead road. Turn right and 20 minutes along it will see you at the Station Hotel for some well-earned refreshment.

Strong walkers, however, may prefer to continue to the Ingleton-Hawes road using Walk 5.14 from *. Here turn left and in about 100 yards you will reach a small lay-by on the right below a little limestone scar. Bear left and climb onto it fairly soon then follow a succession of faint tracks in the direction of the right-hand end of the Ribblehead viaduct where you will join the path up Whernside.

The path, a wide stony track, starts opposite the road junction and swings round the side of the famous viaduct but does not go under it. Follow it first beside the railway line, then across the moor to a bridge across the railway. Now simply follow the walkway up the nose of the moor to the stile, then cross the fence and follow the wall to the summit cairn. From the cairn follow the wall down two steep steps of the ridge. Then bear sharp left to a track that goes down in one zig-zag to the top of the big field above Bruntscar. Again, it's unmistakable and a sign at

Bruntscar directs you to Chapel-le-Dale.

Go left up the main road passing the Old Hill Inn (if it's shut) to a sign and stile 'Footpath to Great Douk Cave'. Follow the path through the pastures, reassured by a signpost at the third stile. The path soon enters the Southerscales Nature Reserve where you simply follow the discreet yellow-topped stakes. As soon as you have passed Braithwaite Wife Hole, the biggest shake hole in the Dales, you will reach a stile that puts you onto the start of a length of new footpath, a walkway composed of boards, much of it tarred and gritted just like a path in a town park. It's very easy walking, but totally out of sympathy with the environment. It ends at the foot of the steep escarpment where a stone staircase helps your upward progress. At the top go through the little gate where, above on the left, you will find a spring of clear cool water, never known to fail. Then follow the path up the steep rocky edge onto the flat top of Ingleborough and the crossed walls at the summit.

The broad flat top can be quite a puzzling place if it's misty. A compass bearing of 60 degrees magnetic north is absolutely essential to leave correctly. Following the left-hand edge brings you to the narrow neck of steep ground that leads to Simon Fell where you take the right fork at the first slight 'levelling' of the ridge. The path curves under Simon Fell as a broad muddy swathe, unmistakable. Some little distance down you come to a section of path that has been drained and resurfaced with what looks like quarry waste as part of the Three Peaks Footpath Scheme. It gives far better going than the badly eroded ground just crossed yet is in keeping with the landscape. It ends some little distance above Nick Pot and a derelict shooting hut and you continue on the eroded peaty path, a reminder of what it was all like before it had 'the treatment'. (Note: More work will probably have been done since 1990 when the check walking was done.) Take the left fork below the hut and follow the wall all the way down until it joins the clear path all the way to the station at Horton. Five minutes along the road sees you back at the car park.

5.11   To High Birkwith, returning via Selside

This walk does not follow the river - there are no right of way paths above Horton - but uses the limestone shelves high above the river. It has exceptionally fine views for a low level walk and is best done this way round. Route finding is tricky in parts. Category B. Time: 4 hours. Map: 1:25,000 Outdoor Leisure 2 Yorkshire Dales Western Area. Park in the car park at Horton-in-Ribblesdale.

Turn left on leaving the car park and continue along the road to the start of a walled lane[1] to the right of the Crown. It's the Pennine Way going north to Hawes. Follow it as far as Sell Gill Barn. This is about a mile and is the first building after a sizeable stream, Sell Gill,[2] but note, the stream may be dry in summer. Turn left here crossing a ladder stile and turn right immediately below the barn. The stiles are obvious through three short fields and then you enter a very long one. At its end there is a stile high on the right, but you keep below the wall corner following the wall to find the next ladder stile, which is crucial for locating the crossing place of a deep-cut gill just before you reach the gill of Birkwith Cave.[3] It's a couple of field lengths from this stile. The walls of the gill seem precipitous but a little path takes you down to the footbridge. Then make towards the wall above the plantation around Birkwith Cave and continue to a gate. Just beyond it you reach the High Birkwith-Old Ing farm road. Turn left here and go down to High Birkwith.

As you turn the corner to the left look out for a stile and finger post to Selside on your right. The way crosses to the plantation (not shown on the map), through it and down the hill to Low Birkwith. Go through the gate to the right of the farm, left into the farmyard and then through a gate opposite. The path follows the stream down to the Ribble, with slit stiles all the way. Here a new bridge, not shown on the map, replaces one that became unsafe. Cross it and bear to the left around the hill opposite and you will come into a walled lane that leads you to the road at Selside.[4] Turn right on the road and then take the first lane[5] on the left, about 100 yards up the hill. (Here, if you want to put in a diversion to Alum Pot see Walk 5.13.) Turn the corner in the lane and go through a gate into a field. Now the way you want is not so clear as the map suggests. Where the cart track turns into the Gill Garth keep straight on and in the next field bear left only a little to find the stile. Beyond it two more stiles put you onto the bridle track that the map shows as going all the way to Clapham, but it is misleading. This track actually swings right to go into a field and the right of way track goes straight on at the point where it starts to curve. There's not much to be seen on the ground at that point but a track soon reappears and leaves this huge field[6] at a gate high on the right. A few minutes walk brings you to the signpost at the top of Sulber Nick where you turn left and follow the broad eroded path all the way down to Horton Station. Go straight ahead on the road and over the bridges to find the car park.

Things of Interest

1. Sell Gill lane was the original road up the valley joining the Lancaster-Richmond turnpike road on Dodd Fell.

2. In normal weather Sell Gill disappears in the stream bed above the cart track in a quite dramatic manner forming Sell Gill Pot. This pothole was explored as early as 1897 by the Yorkshire Ramblers' Club who found a deep shaft leading into a huge chamber, considered to be second in size to the main chamber of Gaping Gill. Below the road there is another entrance, a cave-cum-shaft which leads to the same chamber. The pothole has a total depth of 210 feet.

3. Birkwith Cave is at the head of the ravine and a sizeable stream issues from it. There is a stile into the ravine in the farm side of it and it is not difficult to get down the cave, the mouth of which is impressively large, but quickly becomes impassable.

Directly across the valley a small plantation of conifers above Selside marks the position of Alum Pot.

4. Selside has a fine farmhouse, Shaw House, just opposite the lane where you come onto the main road. Its Georgian doorway is a splendid example, rare in the Dales.

5. The lane is part of the old road to Clapham and the walk on this side of the valley roughly follows its line.

6. In spring and early summer the beautiful mountain pansy is common in this field, and you many find the bird's-eye primrose in the moister patches close to Sulber Nick.

5.12   Horton Station to Settle via Pen-y-ghent

This walk uses the revived Settle-Carlisle line to reach Horton, goes up Pen-y-ghent by the Pennine Way path, continues to Stainforth and returns to Settle by the banks of the Ribble. If you have already done Walk 5.1 you may prefer to reverse it from Stainforth instead of returning by the Ribble. It makes an even better finish on a good day. If you are not so blessed, you may prefer to omit the summit of Pen-y-ghent and start by Walk 5.8b which takes you to a stile below the steep rocky end. Time: About $5^{1}/_{2}$ hours. Category B+. Map: 1:25,000 Outdoor Leisure 2 Yorkshire Dales Western Area.

From the station walk down the road towards the river bridge but cut the corner on wooden pedestrian bridge which brings you to the car park and the start of both Walks 5.8a and 5.8b. Take your pick and continue to the top of Pen-y-ghent or the stile*. At the top cross the wall and turn right, descending by the steep rocky nose. It is full of ledges and there are no problems in reasonable weather. At the bottom you come to the stile* which you reach if you join the main route using Walk 5.8b.

Continue along the wall then bear left along the remade path to the cart track. Turn right here and as you top the first rise take the path to the left, signed Moor Head Lane. This is a fairly new path, created in 1987, not yet well trodden. It follows the wall to Moor Head Lane changing sides part way along, and veers left as it approaches this lane joining it opposite the finger post to Stainforth. From the stile a line of stakes sets you off in the right direction but the route to Stainforth is not well trodden. Look out for stiles, and bear right to a gate just above Stainforth. When you reach tarmac continue to the second road junction and turn right to meet the Settle-Horton road. Turn right and after a couple of hundred yards turn left down a narrow lane that leads you to the river. Cross the ancient packhorse bridge and follow the path downstream to Settle, turning to Walk 5.1 for guidance. When you join the main road the station is a smart 10 minutes, walk away. Turn left, passing toilets, a chippie, shops, a pub and cafes, roughly in that order, on the way. Turn right at the British Rail sign opposite the police station and the station is about 100 yards away on the left.

WALKS AROUND RIBBLEHEAD

5.13   A visit to Alum Pot

Alum Pot is easily reached from Selside by turning up the rough lane just past the last farm at the northern end of the village. There's room to park in it. You will see a notice reminding you that Alum and Diccan pots and Lower Long churn are on private land and that a small fee is payable to cross that land. It gives full instructions as to how to find the farm where it is to be paid.

Having paid your due, go to the end of the lane where there is a stile by the gate. Alum Pot now lies in the clump of conifers a field's length away. The shaft has a wire fence round it; if you go inside take extreme care. The best view is from the end where you arrive. On a fine sunny morning when there is little water running over the lip you will see opposite the large dark cavern where Lower Long Churn Cave joins the open shaft half-way down.

Below it the Slippery Slab leads to a ledge that runs round the shaft and gives access to the Bridge, an enormous slab of limestone that leans across from one wall to the other. A long ladder pitch descends from there to a cascade which tumbles into a deep pool, the end of the pot hole and known as a sump. The water from it reappears at the surface first at Footnaw's Hole, a repulsively muddy pool between the railway and the river, and then goes beneath the Ribble, never mixing with its waters, to appear in Turn Dub close to New House Tarn. Its total depth is 350 feet (107 metres).

Alum Pot was first descended by John Birkbeck of Settle in 1847 by means of Lower Long Churn Cave. This cave is in the same field as Alum Pot, a couple of hundred yards or so along the wall side. Its large cave mouth may invite exploration but a stream is met very soon and deep awkward pools await the would-be explorer. Not recommended.

The Bridge, Alum Pot

5.14   The caves and gills of Upper Ribblesdale

Gale Beck is the accepted source of the Ribble whose many tributaries are called gills. This walk crosses and follows a number of them and makes a diversion to visit three caves, two of them finely situated at the head of their gills. Allow an extra hour for the diversion. Park in a small lay-by close to Ribblehead House, marked on the map but no longer in existence. It is on the Ingleton-Hawes road about ³/₄ mile east of the Horton-in-Ribblesdale junction. Time: 3¹/₂ hours. Category B. Map: 1:25,000 Outdoor Leisure 2 Yorkshire Dales Western Area.

Go through the wicket gate signed to Gauber which is almost opposite the lay-by. Go past the wooden hut to a stile then keep straight on in the same direction towards a distant barn. Cross the stream on a plank bridge and follow the curve of the hill to find a well defined path. Follow it up the hill to a gate on the left close to a wooden electricity pole, then go direct for Gauber Farm coming onto the road by a gate at the right-hand end. Beware of the guard dog. Turn left on the road, then go right in about 100 yards to pass a short row of cottages and follow this lane to Colt Park Farm. Go through a gate on the left and continue through the farm buildings into the hay meadows. A grassy cart track takes you to an isolated barn and just before you reach the next gate turn left to find the stile that takes you into a sort of lane that separates the two parts of Colt Park Wood.[1] When you've gone through the lane into the field turn right and make for the ladder stile below Opposite you will see another ladder stile and another beyond that. Go through these then you will pick up tractor marks in the large field ahead. Follow them diagonally right across the field to a stile by the distant gate.

Turn right and follow the road into the hamlet of Selside. Almost opposite the first house on the right turn left into a wide stony track that passes Selside Farm and continues under the railway. Take the right fork and leave the lane at the finger post that points to Low Birkwith. Bear right in the field curving round the base of the hill to find a good footbridge over the Ribble. Almost immediately cross Coppy Gill and follow it to Low Birkwith. Here pass to the left of the farm, cross the stile beyond the sheepfolds and go steeply up the field to pass through a small plantation before arriving at the road at High Birkwith. Turn left and continue up the rough road towards Old Ing. After a couple of hundred yards turn left on a track that passes above a plantation, but if you want to visit the caves keep straight ahead.

Calf Holes

Diversion to visit the caves

Continue to the junction with a rough track on the right, follow it to the gate but do not go through it. Instead follow the wall down to find a stile that gives access to the gill and Birkwith Cave[2], well worth a look. Return to the farm track and turn right, passing to the left on the Pennine Way. After a few minutes you will come to an iron gate across the track. Immediately beyond it a stile on the right puts you on the very brink of Calf Holes[3] which engulf the stream, an impressive waterfall in wet weather. Continue along the cart track for a few minutes until you come to a stile on the left. Cross it and follow the wall down to its end. Browgill Cave[4] is on the right and it is easy to walk down to it and even penetrate a little way until deep water is met. God's Bridge, the next point of interest on this walk, is a natural bridge so wide that you hardly know you are on a bridge, and is lower down this gill, but there is no

God's Bridge

right of way down the field. You may prefer to retrace your steps to the point where you turned off to visit Birkwith Cave.

The main route, continued
Opposite this junction a faint path crosses the hillside to join the main route where it emerges from a gate. Shortly you will cross God's Bridge then simply follow this well marked track to Nether Lodge*, going between the house and farm buildings onto their access road. Here you will find a signpost. Go straight ahead to Ribblehead, a few yellow-topped posts starting you off in the right direction. A well trodden little path soon develops and takes you to the first stile where you bear left to cross Crutchin Gill, sometimes dry in summer. Continue to a barn, turn right and go over the hill and down to Black Hools barn. Over the second ladder stile turn left and then right through a gateway with a blob of yellow paint. If there is no path, follow the wall at first, pass an isolated ash tree on its left and keep straight ahead to a wall corner. Now you may find a faint path going diagonally left down to the fragile little packhorse bridge[5] over Thorns Gill, the finest gill of them all, its brown peaty waters tumbling from pool to pool in the water-worn limestone rocks. Then just follow the wall up the field to the road, no distance at all from your car.

Things of Interest

1. Colt Park Wood. This apparently ordinary piece of ashwood is something of a rarity. It is growing at an altitude of 1,100 feet - just about as high as trees will grow - and it is growing on a piece of limestone pavement. This unusual combination gives rise to a number of rare plants, particularly mosses. It is managed by the Nature Conservancy and the public is not allowed access.

2. Birkwith Cave has a large entrance from which a stream emerges. Despite its size, it soon becomes very low and eventually ends in a deep lake.

3. Calf Holes' waterfall is about 40 feet high and the water emerges at Browgill Cave. Pot holers often make the through trip though this involves a very narrow passage, and parties can often be seen there.

4. Browgill Cave is another impressive cave opening where the water from Calf Holes emerges, by what route is not known.

5. Thorns Gill bridge. This fragile little packhorse bridge, in its original state without parapets, but at the moment bound together with iron bands, is on an ancient packhorse route from Dent to Horton-in-Ribblesdale and Settle. It is to be repaired and restored by the Park authority.

5.15   Blea Moor and the Dales Way

Blea Moor makes a good upland walk on a poor day. It is in the rain shadow of Whernside and so has better weather, as well as a clearly marked path. As it follows the route of the railway it is a must for any railway enthusiast. Park at Ribblehead, opposite the Horton road junction. Time: 4 hours. Category B. Map: 1:25,000 Outdoor Leisure 2 Yorkshire Dales Western Area. Note that the return by the Dales Way is usually wet.

Start by the green track signposted *Footpath to Whernside*. It joins the rough road that runs under the viaduct, and as it curves to do just this, keep straight on up the steep rise ahead. Continue, hugging the railway for a good mile, passing the former signalman's house at Bleamoor Sidings. The track then swings away from the railway and splits, the left-hand one going to Whernside, the right-hand one going over Blea Moor. (If you are a railway buff and want to see the mouth of the Bleamoor tunnel, divert along the Whernside track, cross the bridge, which also carried the waters of Force Gill on an aqueduct, and follow the railway cutting until you can see it.) Then retrace your steps to the junction and take the cart track that wanders over the moor in the direction of the three big spoil heaps that mark the line of the tunnel. Continue right over the moor by this cart track.

As you start to drop down there are fine views into upper Dentdale. The railway seems so far below it is quite astonishing. Quite soon you will come to a forest road; it is not a right of way and the woodland is private property. The exit gate is locked but climbable and a right turn on the forest road sees you on the main road in about 15 minutes. If your conscience pricks you, or you are a railway buff, continue straight ahead down the fire break. Shortly after the gradient eases, the path bears left to a stile then follows the top of the railway cutting for a time giving a good view of the tunnel mouth. With luck you may hear the rumbles of a train and watch it emerge. Then bear left to a gateway, continue across the footbridge, and through Dent Head Farm where you take their access road onto the main road opposite Dent Head viaduct, another plus for the railway buff. Turn right and grind steeply up the hill for a good 10 minutes to the locked gate, and another 10 along the road to a stile and finger post 'The Dales Way' on the right. Follow this once well-made track, now very wet, until you come in sight of High Gayle farm. Here a finger post to Gearstones directs you above the wall which you follow all the way to the corner above Winshaw farm. It is fairly rough and wet, not much of a path, and is not the original Dales Way, which has been re-routed here. As compensation it has better views of Simon Fell and Ingleborough. When you come to the corner of the wall above the farm, turn left and follow its road down to the Ingleton-Hawes road. Now turn right, and follow the road to your car, because regrettably, there's no more footpath.

Things of Interest

For a full account of the Settle-Carlisle railway see the chapter of that name. Of particular interest on this walk are the two viaducts and the Bleamoor tunnel. It is well known that the Ribblehead Viaduct is the longest at 440 yards, having twenty-four arches with a maximum height of 104 feet. Dent Head is barely half as long but at 100 feet is almost as high. The tunnel is 2,629 yards long and runs along the 1,140-foot contour; a magic figure for many miles of the Settle-Carlisle railway.

6: INGLETON AND CLAPHAM

Walks from Ingleton

6.1 The Glens Walk. Category B 176
6.2 Ingleborough
    a) By Storrs Common from Ingleton. Category B 179
    b) From the Old Hill Inn, Chapel-le-Dale. Category B 179
6.3 Whernside
    a) From the head of Kingsdale. Category B 182
    b) From the Old Hill Inn, Chapel-le-Dale. Category B 182
    c) From Ribblehead. Category B 183
6.4 The Two Peaks Walk. Category A 184
6.5 A walk amongst the caves and pot holes of Kingsdale
    Category B 184

Walks from Clapham

6.6 Ingleborough, Simon Fell and Park Fell. Category A 188
6.7 The Ingleborough Estate Trail. Category C 192
6.8 To the Norber Boulders and Austwick. Category B 193
6.9 To Horton-in-Ribblesdale via the Norber Boulders.
    Category B 194

Other Walks

6.10 Gragareth, Great Coum and Crag Hill. Category B+ 198

INGLETON AND THE GLENS

One could as well try to separate the words 'bread and butter' as try to think of Ingleton and its glens separately. They are unique in the whole of the Yorkshire Dales National Park. Ingleton itself is as old as most villages in the Dales, but thanks to its colliery, quarries and lime-burning its population was raised to over 1,500 at the end of the nineteenth century and it lost its rural character. It has plenty of shops, cafes, pubs and accommodation of all sorts, including a youth hostel. There is camping at Beezleys Farm. Most facilities are open on Sunday even in winter, for Ingleton depends quite heavily on tourism for its livelihood today. There is a car park with toilets and Y.D.N.P. information caravan on the site of the former station.

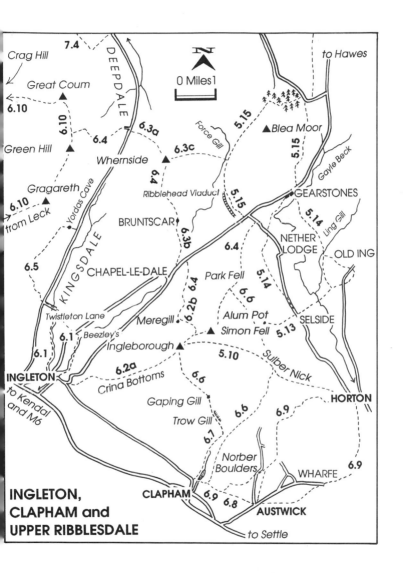

INGLETON,
CLAPHAM and
UPPER RIBBLESDALE

175

WALKS FROM INGLETON

6.1 The Glens Walk

The walk up the gorge of the River Twiss and down the gorge of the River Doe, known as The Glens, is a splendid walk for a bad day because it is sheltered from the wind and the path, though very rough in places, is not boggy. As an added bonus the waterfalls are at their best after rain. Thornton Force in full flood is a sight not soon forgotten. Category B. Time: 2-2½ hours. Map: 1:25,000 Outdoor Leisure 2 Yorkshire Dales Western Area, but hardly needed. You may prefer to park at the start of the Glen, rather than in the free car park. This will save money if there are four of you, as there is an admission charge of 75p per person (summer 1990), whereas car parking costs £2 and includes admission. If you bridle at having to pay to see part of your national heritage, let me assure you it is good value for money.

Having got your ticket simply follow the one and only path, in parts with well-made concrete steps and handrails, until you cross the third bridge into a field. Bear right here to the stile into Twistleton Lane. There you'll find signposts directing you to Beezley Falls. Follow the sign past Scar End farm onto the road opposite the lane to Beezleys Farm, where again more signs point the way down to the river. In one place there is a viewpoint bridge over the stream which is incredibly far below. Don't miss it! As soon as you leave the wooded river valley towards the bottom, the path swings left across the fields to become a tarmac lane that leads to Ingleton in the middle of the main street. Turn right and 5-10 minutes walk sees you at your car.

If you want to do the walk the other way round (and it's just as good), turn left in the main street opposite the Nat. West Bank and then bear right.

Things of Interest

If you are interested in geology or botany there are many examples of the way surface rocks influence the species of plants that will grow. The geology of this little triangle of land is quite unusual. The South Craven Fault crosses the mouth of both glens just above Ingleton village and is the reason why coal occurs there. These Coal Measures are part of the coal-bearing Carboniferous rocks which would be located higher than the top of Ingleborough if they were in their proper place. They

Thornton Force in flood

were lowered some 5,000 feet by the earth movements that caused this fault, and were preserved from the erosion that removed them from land that was much higher than the top of Ingelborough is today.

The very first bit of the walk lies on these Coal Measures but quickly reaches the Great Scar limestone strata which stretch across both glens. At the first bridge as you walk up the River Twiss, the North Craven Fault appears low down in the west bank of the river where it curves to the west but above it are vertical limestone cliffs crowned with yew trees. Below them most of the trees are ash and hazel: Hartstongue and other ferns abound in the moss-covered boulders. All these are typical plants of the limestone which has eroded and fallen from the cliffs above. Higher up very different rocks appear, mudstones and green slates, which can be easily seen at the second bridge. These are the rocks lying below the fault, formerly thought to be of Pre-Cambrian origin, but today are thought to belong to the slightly less old Lower Ordovician Series. These ancient rocks have been sharply folded by many earth movements since they were formed and are now stood on end, which makes them prone to erosion into spectacular gorges like these. The green slate was worked in the old quarry on the left as you approach the bridge and there is a fine chunk of this rock in the footpath its blue-green colour and vertical grain easily seen. From now on the yew and ash trees disappear and are replaced by the oak, for the rock from here right up to Thornton Force is this old rock that breaks down to give the acidic soils suiting the oak, not the ash and the yew.

At Thornton Force the Great Scar limestone can be seen again in quite a dramatic manner making the cap or top layer over which the water pours. The underlying layer of slates is separated from the limestone by a band of softer conglomerated limestone, and this has worn away to make the overhanging lip of the falls. These conglomerates are the rocks of the earliest beds of the Great Scar limestone. Immediately the yew trees are back in view and the oaks disappear, but so do most trees, it's too high and too exposed to the wind here. There are none of the ferns and mosses so common in the lower glen either. They need that cool moist shade that is lacking here and demonstrates that climate matters more than soil in determining what will grow.

The limestone band at the top of Thornton Force does not cross the top of the River Doe where a band of greywacke, another ancient rock, extends across this part of the valley. It is quarried at Skirwith quarry just above and is known as Ingleton granite. The River Doe flows over the Lower Ordovician rocks almost all the way down to the lower part of the glen and the trees there are almost all oak trees, a clear indication of the absence of limestone which reappears as you reach the bottom.

Ingleborough

INGLEBOROUGH, 722 metres (2,375 feet)

Not the highest but certainly the best known peak of the Dales and one of the finest. (Pen-y-ghent and Wild Boar Fell are the other contestants for that honour.) The shortest ascent is from the Old Hill Inn, Chapel-le-Dale, taking barely 1½ hours and a further hour to descend. The route from Clapham (Walk 6.6) is the finest and most varied, but the one from Ingleton is the easiest to follow, bringing you direct to the summit cairn. Recommended if the weather's none too sure of itself.

6.2(a) By Storrs Common from Ingleton

Category B. Time: about 3-3$^{1}/_{2}$ hours return. Map: 1:25,000 Outdoor Leisure 2 Yorkshire Dales Western Area.

Leave the car park by the car exit and turn left and follow the road onto the Hawes road then along that to the last house on the right. The path starts immediately beyond it. It wanders over Storrs Common and eventually comes to the walled lane that leads to Crina Bottom Farm in about 1 mile. As you climb the stile at the end of the lane you will see the summit plateau of Ingleborough and the path clear all the way up to it. Return as you came taking care to check your direction with the compass if it's misty. The summit plateau can be quite a puzzling place.

6.2(b) From the Old Hill Inn, Chapel-le-Dale

Category B. Time: about 2$^{1}/_{2}$-3 hours, the extension is Category B. Map: 1:25,000 Outdoor Leisure 2, Yorkshire Dales Western Area.

Park in the lay-by about 150 yards above the inn then go down the road to a stile marked 'Footpath to Ingleborough and Gt. Douk Cave'. Follow the path through the pastures, reassured by a signpost at the third stile. The path soon enters the Southerscales Nature Reserve where some re-alignment has been done to reduce erosion: simply follow the discreet yellow-topped stakes. In due course you pass Braithwaite Wife Hole, the biggest shake hole in the Dales, but a mere flea bite compared with some on the Continent. You will soon reach a stile that marks the end of the Southerscales Nature Reserve and the start of the Ingleborough (High Lot) Nature Reserve, where the gritstones replace the Carboniferous limestones and the flora changes completely. Because of this change the ground is now peat moorland and the path was an eroded morass in wet weather. As part of the Three Peaks Footpath Project, a walkway composed of boards, much of it tarred and gritted just like a path in a town park, starts here. It's easy walking, but totally out of sympathy with the environment and deadly boring; better switch on your Sony Walkman to get it over with. It ends, thank goodness, at the foot of the steep escarpment where a stone

Ingleborough in winter,
from above Chapel-le-Dale

staircase helps your upward progress. At the top go through the little
gate where, above on the left, you will find a spring of clear cool water,
never known to fail. Then follow the path up the steep rocky edge onto
the flat top of Ingleborough and the crossed walls at the summit.

The broad, flat top is quite a puzzling place if it is at all misty and
a compass bearing is absolutely essential to leave correctly. When you
have gone through the little gate you have a choice of descent routes.
You may retrace your ascent route - dull in the extreme, though it can
be enlivened by a diversion to see Meregill Hole. If you want to do this,
when you have crossed the little stream about half-way down the
walkway you will see a grassy cart track following the stream down.
Follow this track and it will bring you to Meregill Hole which engulfs
the stream and is one of the deepest pot holes in the area. Then continue
to the wall, turn right and follow it to the stile where you rejoin your
ascent route.

A far better return route is to turn right a few feet below the little
gate and follow the well trodden path along the airy edge of the great
hollow of the High Lot Nature Reserve until you come to the wall
where you go down the steep hillside - it is steep too, with no made path
to help or bore you. Just pick your way down and at the wall below cross
the stile on the right. There is a little limestone escarpment ahead with
a sheepfold beyond it. Middle Washfold Cave is just beyond the
sheepfold and the small stream draining the little valley above sinks
into it. From here take the right-hand branch of the path passing first
Little Douk Pot identified by its rowan tree, then on your left the vast
cavity of Great Douk Cave. It is half-hidden by trees in summertime so

that you might not realise what a vast hole it is, not much smaller than Hull Pot on Pen-y-ghent. The water that sinks in Middle Washfold Cave appears in bottom of it. Follow the wall around the hole onto a cart track that brings you to a stile where you turn right and join your outward route reaching your car in 10 minutes.

Extension

If you want to make a full day of it note that this walk meets Walk 6.6 at the little gate at the top of the escarpment. Then follow Walk 6.6 to the signpost on Sulber Nick, turn right and follow the path up the flanks of Simon Fell. The upper part of it has been treated by the Footpath Project, with what looks like quarry waste, and is rough enough to give interesting walking. It climbs easily at first but with ever increasing steepness, though you cut off right to the col just before it really rises on its hind legs. Locate that little gate again and descend by whichever route you please as given above.

Things of Interest

Both of these routes up Ingleborough cross the Great Scar limestone, and in particular the route from the Old Hill Inn shows the big clint fields very well. This way too, you get a better view of the banding of the Yoredale rocks that form the upper part of the mountain. See the Clapham route for notes about the summit and its views.

Meregill Hole is an impressive shaft spanned by a rock bridge and engulfing a stream. There is a lake at the bottom of this shaft, just visible, and held there by a band of clayey shale. Though the shaft attracted the pioneer cavers of the Yorkshire Ramblers' Club as early as 1908, this lake and further waterfalls held up exploration, and it wasn't until the stream was diverted in 1912 that the club was able to reach the bottom. A waterfilled tube of a passage prevents further progress even today. The total depth of this pothole is 565 feet (173 metres), but the mere that gives the pot its name is only 40 feet (12 metres), down. The water appears at God's Bridge, a natural rock bridge that is the start of the River Greta, in the fields below the road.

WHERNSIDE

At 2,415 feet (736 metres), the highest hill in the Park if not the most shapely nor popular. The shortest ascent is from the head of Kingsdale, the best makes a circuit from the Old Hill Inn, Chapel-le-Dale, returning by the 'new' path (not shown on the O.S. map) to Ribblehead, or obviously, from Ribblehead by the 'new' path. They are all Category B walks but in less than perfect conditions go up a grade. All use the 1:25,000 Outdoor Leisure 2, Yorkshire Dales Western Area map.

6.3a   From the head of Kingsdale

Time: $1\frac{1}{2}$-2 hours return. Category B. Park as close as possible to the old quarry just before reaching the top of the road from the Ingleton side, but take care not to obstruct the single width road. The spot height 468 is given on the map just above the quarry.

Walk down the road about 100 yards below the quarry, to the point where a fence meets the road, cross the little stream and pick up a faint path that follows the fence then the wall up the hillside. Where the wall swings left go horizontally right along a stony bank until you come to a small collection of cairns, then go straight up to the summit cairn. The path is clear all the way.

6.3b   From the Old Hill Inn, Chapel-le-Dale

Time: about $3\frac{1}{2}$ hours. Category B.
Park in the lay-by about 150 yards above the Old Hill Inn.

Go down the road to the first lane on the right. It leads to Bruntscar, right at the foot of Whernside. Where the tarmac ends turn right and go over the ladder stile into the field. You will see a well-worn, sometimes boggy path climbing quite steeply up the hillside to the base of the escarpment. Simply follow it. The escarpment has been graced with a set of wooden steps, but the risers are so big that despite a notice asking you to use them, you may prefer to use the escape route to the right. Both routes bring you onto the summit ridge quite some distance from the cairn which lies behind the wall, not obvious in mist. In the summer of 1990 a great deal of path building and restoration work were in progress along this badly eroded part of the route much of which then looked worse than it did before. Nature will heal the scars given time.
    Continue along the summit ridge for about a mile. The path is

Whernside, above
Chapel-le-Dale

pleasantly poised above the blue waters of Greesett Tarn, a haunt of nesting seagulls in springtime. It turns at the wall corner then continues downwards following the fence until the head of Force Gill is reached. At this point the path swings away from the wall and goes across to a stile on the Craven Way, from where it goes straight down the nose of the moor by a length of walkway to reach the Settle-Carlisle railway line below. Having crossed the line by a substantial stone bridge the path wanders across the moor to the former signal box house from where a length of restored path follows the railway line. Leave it after a few minutes going through a short tunnel then follow the cart track to Winterscales Farm where you pick up their tarmac access lane. Turn left at the first junction, right at the junction at Gunnerfleet Farm, then follow the lane to the main road where you turn right and reach your car in less than 10 minutes.

6.3c   From Ribblehead

Time about 3 hours return, for this route does not lend itself to making a circular tour as does route 6b. In dry conditions it is somewhat easier but can be extremely boggy. Category B.

There is plenty of room to park at Ribblehead close to the junction of the B6479, and there is often a refreshment van there, to say nothing of the proximity of the Station Hotel.

The path, a wide stony track, starts opposite the road junction and swings round the side of the famous viaduct but does not go under it. Follow it first besides the railway line, then half a mile beyond the signal box take the left fork across the moor to a bridge across the railway. Now simply follow the walkway up the nose of the moor to the stile, then the fence and wall to the summit cairn. Return as you came.

Things of Interest

The Craven Way, a small part of which is used by routes 6.3b and c is no modern Way, but a very old packhorse track from Dent to Ingleton. It is also known as the Craven Wold. It climbs over the shoulder of Whernside keeping to the limestone strata most of the way and is picked up by walk 6.3b at the stile where it drops down by Force Gill, a fine little waterfall in wet weather. The Way continues under the railway to Winterscales Farm then continues to join the farms that are situated along the base of the steep flanks of Whernside before descending into Kingsdale and Ingleton.

6.4 A Two Peaks Walk

The Three Peaks Walk (No. 5.10) may be more than all but the seasoned walker wants to attempt, but most folk can manage two of them and Ingleborough and Whernside make the best pair. Time: 5 ^{1}/$_2$-6 hours. Category A. Map: 1:25,000 Outdoor Leisure 2 Yorkshire Dales Western Area. Park in the lay-by above the Old Hill Inn, Chapel-le-Dale.

Start by doing Whernside first using route 6.3b which you follow right over Whernside to the point where that walk goes under the railway to Winterscales Farm. Here you keep straight on following the good track to the road at Ribblehead.

Cross the road and go down the Selside road, B6479, for a short mile to the first lane on the right. It passes a short row of former railway cottages and brings you to Colt Park Farm. Keep straight on up the field past the farm and follow the wall up the steep end of Park Fell. As the ground rises to Simon Fell the wall swings to the left, but keep straight on following a vague path until you meet a cross wall. Over the stile the path is very well marked indeed and quickly brings you to the last steep rocky ridge that brings you onto the summit plateau of Ingleborough. Return by either of the routes given in Walk 6.2b.

6.5 A walk amongst the caves and potholes of Kingsdale

Best done on a wet Sunday when there are many potholers around. Pot holes are much more impressive after rain when the dash and rumble of water can be heard far below. Time: 2 hours or a little more if you go into Yordas cave. Category B. Map: 1:25,000 Outdoor Leisure 2 Yorkshire Dales Western Area. Park in Kingsdale where the Twistleton Lane meets the road.

About 100 yards on the Ingleton side of the lane junction there is a ladder stile on the right. There is scarcely any path in the mass of limestone boulders in the field, but make for the next ladder stile on the skyline. Again the same sort of rough going takes you upwards. It is probably best near the wall. Ignore the first gateway and make sure you are on the well marked cart track of the Turbary Road before you turn right through the wall.

Every one of the fields you pass through has caves or potholes in it, but only a few of the best known ones are described here. Soon after you've come into the third field you will see a small stream, quite likely dry. Follow it leftwards and the entrance to Swinsto Pot is in a shallow shake hole or hollow on its right, less than 100 yards from the road. It is a very modest hole, but it is axiomatic in potholing that small entrances have big systems below. Go back to the Turbary Road and continue into the next field. Turn left by the wall and soon you will come to a long line of shake holes running parallel with the road. About a hundred yards along you will find one with a sort of slot-cum-letterbox in the bottom. This is Simpson's Pot. Further along this same field you will see a few rowan trees. They are growing in the top of Rowten Pot, a tremendous chasm. The greater part of it is partially blocked with boulders, but at the western end there is a substantial rock bridge, and on the other side a small open shaft or eye-hole goes plumb down for 200 feet. It is awe inspiring to hear the water far below. Across the road where the water sinks is Rowten Cave and the water soon finds its way into the pot by the side of the road. As you go into the next field you'll soon see another rowan tree. Make over to it. This is Jingling Pot, a long straight drop of 140 feet. Again, the water from the stream sinks into a cave above it, but instead of draining into it, goes into Rowten Pot.

At the next gate the Turbary Road climbs up to a gate on the skyline, and you no longer follow it. Ahead lies the plantation where Yordas Cave is to be found. There is no right of way path to it and it is surrounded by a high, loose very nasty wall. Thus warned you may be quite prepared to go ahead but if not there is no real alternative but to retrace your steps and visit Yordas Cave from the road. (See Note A.)

On the way you pass Bull Pot just below where the next stream sinks. It is a narrow boulder-covered rift.

That wall is best crossed where it climbs over a small escarpment that runs along the field. Then go down the field until you can get easily into the dried-up river bed in the wood. The entrance to the cave is on the left through a stone archway. Provided there are at least two of you, go inside to take a look round, but you will need good lights to see anything of the cave. Wait a few minutes to accustom your eyes to the gloom then go forward to a small stream. Now look up. You are in an impressively high chamber. Turn to the right and follow the right wall. You'll hear a waterfall but it is out of sight in another little chamber at the end of this huge one. Just go on to the apparent end and look round the corner. Retrace your steps as soon as you are satisfied: there is no way downstream.

Now go down to the tarmac road and walk along back to where you are parked. On the way you pass the Valley Entrance to all these potholes. It is within an oil drum sunk in the ground in the field on the right-hand side of the road opposite the lane that leads to Braida Garth. A little further down the road on the left-hand side is Keld Head, a large deep pool draining into the river and much used by cave divers.

Note A

Yordas Cave is easily reached from the Kingsdale road. When driving up the valley it can be identified by the plantation of trees that surrounds it and it is possible to park fairly close to the field gate immediately below the plantation, but take care not to block the single width road. Go up the right-hand side of the field to the second level of the dried-up river bed and the cave is on the left.

Some background information about these caves

The Turbary road that gives access to these potholes and cave today is another ancient track that linked Dent and Ingleton crossing the flanks of Gragareth where it has disappeared in the peat moss. It was also used by the peasants of the villages at the foot of Gragareth to reach the peat cutting grounds there. The right to cut peat on the common land, or the right of turbary to give it its old legal name, was one of the peasants' valuable rights.

The straight sided valley of Kingsdale was carved out of the limestone strata by one of the glaciers of the last Ice Age, right down to the Silurian rocks below it. Its terminal moraine blocked the valley just below Twistleton lane and the melt waters formed a lake behind it. You start this walk on the shoulder of the terminal moraine and walk up the hill for just over 400 feet of height, climbing the entire thickness of the Great Scar Limestone at that point. The Turbary Road happens to run more or less along the line where the gritstone cap of Whernside meets the limestone and this is where the streams are engulfed by the limestone. Exactly where any stream sinks on the day you visit it depends a bit on how much water there is flowing, but all the water from this fellside meets up underground and next sees daylight at Keld Head. A great deal is known about the connections of these caves under the ground.

Swinsto Pot was first explored by the Gritstone Club in 1930 to a depth of 360 feet and more depth to it was found by the University of Leeds Speleological Society in 1962. Simpson's Pot was first explored by the British Speleological Association in 1940, and, like Swinsto, explored further by the University of Leeds S.S. Both of these pots give very popular 'sporting do's' having vertical pitches where rope ladders, or just ropes, are needed, long sections of stooping and crawling in water, as well as passages big enough to walk along. Almost at the end they unite. With proper organisation and plenty of tackle it is possible for potholers to go down one and up the other. Alternatively it is possible to continue into the Kingsdale Master Cave which is almost at the bottom of the limestone layer. This can also be entered direct from the valley by the Valley Entrance, but not easily. Thus it is possible for the well-equipped experienced party to go underground at the level of the Turbary Road and emerge on the tarmac road in the valley.

Rowten Pot was first descended by the Yorkshire Ramblers' Club as long ago as 1897: a formidable undertaking including the climbing of a waterfall pitch 140 feet high using a rope ladder. Today, easier ways of doing it have been found. Its depth is 345 feet and its waters flow into the Kingsdale Master Cave, but the ordinary potholer cannot pass as some of the passages are filled to the roof with water and it needs cave diving gear to pass them. Jingling Pot has a straight smooth shaft of 140 feet in one straight drop from the tree, and again the Yorkshire Ramblers explored this in 1926. Yet again its waters flow into the Kingsdale Master Cave, but the passages are blocked with debris. Yordas Cave, named after a legendary giant, was once a showcave. Its main chamber is big by any standards - 180 feet (55 metres) long,

50 feet (15 metres) wide and 80 feet (20 metres) high. Its formations are high on the walls and roof and are not particularly good, though they take some fanciful shapes.

Keld Head is more than just a pool draining into the river. It is the place where the waters of all these potholes meet the impervious Silurian rocks below the limestone and this forces them to the surface as a massive resurgence. There is a huge underwater cavern about 100 feet, (30 metres) long and passages mostly water-filled continue for about 1,000 feet, (300 metres). All this has been discovered by cave divers.

WALKS FROM CLAPHAM

6.6 Ingleborough, Simon Fell and Park Fell

This is a splendid walk with ever changing views taking about 6 1/2 hours from the Y.D.N.P. car park at Clapham. It can be shortened by returning along Simon Fell Breast to join the longer route at Clapham Lane. Time for this walk, 4 1/2 hours. Both are Category A and need Map: 1:25,000 Outdoor Leisure 2 Yorkshire Dales Western Area.

Turn right on leaving the car park and almost at once cross the beck that divides the village[1]. Turn right then left round a sharp corner, pass the farm buildings and turn right into a rough lane that climbs quite steeply to Clapdale farm. After going through the gate turn right and drop quite steeply into the upper part of Clapdale. Alternatively you can pay your small fee and go through the Ingleborough Estate - see the next walk. Continue past Ingleborough[2] or Clapham Cave as it is also called, through a gate and up the impressive confines of Trow Gill.[3] Emerging from the gill the path follows the wall for almost a mile. Cross the wall at the second stile and follow the broad eroded path to Gaping Gill,[4] a few minutes walk away. You will get the best views of this mighty shaft by going to the right and crossing the stream to regain the main path which is on the left. It is broad and often wet with many boggy places until it reaches the stony flank of Little Ingleborough. Here a bit of excellent new path leads you to the steep stony ascent to the plateau. To find the top with its sheltering cross-walls turn sharp left as soon as you reach it.

The summit of Ingleborough[5] is a tricky place, flat and featureless and so worn by the passage of feet that paths merge into one vast area

The packhorse bridge, Clapham

of eroded ground. If in doubt or if it's misty, check your departing direction by compass: 60 degrees magnetic north. (If you want to return as you came take a bearing of due east.) Following the left-hand edge brings you to the narrow neck of steep ground that leads to Simon Fell. If you are doing the shorter walk keep to the right-hand side and take the right fork at the first slight 'levelling' of the ridge and then turn to Note A. Otherwise keep to the spine of the ridge aiming for the wall in the gap between Ingleborough and Simon Fell. Here you will find a spring of cool water, never known to fail. Enjoy it! Now go through the little gate and descend a few feet to a path that runs along the airy edge of the great hollow of High Lot Nature Reserve. It has the most splendid views towards the Ribblehead Viaduct. Whernside is to the left, Great Coum and Crag Hill are beyond it, and behind them, the Howgills. To the right of Whernside, behind the viaduct, is the escarpment of Wild Boar Fell, and on its right, Mallerstang Edge.

Beyond the stile the path is less well defined until you pick up the guiding wall that runs from Simon Fell right over Park Fell to Colt Park, and you simply follow it all the way. As you drop over the end of Park Fell the view changes dramatically with Upper Ribblesdale at your feet and Pen-y-ghent visible out of the corner of your eye to the right. When you reach the access road to Colt Park Farm turn right on the track to Selside. Follow it through the farm buildings then through the hay meadows to an isolated barn. In the next field, just before you reach the

Park Fell, Simon Fell and Ingleborough,
above Ribblehead Viaduct, seen from Blea Moor. (Walk 5.15)

gate, turn left to a stile that leads to a gap through Colt Park Wood. When you have gone completely through the wood turn sharp right into the field and make for the distant ladder stile. Keep in the same general direction across two more fields, then you find yourself in a large field with the road in sight. Follow the faint cart tracks to the gate by the distant wall to reach the road just above Selside.

Turn right and less than 10 minutes walk brings you to a rough lane on the right that leads to Alum Pot (see Walk 5.13). Turn into it and follow it to its apparent end where it merely does a sharp left-hand bend and becomes pleasantly grassy. In the field ahead the path first follows the wall then disappears. Bear left to find a ladder stile and continue in the same direction to the next one. After the next one you pick up a grassy cart track that the map shows going all the way back to Clapham, but beware! In the middle of this vast field it starts to curve to the right to go through a gate. At this point you keep straight on, and though there's not much to be seen on the ground at first, you will soon find a track to follow. It leaves the field at a gate high on the right and is now well defined almost as far as Sulber Nick where a signpost informs you that it is 3½ miles to Clapham. Follow the track over open pastures* for about a mile, taking the right-hand fork at the first cairned fork and again at the second fork where the track swings quickly right to get into the head of Trow Gill. It then bears left and goes through a gate to become Long Lane. Turn right where this joins Thwaite Lane, duck under the tunnels of Ingleborough Hall and you're in the main street of Clapham, two minutes from your car.

Note A

The path curves under Simon Fell as a broad muddy swathe, unmistakable. Some little distance down you come to a section of path that has been drained and resurfaced with what looks like quarry waste as part of the Three Peaks Footpath Scheme. It gives far better going than the badly eroded ground above yet is in keeping with the landscape. It ends some little distance above Nick Pot and a derelict shooting hut and you continue on the eroded peaty path, a reminder of what it was all like before it had 'the treatment'. Take the left fork below the hut and in due course you'll come to a signpost with the heartening news that it is $3^{1}/_{2}$ miles to Clapham. Turn right here, for you have now joined the main walk.

Things of Interest

1. Clapham is a delightful old village built astride the stream. Its church looks fittingly old but except for the tower was rebuilt early in the nineteenth century by the Farrer family who lived at Ingleborough Hall.

2. Ingleborough Cave is a show cave open to the public. Regular guided tours are available during the summer. The cave originally had a stalagmite barrier at the mouth holding up an under ground lake. It was drained in 1837 by Farrer's workmen and the former level of the lake can be seen very clearly on the formations in the cave.

3. Trow Gill is a very narrow enclosed valley with high rock walls. It was formed by the melt water stream from the glacier on this side of Ingleborough. Today the drainage from Ingleborough runs into Gaping Gill.

4. The yawning chasm of Gaping Gill opens into the deepest pothole shaft in England, a breathtaking 340 feet. It was first descended by the famous French potholer E.A.Martel, using rope ladders and a field telephone to keep touch with his surface helpers. Today it is usual to descend it by a petrol winch, and at holiday times it is often possible to go down for about £2 when one of the major potholing clubs is there. It's highly recommended experience provided you have a good torch a waterproofs. Though the beck is diverted away from the actual line of descent you pass through it briefly. The huge chamber into which you descend like a spider on a thread is 460 feet (140 metres) long, 90 feet (27 metres) wide and 11 feet (33 metres) high. The stream that sinks in the floor of this, the Main Chamber, reappears in Ingleborough

191

Cave some 480 feet lower down the side of Ingleborough. A vast network of passages, caverns, shafts and other entrances into the whole system have been discovered over the years and now amount to more than seven miles.

5. The summit of Ingleborough was once the biggest Iron Age fort in the Pennines and is now an Ancient Monument managed by English Heritage. Its enclosing wall took in the entire summit plateau, but there is little left today except on the side facing Ingleton where there are still some remains of the ditch and rampart. Aerial photos show a great deal more.

6.7 The Ingleborough Estate Trail

In the first edition of this guide book the trail is called the Reginald Farrer Nature Trail, for Reginald Farrer is the best known of the family that used to live at Ingleborough Hall. The pamphlet that described the trail has been reissued under the new name and the return route changed. It can be purchased at the Y.D.N.P. centre in the car park at Clapham and at other Park centres and is not expensive. It gives a detailed account of the many things to be seen on the walk through the estate and about the changes the Farrer family made to the landscape around Ingleborough Hall. There is a small entrance fee for the trail through the grounds of the Ingleborough Estate and only the return is on right of way paths. Even without the information in the trail guide this is a walk well worth its entry money. Time: about 2 hours. Category C, map hardly needed.

Turn right on leaving the car park, and almost at once cross the stream that divides the village. Turn right again then left round a sharp corner and on your right you will see an open farm gate and a notice inviting you to pay your entry fee. Now follow the well kept, wide path past the lake,[1] into the upper grassy valley as far as Ingleborough Cave. Then you may either retrace your steps or, having almost reached the little gate into the woods turn left and climb steeply up the hill to Clapdale farm and follow their access road down the hill where you turn left to regain the starting point of the trail.

Things of Interest

1. This lake was made about 1833 by the Farrer family who owned Ingleborough Hall. They planted the thousands of trees around it and

The summit of Ingleborough, looking across to Whernside
Ingleborough from Crina Bottom

On the Waterfall Walk, Ingleton
Upper Dentdale and the Settle-Carlisle railway

rebuilt much of that end of the village including the church and the tunnels across Thwaite Lane in order to maintain the privacy of the hall and its grounds. Thwaite Lane is an ancient packhorse route, still in use at that time. Reginald Farrer, who was born in 1880, became famous as a writer and plant collector both in Europe and Asia. Many of these plants went to Kew and other great botanic gardens, but some were planted in the hall gardens. Gentiana Farreri a plant well-known among enthusiasts for alpines, is named after him.

6.8 To the Norber Boulders and Austwick

This walk has a strong geological interest. It can be extended to Horton in Ribblesdale to make a full day. See the next walk for details of this. Category B. Time: about 2-2½ hours. Map: 1:25,000 Outdoor Leisure 2 Yorkshire Dales Western Area. Start from the Y.D.N.P. car park at Clapham.

Turn right on leaving the car park and bear right at the top of the village to go under the tunnels.[1] Where the lane forks, take the right-hand one, and in about a mile you will find a ladder stile on your left. Cross it and aim at the wall corner beneath the impressive limestone crag. Follow the wall to a finger post, passing amongst quite a number of dark slatey boulders scattered about the grass. These are just a few of the Norber boulders,[2] but the biggest and best are higher up the hill. At the finger post turn left up the grass gully and you will see any number of them, some perched on little limestone tables. Have a look

Norber Boulders

193

round then retrace your steps to the finger post.

Even if you are only doing the short walk to the boulders ignore the sign to Austwick - unless it suddenly pours down, for this is a short direct way to the tarmac road to Austwick, a sort of emergency exit. The proper walk continues in the general direction of the finger that points to Crummack, but don't be misled by the many animal tracks.

Keep straight ahead for 50-70 yards then bear right a little to find the ladder stile. Follow the path below a little limestone cliff, Nappa Scar, and spare a moment to examine it fairly closely.[3] Continue to the wall and follow it to the road to Crummackdale Farm. Straight across the road is another stile. Cross it, and turn right. The path drops fairly steeply down the field at first to Norber Sike which is crossed by an ancient clapper bridge, and then follows the wall to Thwaite Lane. Go straight across this and again follow the wall to Town Head. Turn right when you meet the main road through the village and a few minutes walk will bring you to the village cross. Go straight on and keep a lookout for the start of the path back to Clapham, marked by a signpost between the houses on the right. The way is obvious except in the second field. Make for the venerable ash tree and from there you should be able to spot the slit stile in the opposite wall. As you come into the farmyard close to the car park don't be tempted to climb the fence into it. Go into the fenced path opposite and in just a few yards you'll find the stile.

6.9 To Horton in Ribblesdale via the Norber Boulders
A fine geologically based extension of the previous walk taking a total of 6-8 hours depending very much on how long you spend looking at things. Category B but long. Map: 1:25,000 Leisure 2 Yorkshire Dales Western Area.

Park in the Y.D.N.P. car park at Clapham and follow the previous walk as far as the road to Crummackdale Farm. Cross the stile opposite and instead of turning right, turn left. Two field lengths and obvious stiles will bring you to another bit of tarmac. Go straight across and up the pastures. At first there is a faint path that soon disappears, but as you go over the crown of the hill the ladder stile by Austwick Beck is easy to spot. Cross the beck and on the right is a three-star site for lunch - fairly sheltered and sunny with a fine view across to the Bowland fells. Otherwise, turn right on the lane and left at a junction in less than 100 yards. This green walled lane takes you delightfully up Crummackdale and finally swings right up a side valley and ends at a ruined shooting hut. The path itself continues very clearly up the valley to the limestone escarpment where you bear diagonally left to a cairn on the edge of a little clint field. The track continues through a line of shooting butts bearing right to a ladder stile in the wall.[4] Over the stile turn left and follow the path to the next stile, then bear diagonally right on a faint path to join the Three Peaks path from Ingleborough to Horton, just above a large gap in a wall. It is well trodden all the way to the road[5] crossing the railway en route. Go straight ahead to the wooden footbridge by the road bridge. The slit stile to the river bank is on its right.

However, you may want refreshments at this stage. Maybe you home in on The Crown if the hour is right. If not, go to the Pen-y-ghent Cafe, a veritable haven for the weary and hungry. Just over that wooden footbridge, through the car park (toilets) and you'll find it in less than 100 yards. Sooner or later - but not too late, there's much to be done yet - come back to that stile.

The footpath is obvious most of the way to Cragghill Farm, for it is part of the Ribble Way and well used. It follows the river bank[6] closely and is a first rate stretch of riverside walking. As you approach the farm keep to its left on the very brink of the river and continue to follow the bank until you reach a finger post that directs you across the field to a gate where you enter a walled lane, often deep in water in wet weather. The lane leads you under the railway onto a tarmac road leading to those huge quarries that destroy a whole hillside. Turn left and follow the road to a T-junction close to the pub at Helwith Bridge.

Here you turn right and launch onto an unfortunate 1 1/2 miles of road. The quarries have been greatly enlarged[7] since the 1984 edition of the map was published and although the footpaths have been diverted and some landscaping done, the footpath route used in the first edition of this book is no longer worth while. Continue to a lane on the left that leads to Jop Ridding. Keep straight on past the farm to the stile and follow the line of the wall[8] until you come to a gate that leads you onto a walled lane, full of wild roses in June and July. Turn left at the T-junction, and shortly afterwards you will come to an offset cross roads of lanes. If you have time (and energy) to have a look at Austwick[9] take the right-hand one which leads you into the head of the village. Otherwise go straight across and follow this to the road at Austwick

Bridge. Turn right and a minute or two sees you at the tiny village green with its cross and village shop opposite. Turn left here and keep a look out for a signpost on the right between the houses that mark the start of the path back to Clapham. The way is obvious, but see the previous walk if you need guidance.

Things of Interest for both these walks

1. See Walk 6.7 for something about Clapham village and the tunnels.

2. The Norber boulders are famous amongst geologists. The early observers of the 'natural curiosities' of the Dales could not understand how these dark slatey boulders, so different from the surrounding limestone, came to be there. It was only as the effects of the Ice Age came to be understood that it was realised that these chunks of rock must have been torn off the western slopes of Crummackdale where the basement rocks of Silurian slates outcrop, and where carried by the ice to be deposited here when it melted. Those perched on little limestone plinths are where the boulder protected the limestone underneath it from the slow, eroding effect of the weather. Elsewhere the limestone has been slowly but surely dissolved away by the rain in the course of these 10,000 years.

3. Nappa Scar looks just like any other limestone cliff until you look closely, especially at the base at the far end. Here you will see it is a deep band of conglomerate. Chunks of Silurian slate and what look like shells are embedded in. Other bands look like the usual Carboniferous limestone. Here you are very close to the bed of Silurian slate - it can be seen in the bed of the stream below - and the earliest layers of Carboniferous limestone are usually of this mixed material, whilst later ones are very pure. This band of dark rock is the first one you see of the Silurian slate, the bed rock of the valley whose flanks are of white Carboniferous limestone. Beyond it more slatey rock outcrops on the ground and continues to do so right up to the shooting hut. Above this the rock is limestone. Field walls are always a sure indication of the rocks beneath, and you will see the change. The bed of Silurian slate is the cause of the large stream in the valley: in valleys with limestone floors streams tend to disappear in summer.

4. If you do this walk in early summer have a good look at the vegetation. Close to the wall it is full of little flowers - daises, dandelions, thistles, clover, vetches, buttercups, even the occasional early purple orchid. A few yards away to the right is a clint field of bare

limestone with heather growing amongst it. This is most unusual. Heather is a plant of the gritstone moorlands, it won't grow where there is lime, so how does it manage to do so here? The plants close to the wall are characteristic of sheep-grazed limestone pasture. The explanation is that in the clint field, which is a very open one with large gaps, rain has leached the lime from the top layers of soil and iron salts present have formed an impermeable layer just below the level of the top soil, thus destroying natural drainage. This allows sphagnum and other mosses to grow. If you look below the heather you'll find them. As they die off the level of the soil is raised and drainage improves, but because it is raised, it does not receive water running off the adjacent limestone. Therefore the soil stays acid and heather will grow.

5. This path has some unexpected uphill bits in it. This is where it is climbing up and over and round a set of drumlins left by the retreating glaciers of the last Ice Age. If you look up and across the Ribble Valley from here you'll see many more of them, a veritable 'basket of eggs'.

6. There are a number of willow trees growing along the river bank and you will see the two sorts growing side by side. The sallow willow from which cricket bats are made has long strap-like leaves, whereas the goat willow has broad rounded leaves like big salt spoons. Both sorts have pussy catkins. As they hybridise freely you'll see some that are neither one thing nor the other.

7. Exactly what you will see depends on the state of quarrying, but two things are unmistakable; the rock is not limestone like the little crag perched over the quarry, and its strata sweep upwards whilst the limestone's is horizontal. The material of the vertical strata is the ancient Silurian slate, the same as is found in Crummackdale and which covers a small area round here, down to the North Craven Fault. You can see the same thing behind the row of houses where the horizontal Carboniferous limestone is sitting on the vertical slates. This, in geological terms, is an unconformity, not because of the change in direction of the strata, but because a whole set of rocks, the Devonian sandstones, is absent. It should be between the slates and the limestone, but in the aeons of time that passed between its deposition and the deposition of the limestone, it was weathered away in the Dales. As its name suggests it is found in its true order in Devon.

8. Towards the end of this wall the hillside has a queer lumpy look about it. It's the site of a large number of tiny quarries, now weathered and grown over. They are very old and it is possible they were quarried

for the stone to build Austwick village.

9.   Austwick is a most attractive and unspoiled village. The name ending in wick suggest it was founded by the Norsemen. Most of the houses were built between the seventeenth and eighteenth centuries, but Austwick Hall has parts that are much older. It was a fortified manor house and had a pele tower as protection against the Scots raiders who threatened Craven so much after the Battle of Bannockburn. The church is Victorian.

Crummackdale, with Ingleborough behind

OTHER WALKS

6.10   Gragareth, Great Coum and Crag Hill

These three hills form the western boundary of the Yorkshire Dales National Park to the north-west of Ingleton. On a good day the latter pair offers quite the finest panorama in the whole of the Park. They are, however, best done from t'other place, Lancashire, as they form a natural circuit of upper Easegill.

The walk starts at the top of the road that goes to Leck Fell House from the village of Leck. This road leaves the A65 at Cowan Bridge, 4½ miles from Ingleton. There are two good parking spots towards the end of the road at an approximate height of 1,300 feet. Category: B+,

Map: 1:25,000 Outdoor Leisure 2 Yorkshire Dales Western Area. The walk is very wet in parts and best done this way round. Time: 4 hours, but note this does not give the road approach, for which the 1:50,000 map sheet 97 is useful.

Walk up the road to the point where it drops to Leck Fell House then go straight ahead through the gate onto the fell road. Continue for about ¹/₄ mile until you are below a grassy break in the band of stones which lies across the hillside. From here a faint path leads up to the collection of cairns known as the Three Men of Gragareth. From them a path, faint at times, continues straight up the hillside to the trig point from where there is a fine view of the western part of the Lake District and Morecambe Bay, though the best is yet to come. Continue towards the wall and then follow the path alongside it to Great Coum, passing over the modest little Green Hill on the way. In the dip beyond it follow the tractor marks to the gate on the left and thence to the top. The cairn is over the wall and there's no stile so it is not worth crossing over though Great Coum is the highest of the three, 687 metres (2,253 feet). From here the vast panorama extends from Lovely Seat - which divides Wensleydale from Swaledale - to Black Combe, the most westerley outlier of the Lake District. Whernside blots out the views of Pen-y-ghent and its nearby fells, but those were well enough seen from Gragareth. Continue to Crag Hill with its trig point, reached by stepping over the fence, and the view is extended to Morecambe Bay. It's magnificent in the late afternoon with the sun glinting on the water.

Descend by the fence towards Bullpot Farm, out of sight for quite a time, eventually identified by its sheltering trees. A little path starts you off then joins a set of tractor marks that winds down the fell and in due course you will come to a broken-down wall on your left. Follow this down to the first cross wall, step over the fence on your left, and continue by the wall until you meet the track from Bullpot Farm that goes over the moor to Easegill. It is marked by stakes and is easy to follow even in thick weather. The descent into the gill is steep and surrounded by a fence, best crossed to the left, and the decrepit bridge left severely alone. In the corner, on the left at the foot of a little cliff, is a square shaft in the boulders. This is County Pot and is the main way into the maze of caves below. The gill is normally dry: cross it and continue up the field making towards the wall, pass through a gate in a wire fence and continue to the wall corner. Climb quite steeply up this rough field to a gate high up the wall. From here a track takes you back to the farm and the road.

Things of Interest

Yorkshire is commonly thought of as the home of potholing; however, beneath Easegill there is arguably the finest collection of caves and potholes in the British Isles, BUT they are in Lancashire! The Carboniferous limestone in which Yorkshire's great caves and potholes are located extends under this upland valley - so much for county boundaries and geological land forms. The stream sinks underground well upstream of the point where you cross the gill and its waters have eroded a vast collection of passages and shafts, some long since devoid of water and thickly coated with clay, others with a stream running through them. They were discovered by members of the Red Rose Pothole Cub in the late 1940s. The story goes that one of their members was sitting on the moor not far from the farm on a warm windless day and noticed a tuft of grass at his feet wafting about. This showed him that there was an air current rising from below ground, so he pulled out the tuft of grass and quickly revealed a deep shaft that was found to lead into some very extensive caves, which were named Lancaster Hole. At about the same time a way into a cave system near County Pot was discovered, and in due course it was found that this and the Lancaster Hole shaft were two entrances to the same vast cave system. Bullpot Farm was used as a base for exploration in these early days of discovery, for the farmer there was a hospitable chap and allowed people to use his barn. Today it is the headquarters of the Red Rose Pot Hole Club and the focus of potholing in the area. The route across the moor was marked by stakes in the early days of exploration because of the problems encountered in mist or darkness by returning potholers who were often wet through and tired. Cases of hypothermia were not unknown when people had wandered around for a long time looking for the farm.

7: DENTDALE AND GARSDALE

Walks in Dentdale

7.1   The riverside to Tommy Bridge. Category C 204
7.2   The Dales Way and Gawthrop. Category C 205
7.3   The Dales Way from Ewegales Bridge to Dent.
      Category B+ 205
7.4   Flinter Gill and Deepdale. Category B 209
7.5   Great Knoutberry Fell. Category B 211
7.6   Whernside from Dent. Category A 213

Walks in Garsdale

7.7   Frostrow Fell and the River Clough. Category C 214
7.8   A look at Grisedale. Category C 216
7.9   Baugh Fell. Category A 217
7.10 Garsdale Station to Kirkby Stephen Station
      via Wild Boar Fell. Category A 219

ABOUT DENT AND DENTDALE

If you come here direct from Wharfedale and have an observant eye for the fields and farms, you will notice the difference between the two dales. Wharfedale was heavily settled by the Anglo-Saxons whose ploughing methods produced the lynchets or terraces in so many fields, and was the cause of the many compact villages. The Anglo-Saxons never reached Dentdale; it was left to the Irish-Norse colonisers of the ninth and tenth centuries who arrived from the West to settle this valley. They were sheep farmers, not arable farmers, and left no mark except the scattered farms in the valley. They were followed by the Normans, who, judging by the Norman arch in the church door, founded the settlement of Dent, once very much bigger than it is today. At the end of the eighteenth century it was bigger than Sedbergh and the 'capital' of the western Dales. Its prosperity was based partly on farming and quarrying but mainly on hand knitted stockings and caps usually made by the womenfolk who would gather round the fireside whilst one of the group read to them, or in galleries along the house fronts, but these have now all disappeared. Dent has retained many of its old houses and cobbled streets, but it is a thousand pities there is no by-pass to it. Its

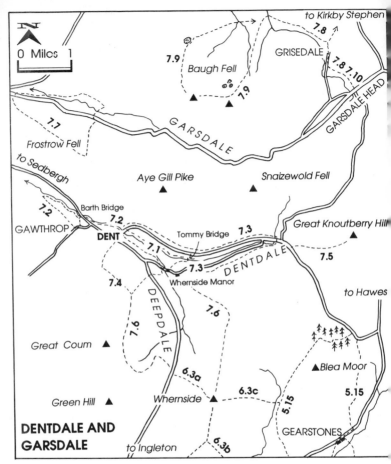

DENTDALE AND GARSDALE

most famous son is Adam Sedgwick (1785-1873) who became Professor of Geology at St John's College, Cambridge. He was the first to suggest that 'foreign' rocks in the Dales such as the Norber Boulders (see Walk 6.8) had been carried there by the glaciers of the last Ice Age, and he contributed much of our early knowledge of that period. He is commemorated by a fountain made from a huge block of Shap granite in the main street. Today tourism is increasingly important. The village has two pubs, two camp and caravan sites, shops and some accommodation.

Dent, with the Adam Sedgwick Memorial

Several good walks start from Dent Village. The car park is on the left as you come in from Sedbergh, and there are toilets and a picnic area. All of these walks have sections through the valley hay fields. In May, June and July it is essential to walk in single file to cause as little damage to the grass crop as possible. In the Dales grass is just as much a crop as corn is elsewhere. It is well to remember that if it has rained recently, this long grass can be very wetting. Map: 1:25,000 Outdoor Leisure 2 Yorkshire Dales Western Area covers all the walks.

WALKS IN DENTDALE

Both the upstream and downstream walks can be shortened if required and both have good views up and down the dale. Both are Category C, and overtrousers are worthwhile after rain when the hay is ready for cutting.

7.1 The riverside to Tommy Bridge

Time: 1¹/₂ hours or 1 hour for the short version.

Turn left on leaving the car park and wander through the village taking time to look at Adam Sedgwick's monument, the cobbled main street and the church. Then make your way to Church Bridge on the 'main' road. Go through the stile opposite and follow the path up Keld Beck to Double Croft. It is well marked and the stiles are waymarked. Go straight across the lane at Double Croft into the next field. At the end of it you come to another footpath at right angles, and if you want the short version, turn left (see note A). Otherwise, turn right and continue to the road by the path. Turn left on the road, ignoring the waymarks opposite. Less than 100 yards away, immediately past Mill Bridge Farm, is the stile you want. No path is to be seen in this field, but climb up towards a couple of trees and then make towards the far wall. Don't go through the gateway, but turn right and follow the wall down the hill. There you will find a line of stiles that brings you to Tommy Bridge. Cross the bridge and turn left. The path is not always visible, but it hugs the river bank and all the stiles are waymarked. Just as you think it is going to take you back to Dent, a finger post directs you very firmly to the right to a stile which takes you quickly to the road. Regrettably there are no more footpaths, but 20 minutes along the lane back to the car is a small price to pay for so excellent a walk.

Note A

Follow the path down to the river bank, then follow the flood bank of the river all the way to Keld Beck. At a barn close to Keld Beck cross the beck, turn right and a couple of hundred yards sees you on the road at Church Bridge.

Things of Interest

This walk goes along the river flats that are naturally prone to flooding; note that all the farms and buildings are well back on the first rising ground of the valley sides. Ground such as this always has a rich soil and there is a wider variety of plants and trees than in many of the dales, elm and beech, for example, are quite common, so is meadow cranesbill and salad burnet. Dentdale is known for its lush vegetation.

Mill Bridge was once a corn-mill taking its water from sluices in Deepdale Beck. Oats were grown in the dale until about 100 years ago and these were ground for flour and meal.

7.2 The Dales Way and Gawthrop

Quite a bit longer than the first walk, and best done this way round for the sake of the views from the lane. Time: 2½ hours, 1½ hours for the short version. Category C.

From the car park go straight down through the fields to the river, turn left and follow the river bank to the road. The path to Barth Bridge continues a mere 50-70 yards further on and is easy to find all the way. At the bridge turn left on the road and go through a scarcely visible slit stile at the first gate on the right. Follow the hedge side to find the next stile to the left by a small stone building, then go straight up by the beckside only leaving it to go to the gate by the cottages. Go up the tarmac road where you will find the village shop. If you want the short walk, now turn to Note A. Otherwise follow the road past the shop, take the right fork and follow this very pleasant lane through the farms gently down the hill. When you've passed the lane to Dillicar and gone over a humped-back bridge, turn right into the field to return by the Dales Way to Barth Bridge. The path follows the river bank very closely all the way, only leaving it by 20 yards or so to find the bridge to cross a stream. When you reach Barth Bridge return to Dent as you came.

Note A

Go left just a few yards, then right up a lane to the first fork on the left. The field path to Dent starts at the end of it. It is not well marked but the stiles are all there. Go gently downhill to Mill Beck Farm, between the buildings and cross three more fields by a faint path to emerge on the Flinter Gill Lane. Turn left and a few minutes sees you in Dent.

7.3 The Dales Way from Ewegales Bridge to Dent

The Dales Way enters Dentdale at the very head of the valley but unfortunately then follows the road for a good two miles. However, from shortly after Ewegales Bridge it follows field tracks and riverside paths right into Dent, a first class bit of valley walking, but obviously a linear walk. In the absence of a transport manager a circular walk can be made using field paths linking the farms on the north side of the valley. It is quite long and involves a lot of painstaking route finding between these farms, so many people may prefer to do it in two halves starting the upper half at the Ibbeth Peril car park. This is some

3¹/₂ miles from Dent on the Ribblehead road. The link from this car park to the route and the return to Dent on completion of the outward leg are given at the end of the walk proper. Category B+ because of its length, time about 6 hours.

NOTE. Few of the paths on the outward leg are visible and great care must be taken to follow the instructions particularly through the hamlets that are on the route, otherwise much time will be wasted. The O.S. map is of very limited value in passing through these hamlets. The return along the Dales Way is very well trodden and easy to follow. Map: 1:25,000 Outdoor Leisure 2 Yorkshire Dales Western Area.

Dent to Bankland
Turn left on leaving the car park and take the left fork in the village. Cross Church Bridge and go through the stile on the left-hand side, following the riverside path through the fields to the road. Turn left and shortly take the first lane on the right, signposted to High Hall Rare Breeds Farm. Turn right 20 or 30 yards up this lane in front of the 'Atco' building, go through a gate into the fields and continue straight across through a line of gateways until you reach a farm access road. At the point where it curves towards the house you will find a slit stile and from it you can see a gateway ahead just below Dee View. This gateway has a flanking yellow waymark and you will find other reassuring waymarks as you go.

Make for the obvious stile, pass in front of the house and go left into the head of the tiny stream. It is rather awkward to cross but then the way is clear to another gate at Hall Bank. (None of these houses have their names visible: they are on their roadside gates, so it is not easy to know where you have got to.) Go between their buildings and leave by a slit stile on the left, following the hedge to a slab footbridge onto the access road to Well Head. Follow the road past the farm and continue towards the next collection of buildings, Backstonegill, whose barns were being converted to dwellings in 1990. Aim for the low side of them to pick up the end of their access road and at the T-junction ahead turn left. Go between the buildings, cross a good footbridge and enter a walled lane straight ahead. This quickly brings you to another collection of buildings. Keep straight on into the field and follow the hedge to reach Scotchergill's access road. You now have fine views into Deepdale, flanked by Whernside on the left and dominated by Great Coum on the right. Follow the access road in front of the buildings then through two slit stiles to reach the back of High Chapel, a derelict farmstead.

The next two slit stiles are visible ahead and lead you to the access road to Peggleswright which you follow to Cross House. As soon as you have gone through the gate behind the house go through the gate on the left, head up to the wall corner and follow the hedge to a gate onto the access road to Bankland. Now turn right and follow this to the road.

Bankland to Cowgill.

Turn left on the road and continue for about a mile to the start of the farm access road to Broadfield House, which is signposted *Footpath to Cowgill.* Follow the access road to Broadfield House, unusually large for Dentdale and with an imposing classical porch on its obviously newer wing. At Broadfield House many other buildings are scattered around and care is needed to find your way through them. Go through the gate at the end of the house, turn right, and go left behind the next house to find a slit stile right in the corner by the house. Now go through the gate on the right of the house ahead, down the short length of lane to the barn then left into the field on a grassy cart track. In the second field follow the wall to find a step stile over the fence to the white-painted house, Hollins, then go through the gate opposite. Continue along the back of the farm, turn left to go through another gate onto a cart track. Pass in front of the next house and continue onto the access road to Broadmire. Follow this down to its first tight bend then keep straight on to a short length of wall where you will find a hidden slit stile. Now bear diagonally right across the field to find a good wooden footbridge with red waymarks into the hamlet of Spice Gill.

The tricky part is now over and you have time to appreciate the view ahead - the mass of Widdale Fell fills the head of the valley and is crossed by the line of the railway. More than likely you will see a train on it during the time it is within sight. Turn left past the first building and continue into the fields where you pass through two slit stiles and then head to the right to cross two step stiles over fences in quick succession. Now turn left to find another slit stile and left again through two gates in quick succession then aim diagonally right for a distant slit stile. (All this sounds a bit complex but it is easy when you are actually doing it.) Two more slit stiles put you onto a farm access road which you cross, following the wall to yet another slit stile in the corner. Now bear left across the field to a slit stile by a gate where you arrive in a lane.

Turn right and a couple of hundred yards walk brings you to Cowgill Church on the road.

Cowgill Church to Dent.

Turn right on the road, cross Ewegales Bridge and continue along the road for about ½ mile to a gate with a signpost to Laithe Bank. Follow the wide green track below the buildings into the plantation. A well trodden, clayey path brings you to Little Town where the path has been diverted to the right to pass below the buildings before it re-enters the gloomy plantation. On emerging follow the well trodden path passing a barn to reach a farm access road. Turn left on this for a mere 20 yards or so then cut across the field at a waymark to a stile by a tree and continue through a hayfield to a walled lane leading to Hackergill Farm. Turn left in the lane, pass to the right of another house and head for a gate with a signpost. Turn right and pass behind the next house to emerge at West Clint. Follow the access road until it bends to the right then go straight on through a gateway. Keep straight on to the next farm access road then turn down it to reach the tarmac road.

Turn left on the road and continue for about 200 yards to a gate with a sign to Lenny's Leap on the right. Follow the well trodden path to the footbridge over the River Dee, here deep cut in a mini-limestone canyon which presumably one Lenny leapt across. Having crossed the bridge turn left and follow the banks of the river, often devoid of water which has sunk beneath the limestone, to Tommy Bridge, a good half mile. Cross the bridge and turn right avoiding the length of wire, to locate the stile to the left of the gate. Climb up the hill following the wall to the top of the rise then strike across the field to the far right corner to find the stile onto the road. Turn right and in a few yards you will see a finger post to Church Bridge. Turn into this lane and follow it alongside Deepdale Beck to its junction with the River Dee. Now follow the flood bank of the river until you reach a sign directing you to the left, cross Keld beck, turn right and a couple of hundred yards sees you at Church Bridge. Retrace your steps to the car park.

Joining the walk from the Ibbeth Peril car park

Turn left on the road and simply follow it for a few hundred yards to the start of the farm access road to Broadfield House where you pick up the main walk. If you are doing the upper part only, having crossed the bridge at Lenny's Leap go straight up the field to a gate onto the road.

Turn right here and continue for a short mile to the car park.

Returning to the Ibbeth Peril car park
Although there is a footbridge and path from the car park to the road on the opposite side of the valley there is no path between the Dales Way and the road. This is unfortunate as it entails almost a mile of road walking after the bridge below Basil Busk has been crossed. However, to find this bridge, continue along the Dales Way until it joins the road in the main walk, then after about 100 yards turn right into the field at a finger post. After crossing the bridge climb steeply up the field to its left-hand corner to find the stile onto the road then turn right.

Return to Dent from Bankland
Turn left along the road and continue as far as a finger post to Lenny's Leap, just a couple of hundred yards, follow the path down to the bridge and turn right before you cross it. You have now joined the return path.

Things of Interest
The line of farms that extends right up the valley and which you follow on this walk were almost surely the first farms built outside the village of Dent, for they are on the south-facing side of the valley, much more favourably situated than the north-facing slopes. These were built in Victorian times, indeed one of them has a date stone 1868.

Backstone is a word associated with life in earlier centuries, when people were self sufficient. The wet climate of Dentdale meant that wheat could not be grown, and oats do not make good bread. Instead, oatmeal was made into 'clapp bread' which was baked on stone pushed onto the fire. This stone was called a backstone. They were made out of a slately stone that could be hollowed out a little and suitable stone was evidently found in this gill. There is a backstone in the museum in Hawes.

The bridge at Cowgill has a plaque recording a repair made in the early years of the eighteenth century.

Many of the fields you pass through on this walk are hay fields in early summer, rich with flowers, for they have never been reseeded.

7.4 Flinter Gill and Deepdale
This is a fairly strenuous walk climbing very steeply up to the old moorland road, the Occupation Road, that runs around the shoulder of

Great Coum to the head of Kingsdale at about the 1,400 foot contour. Dent itself is about 500 feet above sea level. The walk has plenty of variety and very good views. Category B. Time: about 3 hours.

If you first want to wander through the quaint village of Dent, turn left on leaving the car park and continue along the main road to the Sedgwick memorial, a rugged block of granite. Fork right here and right again after about 50 yards. This road takes you to the village green which you can reach directly from the car park by going straight across the road. Here there is a finger post to Flinter Gill. The road is metalled at first but rapidly becomes a rough lane winding its way steeply up the hill. It eases off a bit and then meets a broad stony lane. Turn left on this and follow it contouring along the fell until you come to a T-junction. Turn left here and follow this lane down to the Deepdale road at Low Nun House.

Cut straight across the road into the field and down the hedge side to the next gate. Pass through this and go straight down to the gate at the left-hand side of the farm buildings (it's marked) and follow the line of stiles through the fields. Drop slightly right to go into the wood, where there is a little notice to guide you, and then turn left, when 50 yards will see you on the road at Mill Beck Bridge. Turn left on the road and just across you will see the signpost, path to 'Church Bridge'. Keep straight on when you come to a branch that goes left. Your path follows the river flood bank all the way to Keld Beck, easy to walk and easy to follow. You'll soon see Dent Church ahead. At a barn close to Keld Beck where the flood banking ends, cross the beck, turn right and a couple of hundred yards sees you on the road just out of Dent.

Things of Interest

The track up Flinter Gill is part of an old packhorse way to the port of Lancaster, via Ingleton. It was later incorporated into the Occupation Road, built in 1859 for the newly enclosed (ie. 'occupied') land above Dent. Dent marble, a black highly fossilised limestone that takes a good polish, was quarried at Binks Quarry further along it. There's at least one fireplace in the youth hostel made from it. The high level portion of the route has magnificent views. Whernside lies across the ravine of Deepdale. At the head of Dentdale the line of the Settle-Carlisle railway can be made out crossing the fell, 1,100 feet above sea level here. Straight across the valley is Aye Gill Pike dividing Dentdale from

Garsdale. Behind you to the left are the rounded hills of the Sedbergh Langdales.

7.5 Great Knoutberry Fell, 671 metres (2,203 feet)

Widdale Fell lies sandwiched between the upper valley of the Ure, the Dee and the Clough. One might expect a good walk along its length, but not so. Its top is wet, boggy, and full of peat hags - just not worth the effort, except for the south western end, Great Knoutberry Fell, which happens to be the highest point. It's a superb viewpoint, the best in the Yorkshire Dales National Park, and worth saving for a clear day. The best ascent is by Arten Gill and it is just possible to park in the corner at Stonehouse Bridge where the track up the gill starts. Take care not to obstruct the cart track at the bridge. Category B. Time: 2½-3 hours return. Map: 1:25,000 Outdoor Leisure 2 Yorkshire Dales Western Areas.

Cross the bridge and go straight ahead up the lane, past the houses and under the viaduct, possibly the most impressive one on the Settle-Carlisle line. Continue up the walled lane, wet and stony in parts, pleasantly grassy in others, until it curves sharply left at the top of the gill. Then keep straight ahead to the wall corner 200 yards ahead. Turn left and follow the little track besides the wall to the flat top, crowned by a well built cairn. Now enjoy the wide panorama spread before you.

Where to start? To the south-south-east, quite distinctive, is Pen-y-ghent, and Ingleborough. Between them in the background is the whale back of Pendle Hill. Next comes Whernside and the long low line of

Great Knoutberry Fell from Blea Moor

hills between it and Ingleborough are the Bowlands. Right of Whernside are Great Coum and Middleton Fell which rises out of Dentdale. Aye Gill Pike is the insignificant ridge you see below you when you look straight down the wire fence, and behind it are the Lake District hills. At the far left of them there's Black Combe, and you can make out the Langdale Pikes well to the right. The shapeless mass of East Baugh Fell cuts them off on the right. Wild Boar Fell is the escarpment hill to its right, and right again is Mallerstang Edge. Between them, far away, are the northern Pennines. Now the view loses some of its drama. Great Shunner Fell stands clear enough above Wensleydale, and at the end of this dale, the distant Cleveland Hills. Right again is Dodd Fell merging into the low hills at the head of Ribblesdale which complete the panorama.

One more point before you retrace your steps to the road. If you're there on a day when early rain has cleared to sunshine, you will notice that the landscape between Pen-y-ghent and Ingleborough is often grey and cloud shadowed, whilst if you look down Wensleydale, it's bathed in sunshine. This is the effect the Pennines have on rain coming from the west - and you now know why no true Lancastrian ever goes without his raincoat!

When you were looking round the panorama you may have noticed Wold Fell below you as a flat bright green area. This is because it's limestone and the rest of the land around is gritstone. It gives much better grazing for sheep and walls for shelter for them.

Finally, Arten Gill was the home of the Dent marble cutting and polishing industry in the last century. Highly fossilised limestone was quarried high up Arten Gill on the left, and a black limestone was quarried near Dent Head. Both of them were cut and polished to make quite beautiful fireplace surrounds and the like at a small works in the bottom of the gill whose waters were dammed to feed a water-wheel that powered the cutting and polishing machinery. Coloured Italian marble was also imported for cutting and polishing and eventually, being cheaper, contributed to the closure of the industry. Nothing is left of the works today, but some of their production can be seen in local houses, including Dent Youth Hostel. The viaduct is not quite the highest one on the Settle-Carlisle line though at 117 feet it tops the Ribblehead one by 13 feet but is just half as long. It's probably more dramatically situated though, spanning the deep-cut Arten Gill.

7.6 Whernside from Dent

It could hardly be said that Whernside dominates Dent: on the contrary, it can hardly be seen. This is one reason why its ascent is not nearly so popular as from Ribblehead, the other is that is it a long haul, much of it virtually trackless. But to escape the crowds it is perfect. Category A, note that the return is usually very wet in parts. Time: 6½-7 hours, add on another hour if you put in Great Coum. Map: 1:25,000 Outdoor Leisure 2 Yorkshire Dales Western Area. Start at Mill Bridge where there is room to park two or three cars with care.

Walk up the road to the little chapel on the corner, turn up this road and after about ¼ mile turn left into a short length of walled lane. At its end continue past two little radio/television huts then up the broad, eroded track that climbs quite steeply up the brow of the fell. Higher up it becomes walled and at the end of this section turn right following a thready track by the wall. At its end continue in much the same direction keeping well to the left of the cairns. You should pass just to the left of one of the beautiful little Whernside Tarns and then pick up a well marked track that leads you to a wire fence. Climb a stile, turn right and continue to the trig point which is on the other side of a wall, through access gaps.

As the highest point in the Yorkshire Dales National Park Whernside commands a wide view. Ingleborough and Pen-y-ghent are unmistakable. On the other side is the long moorland ridge of Great Coum and Gragareth. To the right of them are the Howgills and, if it is clear, the Lakeland hills. Further right still the hills of Wensleydale tend to merge into an inseparable mass.

From the trig point a few cairns and a faint track start you on the descent to the Kingsdale Road. Go straight down, keeping left of a fence to the road. Turn right and at the top of the hill a wide walled lane - the Occupation Road - goes off on the left. It contours round the fells very neatly but where it crosses Foul Moss it is particularly wet and boggy.

Diversion to Great Coum

When the track has turned to the right for the second time, at the second wall coming down the fell from the left, you can divert to put in Great Coum if you wish, a very good viewpoint. The return to the track over Crag End involves some rough going. Take care not to overshoot the

213

junction for Nun House Outrake.

Carry on for about 1½ miles to this unmistakable junction, turn right and follow the rough, stony lane steeply down to the Deepdale Road. Go straight across to the track to Scow finding the stile at the left-hand side of the buildings. Drop down just a little and follow a line of stiles parallel to the stream for about ½ mile. Keep a sharp look out for the little path down the steep bank that takes you direct to Mill Bridge. It's no disaster if you miss it: stiles continue to the road ahead.

WALKS IN GARSDALE

Garsdale, steep-sided and narrow, does not offer the walker much scope. It has some riverside paths but all too often there are no convenient alternatives to make that highly desirable circular walk. Its flanks, Baugh Fell and Aye Gill Pike are steep and unwelcoming. Therefore this guidebook only offers three walks: a first rate riverside walk; Grisedale, an upland valley of quality; and Baugh Fell itself, which as a 2,000-footer cannot be ignored. There is no village in the valley, only a couple of tiny hamlets and some scattered farms.

7.7 Frostrow Fell and the River Clough

Frostrow Fell is the extension of Age Gill Pike towards Sedbergh. Despite what the map says the paths on it have almost disappeared and considerable care is needed to navigate, but the penalty for failure is small. The return by the riverside path is excellent for the Clough has a quality the neighbouring Rawthey lacks. Because the riverside walk is so good a shorter easier start is given as an alternative to Frostrow, but note its return is uphill. The longer walk is Category B and takes about 2½-3 hours. The shorter one is Category C and takes about 2 hours. Map: Sedbergh footpath map, or 1:25,000 Outdoor Leisure 2 Yorkshire Dales Western Area. For both walks park at the end of the unfenced section of the A684 about 2½ miles from Sedbergh.

The Longer Route via Frostrow

Go up the road for about 100 yards to a cattle grid where the bridle path to Dent starts on the right. It disappears after about a couple of hundred yards, but just follow the general direction of the wall on your left. When you've been going for about 30 minutes and crossed a small stream you will be able to see a wall ahead to the right. Head in that direction, but it is not necessary to climb up to it. Follow the general direction of the stream, on you right and you will find a cart track. Stick to it even though it is faint and don't follow the stream which will take you back to Garsdale. When you see a field that is much greener than the rest, bear left, pass an isolated barn and you will find a track that steadily improves and leads you down to Side Farm. Turn right into the farmyard, go through the gate beyond the barn and *then* turn left at the signpost.* Follow the edge of the field to a gateway, then go straight down to find a stile in a bit of wall, pass a tiny round pond and climb up to the road. The next stile is almost directly across the road. Bear left a bit down the next two fields to find the stile between the buildings of the Pennine Tweed Mill. Follow its lane to the road by the bridge, cross the bridge, and immediately you will find a stile on the right. There's no path, but follow the river bank closely to find the stiles. At a sharp bend where there are a couple of houses close to the river, the path - such as it is - climbs gently away from the river. It crosses a low earth bank and then two more stiles before entering a long field beyond whose end you see a barn. Aim for that barn and you will find a stile into a lane with a signpost to Danny Bridge, which is just below where you are parked. This lane curves round to the left at first gently then more sharply. Keep a look-out for a finger post ahead at this point, and turn right behind the wall there. Follow the wall through three fields to High Fawes, turn right on their access road and go through the gate at its end. Then go diagonally left down the field to find a pair of stiles into the field below and fight your way through gorse and brambles to the road at Danny Bridge, when 5 minutes walk up the road to the right returns you to your car.

NOTE: THE SEDGWICK GEOLOGICAL TRAIL starts at Danny Bridge and continues downstream for a short half mile before returning by a marked route to the car park. It is of very considerable interest to geologically minded walkers as the changes in rock structures that mark the Dent Fault are exposed in the stream bed. The explanatory leaflet, available at YDNP centres, is essential to appreciate the finer points of the trail.

The short route via Side Farm

Walk down the road for a good half mile, almost to the little roadside chapel. Just before it there is a little footbridge over the stream and this is where the footpath starts. Go between the houses and through a gate, follow the wall to the next gate where you turn right. Turn left at the next gate and left after the barn, and, here's the crucial one, turn right at a signpost *before* you go through the gate to Side Farm. Now you join the previous route at *.

Things of Interest

Garsdale, like its neighbours Dentdale and the valley of the Rawthey, escaped colonisation by the Anglo-Saxons. Nowhere will you see that hallmark of their agriculture, lynchets. Like the other two, Garsdale was colonised much later by the Irish-Norse coming from Ireland and the Isle of Man. The dale was a wild and isolated place until the building of the turnpike road in the early years of the nineteenth century, and this road is now the main highway between east Yorkshire and the Lake District. Pennine Tweed Mills is one of the many water-powered spinning mills built about this time. The mill can be seen from the footpath and the line of the water leat running upstream to a deep pool can still be traced.

GRISEDALE AND BAUGH FELL 675 metres, (2,216 feet)

Though Garsdale has so little to offer the walker, it does have a remote upland recess, hidden from the dale and the rest of the world by 500 feet and more of steep fellside. This is Grisedale, once the home of a dozen families, now almost deserted. Its green intake fields are slowly reverting to the moor, becoming rush-grown and brown. Nevertheless, it is still, in summer, a green oasis folded in the moorland wastes of Baugh Fell and Swarth Fell. There is one pleasant beckside footpath that can make a family outing and another that leads eventually to Baugh Fell. Baugh Fell is another kettle of fish, trackless, usually wet or very wet moor, quite hard going.

7.8 A look at Grisedale

Parking is no longer permitted in this hidden upland valley, and you must try to park in the lane which branches off the A684 to Garsdale Station, though this is not easy. The walk starts opposite this lane at a little gate. Time: 2-2½ hours. Category C. Map: 1:25,000 Pathfinder map No. 617, sheet SD 69/79. The 1:50,000 Wensleydale and Wharfedale sheet 98 covers the area but it is of very limited value.

From the little gate follow the faint path to the gate but don't use it, go through the stile a mere 20-30 yards further up the wall. Here a finger post shows you the line to take across the wet mossy field ahead. Note this line carefully. You'll find a similar finger post at the next stile and at almost every subsequent one, though in many places there is a little track to follow. There are no problems given a bit of observation and in due course you will arrive on the road at Moor Rigg. Straight across the road is a finger post to Round Ing, a deserted moorland farm, and again you follow a line of stiles and finger posts leading to a faint path that runs pleasantly close to Grisedale Beck. In due course you will come to a well arched stone bridge and a cart track leading to Scale, now abandoned as so many of these farms are. Just before the bridge turn right along a little track that climbs steeply up the hillside, and again, follow the direction of the signpost at the top of the steep bank keeping above the stream on the bank. In the distance is a ruin, standing forlorn in a group of dying trees. This is Round Ing, the final outpost of man in this valley, an incredibly bleak place on a bad day. Imagine, if you can, the sort of life the family used to lead.

From it a little track leads up the field and fizzles out. Bear right and a distant finger post comes into view. From it aim at the right-hand end of a plantation on the hillside above to pick up a grassy cart track where you turn right. It steadily improves and leads you across the moor and, if you stay on it, over to the Eden Valley. So when the wall that accompanies it drops down to the right, you do so too, to reach the first house very shortly. Now simply follow the road down to Moor Rigg and either retrace your steps across the moor to the main road, or follow the lane down to the main road, taking care to turn left at the junction. This is rather tedious but if you've had enough route finding for one day can be a relief.

7.9 Baugh Fell

Those made of sterner stuff may continue up Baugh Fell. Not recommended except on a good clear day, and it's something of a collector's piece. Category A. Time: 5 hours. Map: As above, and 1:25,000 Outdoor Leisure 2 Yorkshire Dales Western Area covers part of it.

Park and start as for the previous walk and when you reach the road turn right and continue to the last farm where you bear left along the wall to find a good cart track. Follow this beyond the plantation to Round Ing, a forlorn ruin in a clump of dying trees. Behind it is a gate onto the open moor. There is a bit of a track at first, but it fizzles out. Keep going up the right-hand side of the stream crossing two side streams, one of which contains a sheepfold, until you come onto the low ridge of moor that separates Grisedale Beck from the infant River Rawthey. There is a band of limestone here and although it all looks very much alike, you may be able to identify the place by a couple of shallow potholes. They are marked 'cave' on the 1:25,000 map. On your left are three streams coming down Baugh Fell. Turn sharply towards them and climb the fellside roughly by the middle one. There's no real landmark to aim at, but bear slightly right if in doubt. You will come to a collection of four or more shallow peaty tarns and around them much heavy ground. Just keep on aiming for the wall where it's a bit better. The first top you come to will probably be Tarn Rigg Hill but it's not the true top. Turn right and follow the wall for around 10 minutes to the next rise, Knoutberry How, where you will find the O.S. cairn. Views to the south include Whernside, Great Coum, Middleton Fell and the head of Morecambe Bay with the Lake District behind. Widdale Fell lies across the other side of Garsdale and Great Shunner Fell well to the left. The Sedbergh Howgills are not so impressive - you're too high here and Aye Gill Pike has sunk without a trace.

When you are ready to return, either retrace your steps or if you have a taste for trackless moorland, bear away to the west towards West Baugh Fell Tarn. Here go half right down the long shoulder to the bend in the infant Rawthey, cross it well before the bend - not easy - and from there make a way across the moor to the gate in the intake wall by the ruined farm. Then retrace your steps. Returning to Grisedale by following the summit wall eastwards is not recommended because afforestation has blocked the track that leads past High Laithe to the road.

Things of Interest

Grisedale is an example of the abandonment of farms on marginal hill land. Before the First World War sixteen families lived in the valley and made a living from farming. In the hard times of the 1930s eight of them left the valley, and the privations of the hard winter of 1947 when the people of the valley were cut off by continuous frost and snow for seven weeks obliged another four to leave. Even in the November snows of 1990 the valley was cut off for five days. Today all the land is farmed by one man who, though born and bred there, does not live in the valley but close by, coming up daily to tend his animals. None of the other houses are occupied by farming families but by people who enjoy its isoliaton.

The story of the dale is sensitively told in the book, *The Dale that Died,* by Atkinson.

7.10   Garsdale Station to Kirkby Stephen Station via Wild Boar Fell

Perhaps the best 'railway' walk in this book, given a good day, and one that can be done by even a moderate walker in time to catch the evening train from Kirkby Stephen to places on the line to Leeds. There is ample parking at Kirkby Stephen station for those who prefer to be free from the pressure of catching a train. The route is tracked, if faintly, all the way, and there are no route finding problems once you have climbed out of Grisedale - and those are small. Note that Kirkby Stephen station is about 1 1/2 uphill miles out of the town and that the nearest place for refreshments is the Croglin Castle Hotel which is opposite the Nateby road end. That is only 3/4 mile uphill back to the station! Time: 6-7 hours including stops. Category A. Maps: 1:50,000 Landranger Series sheets 91 and 98. Sheet SD 69/79, No. 617 of the 1:25,000 Pathfinder Series is useful for getting out of Grisedale but is not essential.

Go down to the road from the station and through the little gate opposite, the start of Walk 7.8, which you follow until it meets the road at Moor Rigg. Now turn right and follow the tarmac to its end at East House, then continue on the rough cart track that goes between Turner Hill and White Birks Common. It soon disappears, but at the top of the rise turn left following the fence over the common. Cut the corner at the first bend aiming at a fence junction well ahead where you will find a stile. Here you start the long pull up the end of Swarth Fell, following a faint track beside the fence. Continue to the main top a short mile away, and then Wild Boar Fell awaits you. The track that can be seen veering away to the right from the fence does not go to the true top but to a collection of cairns on the eastern escarpment. In thick weather, or if you fear you are short of time, it is better to follow the fence to these cairns rather than this track and forget about the true top. (To find the true top, follow the fence to a gate, go through it, and make straight ahead over the moor to the top, a circle of walls around the trig point on the north-west edge. A well trodden path will take you back to a bold cairn at the start of the descent. This is very straightforward in clear weather.) From the cairns continue along the escarpment, a magnificently airy situation. From its end a good track leads right over Little Fell and then picks up and follows a wall for a considerable distance. When you have passed a little gate look out for a branch path to the left, then follow this right over the gentle rise ahead to the tarmac fell road. Turn left along the road for about $\frac{1}{2}$ mile, and having passed a limekiln with a mouth that looks a bit like a minature railway tunnel, turn right into the rough pasture just above it. Head up to the wall and follow the tractor marks beside it for almost a mile then veer right to reach the road close to a wood. Turn left on this road, right at the next two road junctions, and a good 10 minutes walk sees you at the station.

Things of Interest

See Walks 7.8 and 7.9 for more about Grisedale and page 283 (Things of interest, 2) for a note about the geology of the area. The rough ground where you pass two limekilns is another area of Permian limestone which was worked and burnt to make quick lime. The many humps and hollows in the field are the result of this casual tearing up of the ground for limestone, probably late in the eighteenth century.

8: SEDBERGH AND THE HOWGILLS

The Walks
8.1 The Rawthey Way returning by Underbank. Category C 224
8.2 Millthrop, Pennine Tweed Mills and the Rawthey Way.
     Category C 225
8.3 From Sedbergh to Dent and back. Category B 226

Walks on the Howgills
     The geology and character of the Howgills 228
8.4 Winder, Arant Haw and the Calf. Category A 229
8.5 A visit to Cautley Spout. Category C 232
8.6 Yarlside, Kensgriff, Randygill Top and Harter Fell.
     Category A 232
8.7 All the 2,000-ft tops of the Howgills. Category A+ 234
8.8 Carlin Gill, Black Force and the Calf. Category B 235
8.9 The northern side of the Howgills. Category A 236

ABOUT SEDBERGH

Sedbergh is fortunate in having a long stretch of riverside footpath called the Rawthey Way. It is also the starting point for walking on the Howgills, some of which must be amongst the least visited of the fells within the Yorkshire Dales National Park. This is no reflection on their quality, but rather upon their former inaccessibility. The M6 has now completely changed this. Leaving it at junction 37 Sedbergh is only a few minutes drive along the A684. The town has two good car parks. The one in Joss Lane is the best starting point for the Howgills and is at the end of the main road through the town's one-way system, on the left-hand side. It has toilets and the Yorkshire Dales National Park Centre is adjacent. This car park is also used for the Wednesday market and is then closed, of course. In that case, turn down the Dent road and use the one in Loftus Lane. In any case, it is just as handy for the Rawthey Way walks.

The town is a very ancient place. It is mentioned in the Domesday Book and had a motte and bailey type castle. As is usually the case for these early structures, only the earthworks are left. They are crowned with trees and the big mound can be seen quite well from the junction of Main Street and Back Lane, behind the council houses. Marked 'Castlehaw' on the map, there is no public access to it. The influence of the Normans can be seen in the architecture of the church: its north porch and door have simple Norman arches. The influence of the Norsemen who came to this part of the Dales somewhat earlier, is less obvious: the isolated nature of the farms in the Rawthey valley and in Dentdale, and place names like Branthwaite, Settleback, Dowbiggin to name but a few.

Probably the most far reaching event in Sedbergh's history was the founding in 1525 of a school by a Roger Lupton, a native of the parish, who endowed it with scholarships and fellowships at St John's College, Cambridge. The school has had its ups and downs and produced a number of famous scholars including Adam Sedgwick, the geologist. This foundation became the public school so well known today, and is probably the most important influence in the town both culturally and economically. Its early buildings have long disappeared, the oldest one remaining being the School Library at the junction of Back Lane and Loftus Lane. It has the date 1716 over the doorway and is built in a Neo-Classical style that was a departure from the local one and considerably in advance of the times here.

Another important event was the 1761 Turnpike Act which caused the Askrigg to Kendal and the Lancaster to Kirkby Stephen roads to be built. Both of them went through Sedbergh and so it grew at the expense of Dent, at that time the more important of the two places. It was at this time that the cobbled yards, for example Weaver's Yard which opens unobtrusively off Main Street, were built, crammed with tiny cottages,many of which housed spinners and knitters who worked in their homes. Spinning was often carried out on galleries outside the house, a kind of veranda. Just one of them remains, in Railtons Yard, now sadly not much to look at since the house is empty and semi-derelict. It is to be hoped that at some future date it will be restored, because it would be a pity to let the last spinning gallery disappear. Hand spinning and knitting became obsolete as general mechanisation of the industry came along. Mills were built at Birks, Milthrop and Howgill. Woollen mills were built at Hebblethwaithe Hall in 1792, driven by water power and Sedbergh, like Dent, employed many people in this industry.

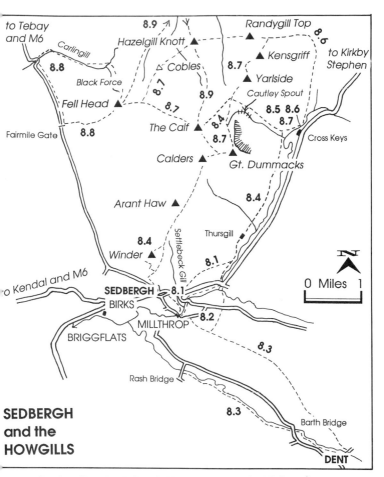

MAPS FOR SEDBERGH AND THE HOWGILLS

Sedbergh is in the very corner of the 1:25,000 Outdoor Leisure Map No. 2 which is of no value in this area. Sheets 97 and 98 of the 1:50,000 Landranger Series cover all the walks, but have their limitations. The Sedbergh and Baugh Fell 1:25,000 Pathfinder map sheet SD 69/79 is a good investment considering its value on other walks even though it does not cover the northern fringe of the Howgills. For the valley footpaths the Sedbergh [Dent] Stile map is useful and cheap but the Sedbergh [Howgills] Stile map covers no more than the pathfinder map. The 140,000 Harvey Map of the Howgill Fells is a useful supplement to the 150,000 maps and does cover the northern fringes.

The Valley Walks

The Rawthey Way is a fine riverside path that can be incorporated in a number of walks of which just two are given.

8.1 The Rawthey Way, returning by Underbank

A truly rural walk, unlike the second riverside walk. Time: about 2 hours, 30-40 minutes for the short version. Category C.

Turn left along the main road from the Joss Lane car park. Look right at the first road junction and across the road is a cart track signed, 'Field Path to Millthrop'. Take this track and keep straight on through a swing gate where the cart track goes left to the Old Vicarage. Cross the private road ahead and descend a little to a narrow stile. Pass through this, turn right and then through another stile following a well defined path to the Millthrop road close to the river bridge. Cross the bridge and you will find this part of the Rawthey Way starting on the left-hand side. It follows the river quite closely all the way to the next road bridge, and can be very muddy in wet weather.

If you are taking the shorter route, cross the bridge and find the start of the return riverside path on the left. After a while it leaves the river bank and swings up to the stile on the hill above the river, from where you retrace your steps to the car park.

If you are taking the longer route, cross the bridge and the road and the Rawthey Way continues on the other bank of the river. There's quite a change in character here. First the path is narrowly penned between a hedge and the trees of the river bank, then it opens out into pastures and almost disappears. There's no problem, simply follow the river to find all the stiles. Cross the road at the next bridge, and though the path follows the river at first, it leaves it following the line of the fence into the stock yard of the Buck Bank Farm and then onto the lane. Turn right and after about 200 yards there is a signpost on the left to Underbank.

From now on there is very little path but those all-important stiles are present and keep you on route. Look carefully for them. Start by going straight up the field past the breeding kennels of the house. A chorus of dogs will assail your ears. As soon as you are through the stile

Sedbergh and the Howgills
The Lower Falls at Aysgarth

The great cairns on Nine Standards Rigg
Below Kisdon, Swaledale

at the end of the kennels bear left and climb up sufficiently to get round the end of a wall, then cross the field dropping a little to the far bottom corner. This stile is decrepit and difficult to see, but the next one is obvious. From it bear right to the farm, Hollen Hall, a fine old building with massive rounded chimney stacks and a date stone, 1732. Here there is a set of notices in red directing you the correct way in front of the house and into the fields again. Drop down a little and cross the stream by a good bridge and go straight along a wall side to the next farm, Stone Hall, another fine old building with a two-storey porch. Go onto the road here and follow it until it makes a sharp bend left. In the corner on the right, hidden by the massive trunk of an old elm tree, is the stile you want. Immediately turn left and follow the wall down to another streamlet and bridge, then go up to Underbank. Go through its iron gates and follow the lane through its buildings. This lane now becomes Thorns Lane and leads behind Balliol School. As it starts to drop down back to Sedbergh a narrow path goes off on the right behind some council houses. It neatly cuts off a corner onto the main road a couple of hundred yards from Joss Lane car park.

8.2 Millthrop, Pennine Tweed Mills and the Rawthey Way
A walk of considerable variety and good views considering so little height is made. Park in Joss Lane car park. Category C. Time: about 2 hours.

This walk uses the same start as Walk 8.1 as far as Millthrop Bridge. Take the first road on the left, then first left again and having passed the houses, look for a seat by a stile and signpost on the right. Follow the track which is between walls most of the way to the stream and cross it quite easily at the finger post. The path becomes indistinct. Cross an earth bank and follow it up the hill to a wall and follow the wall back to the stream. After crossing two stiles keep an eye open for the next one on the other side of the stream. Cross it and go up a biggish field towards High Side Farm.[1] The gate is to the right of the buildings. Turn left by the side of the shippon and follow the wall round the edge of this field into the next one, then left onto a cart track which takes you onto the lane under an unusual archway linking house and farm buildings. Turn right and follow the tarmac to its end at Side Farm. Turn left into the farm and go in front of the house and barn beyond. At the next gate there is a parting of the ways. Take care! Go through it and *then* turn left. The track follows the wall, cuts straight down the next field to the only bit of wall left in the hedgerow, passes a little pond[2] and climbs up to the road. The next stile is 20 yards away to the left. Now bear slightly left towards the buildings[3] and go over the lane between them.

Turn right on the road and take the left fork over the river when you will arrive at the Kirkby Stephen road at Straight Bridge. Cross the bridge and pick up the Rawthey Way on the other side. There's not much of a path, simply follow the river bank to find the stiles. When you reach the road at the next bridge go straight across it to continue the Way, and after crossing a little arm of the river, climb up right to pick up your outward route about 5 minutes from the car park.

Things of Interest
1.   High Side is an example of the abandoned farms to be found scattered throughout the Dales. Too far from the amenities of life such as electricity and a tarmac road, with only primitive buildings for his animals, the occupier has not been able to move with the times and has abandoned the buildings, though the land is still farmed.
2.   The pond is a former quarry.
3.   Pennine Tweeds occupies the buildings of a former water powered woollen spinning mill.

8.3 From Sedbergh to Dent and back
This walk goes over Frostrow and returns by the Dales Way. It uses parts of several of the other walks in the book, some in reverse, but all are put together here as a coherent whole. Time: 5-6 hours walking plus time spent in Dent. Do not expect to get a bus back or you'll wait until next Wednesday. Category B. Map: Sedbergh (Dent) footpath map or 1:25,000 Outdoor Leisure 2 Yorkshire Dales Western Area.

The outward route
Turn left along the main road from the Joss Lane car park. Cross the road at the first road junction and you will see a cart track signed 'Field Path to Millthrop'. Follow this track and keep straight on through a swing gate where the cart track goes left to the Old Vicarage. Cross the private road ahead and descend a little to a narrow stile. Go through this, turn right and then go through another stile following a well defined path to the Millthrop road close to the river bridge. Cross the bridge, turn left on the road to Millthrop and left again at the T-junction.

Follow this lane until you see a stile with a finger post on the right. Go up this field to enter a narrow lane, and at the end of it take the stile immediately left of the gate. Follow the hedge to a gate and then a stile. Straight across the field there is another gate and then the next stile is in the bottom right-hand corner. Very shortly it brings you onto a farm road. Follow this until it turns left through a gate, then you keep straight on into a short walled lane that brings you onto the road.

Follow the road up the hill for about ½ mile to where it ends at Side Farm.

The cart track that you want goes to the right of the farm straight onto the fell. It soon crosses a small stream, then forks where you take the right-hand one, and continues in the general direction of a barn. Before it gets there it becomes faint and veers to the right. Take care to keep to the right of the valley that lies beyond the barn and continue right the way up to the wall that runs along the top of Frostrow. Turn left and follow the wall to a gate and sheepfold.

At this point take stock of the time and weather, for from here you can shorten the day by about ½ hour, though you will not have been to Dent. Take heart though, the return is easier and quicker. If you are faint-hearted for any reason simply keep in this green lane to Lunds, turn right on the access road and follow it to the main road 100 yards from Barth Bridge where you can pick up the return route.

Once through the sheepfold you will see two gates side by side on the left. Go through the right-hand one and take a line through the obvious gateways to Roantree. From now onwards there are fine views of Dent backed by Whernside and Crag Hill. The stile at Roantree is 3-4 yards from the near end of the buildings. It is topped with old timber and is scarcely recognisable as a stile but not difficult to cross. Follow the wall down to a wall junction (the O.S. map shows the path on the other side of the wall, the Stile map shows it correctly,) and cross the stile there, then head towards the wall. Now follow the little ravine down by an ever broadening track to a couple of barns where a finger post directs you into the fields. Two slit stiles show the way ahead, then bear right to a step stile over a fence and left again to another slit stile. Make towards a patch of very open woodland, cross a very wet area beyond it and you will see two barns. Go between them, turn right and then left through a slit stile opposite a third one. Beyond are two more easily seen stiles, then strike across to a gate in the corner which brings you within sight of High Hall. Follow its access road to the minor road by the river. Turn left and just as the wall on the right ends, look for a stile that takes you directly to Church Bridge on the edge of the village.

The return route
Leave the village by the main Sedbergh road. After a few minutes it comes right up to the river. Here you will find a footpath to Barth Bridge, plain to follow. Go straight across the road and pick up the riverside path on the other side. Except in one place where it diverts to find a bridge across a side stream it hugs the river bank all the way to just beyond Dillicar where it joins a very minor road at the river bank. Now follow this road pleasantly to Rash Bridge, the first bridge over the river below Barth bridge. Turn right on the road over the river bridge, and pick up the Dales Way signpost just before the next farm. Climb quite steeply up the long field to the ladder stile in the left-hand corner and again find the next stile in the top left-hand corner. It puts you on a bridleway which soon forks. Take the right-hand one. At the next stile you will have a fine view of Sedbergh and the Howgills, even better when you top the little rise ahead. From here you will see a green golf hut below. Make for it and follow the lane from it back to Millthrop and the river bank from where you retrace your steps to the car park.

Things of Interest
See the various things of interest listed in Walks 8.1 and 7.7.

WALKS ON THE HOWGILLS

The geology and character of the Howgills
The Howgills are quite different both in appearance and geology from the rest of the fells of the Yorkshire Dales National Park. These rounded grassy hills are made of Silurian and Ordovician slates, grits and mudstones which only appear at the surface in the Dales proper in a very limited area around Clapham and Horton in Ribblesdale, and play no part in determining the shapes of the fells and moors thereabout. Here they dominate and have produced shapes more akin to those of the eastern Lake District - being made of the same series of rocks - than the Dales. The Howgills were glaciated but not so severely as the Lakeland hills except at Cautley Spout where a combination of mudstone, which as its name suggests is a soft rock, and glaciation, produced the great black cliff in a miniature corrie, reminiscent of Wales or even Scotland.

The Howgills are separated from the Dales' geological structures by the North Dent Fault which runs roughly across the mouth of Dentdale and along the Rawthey valley on the south-east side. This means that Dentdale and Garsdale have limestone floors and their fells are built up of the Yoredale Series and have a gritstone cap if high enough.

Because the Howgills are well rounded hills they are better drained than the high flat moorland tops and so are free from bog. Free too from heather, as they have too high a rainfall, and being predominantly grass, give very good walking. They rise to over 2,000 feet in eight places and the highest point is The Calf, 2,220 feet (671 metres). The walking may be easy but the route finding can be tricky except on Walk 8.4. There are too many similar-looking rounded knolls linked by a confusing number of animal, tractor and bridle paths, too few landmarks and a complete absence of walls. The whole area is best left alone in poor weather unless considerable experience in map and compass work has been gained.

Five walks covering various parts of the Howgills are given together with the classic traverse of the eight 2,000 - foot tops. Necessarily these walks have different starting points.

8.4 Winder, Arant Haw and the Calf

Winder is the nearest of the Howgills to Sedbergh and is a splendid view point. The Calf, 2,217 feet (676 metres), is the high point of the group. A short return is given from Winder and this version is Category B taking about 2 hours. The entire walk is Category A and will take 6-7 hours, returning by field paths down the Rawthey valley from the Cross Keys, a temperance hotel. Maps: for preference use Pathfinder sheet SD69/70, otherwise sheets 97 and 98 of the Landranger Series.

From Joss Lane go along the main road towards Kendal until you come to Howgill Lane. Turn up this and follow it to the de-restriction signs. It is also possible to park around here. At the de-restriction signs take the lane to the right that leads to Lockbank Farm. At the farm go through the farmyard gate on the right and through the next gate onto the open fell, turn left and follow the wall side just past the top of a small wood. After crossing a tiny stream bear right. The path is vague to start with but quickly becomes a broad grassy track that climbs reasonably easily to the top. The views are excellent. Sedbergh is at your feet dominated by the buildings of the school. To the south lies the spread

Arant How

of the fells of the North West Dales. Most prominent to the left is East Baugh Fell and to its right Aye Gill Pike. Garsdale lies between them. To the right of Aye Gill Pike is Dentdale and the end of Great Coum. Then comes the Lune valley, and well to the right, the fells of the eastern Lake District.

Continue in the same direction until you have lost a bit of height as you come into the top of Settlebeck Gill. Here a broad grassy track comes up from the right.

The short return
Turn sharply onto it and follow it down to the intake wall. A swing gate takes you onto the fields not far above the car park. Go down the field and the lane below it to the farm, bear right on a cart track, go through the gate onto the road, turn left at the first cross roads, and you're in the car park.

Otherwise continue along the broad grassy track which traverses below Arant Haw, picks up a wire fence and makes the first top, Calders. Continue, bearing left a little to the narrow neck of fell that leads to Bram Rigg top. Once over this keep in the same direction and drop down a little before climbing up to The Calf. From the trig point a good path starts in the direction of the col but in fact descends into Bowderdale. Some 10-15 minutes along it a path goes off on the right and leads towards Cautley Spout. This is the way you go. Under no circumstances attempt to descend the stream which shortly plunges over the great waterfall of Cautley Spout. Stay on the fellside all the way down into the valley. If you fail to spot this path and find yourself in Bowderdale simply climb back over the col. It isn't as bad as it looks.

When you are almost down to the River Rawthey, keep a look-out to the right for a track going off across a plank bridge over Cautley Holme Beck for this is where you start the return to Sedbergh through the fields. This path forks as you come to a barn, keep right and on the top side of a wall until you come to a gate in it. Go through this, but keep in the same direction to a gateway into the next field. Keep at much the same level here until you've crossed the stile, then make slightly upwards to find the way out at the junction of two streams. The path continues along the top side of a hedge past the farms at Steps End right the way to Fawcett Bank. Here it goes below the farm and joins that farm's bridleway approach road. Follow this to the tarmac road at Thursgill.

About ¼ mile along the road there is a sign to Underbank. You may take this if you wish, see Walk 8.1. for the details, but it is quicker and easier to follow the Rawthey Way by the river. To find the start, go a little further to Buck Bank and turn left through the stock yard which is just past the farmhouse. Once through the stock yard keep to the right of the hedge right down to the river bank. The path now follows the river for some miles. Leave it at the second bridge and take the road into Sedbergh, 10 minutes' walk at the most.

Walks started from the Cross Keys Temperance Hotel
This hotel is on the Kirkby Stephen road, the A683 about 4-5 miles from Sedbergh. There is a small parking space immediately past the hotel.

Cautley Spout, upper falls, with The Calf behind

8.5 A visit to Cautley Spout

Category C only in dry conditions. Allow anything from an hour to an afternoon to enjoy this fine upland valley. No map needed.

A footpath starts from the far end of the parking space and crosses the River Rawthey on a good bridge. Turn left and follow the cart track into the valley below Cautley Crag, a most impressive place to be in the late afternoon sun with the crag beetling and black above, or on a wet day with the long foaming cataract of the Spout. Wander about as you please, keeping on the right-hand side of the main stream. There is a path going quite some way up the right-hand side of the Spout and this gives you good views of the waterfalls. Return as you came.

8.6 Yarlside, Kensgriff, Randygill Top and Harter Fell

These three hills are probably the finest of the Howgills - two of them are 2,000-footers - yet they are outside the park area. This is no excuse for omitting them from this book. On their own there is not enough to make a full day for even an average walker, but if extended over Green Bell to Harter Fell it makes a fine circuit. Like the rest of the Howgills it is not recommended except in clear weather. If the little lay-by at the Cross Keys is full, use the one higher up the road, it's handy for the return. Category A. Time: about 6 hours. Map: 1:50,000 sheets nos 91 and 98.

Start as for the previous walk. At the base of the Spout take the green track through the bracken that leads over to Bowderdale. At the col climb steadily up the flank of the fell on the right, making towards the head of the gill and then to the top of Yarlside, 2,047 feet. The way ahead is now seen with some distressing clarity. Kensgriff is deep down below and Randygill Top soars far above it. Take heart, the height lost here is less than 400 feet, and trivial after that until the last climb of the day. However, do not leap over the edge in your haste to get to Kensgriff or you will find yourself on some exceedingly nasty ground. Traverse the edge for about 5 minutes; don't be in any hurry to go down and you'll find it much easier.

A little path takes you over Kensgriff and most of the way up Randygill Top. If it is less than perfectly clear, note that Randygill Top is at the west end of the ridge ahead and you will need to take a compass bearing to find the base of Green Bell. This top fails to reach the 2,000 feet mark by only 15 feet but has a trig point and is a very fine viewpoint for the Pennines from Cross Fell to Wild Boar Fell.

From it retrace your steps a little and pick up the broad ridge of Grere Fell that runs down to the road from Ravenstonedale to Adamthwaite Farm. Keep to the left-hand side of the ridge - there's no path just a few sheep tracks - to drop off it onto the high point of the road from Ravenstonedale to Adamthwaite Farm. Harter Fell lies straight across the road and 30 minutes' walk will see you up, though there's no track. Being set out a little from the Howgills it has surprisingly good view of them. Leave the top in an approximately south-westerly direction and you will pick up a good cart track. (You could of course, treat Harter Fell as an optional extra, for you can pick up this cart track on the left a few hundred yards down the road (yes it's tarmac) to Adamthwaite.)

Turn left and follow it towards Murthwaite Farm. Some 50 yards before the first farm buildings turn off to the right passing an isolated barn and continue down the hill following the fence and then bear right into the wood. There's no real path though you may pick up a hollow way that was the original bridle path. Towards the bottom it disappears and leaves you to struggle through bushes. Don't be tempted to break out left or right into those green fields, for you have to cross the formidable Wandale Beck, best done at the ford at the very bottom tip of the wood, where a sheep catcher and some well placed stones help.

From Cautley Crags, looking to Yarlside, with the Pennines behind

Once you're across go along the lane that goes up to Narthwaite. If you're parked at the Cross Keys follow this lane to the sharp bend where a path goes off between two buildings, down the hill and passes between two more barns. Then it swings right below the wall to find the little bridge and finally drops down the hill to the bridge back to the Cross Keys. If you are parked in the lay-by, turn left as you join the lane, cross the bridge and your car is in sight.

8.7 All the 2,000ft tops of the Howgills

This is without doubt the finest walk in the Howgills, taking in eight separate tops over 2,000 feet. They are: Calders, Great Dummacks, Bram Rigg, The Calf, Yarlside, Randygill top, White Fell Head and Fell Head. They are arranged in the shape of a wide V with Sedbergh at the point of the V so their traverse presents some nice problems. You either have to retrace your steps or face some pretty rough going across the 'grain' of the country. It's most easily done from the Cross Keys Hotel and is best not attempted without some prior knowledge of the area and a clear day. Category A+. Time: about 8 hours. Maps: 1:50,000 sheets 91,97,98 and Harvey Map Services Ltd 'The Howgill Fells' scale 1:40,000.

Follow the line of the previous walk, stomping up Yarlside, over Kensgriff - not a 2,000-footer but you might as well throw it in - and on to Randygill Top which is the end of the right-hand part of the V. All these are short and sharp. Now plunge straight down to the stream, have lunch and think about what you prefer to do next. If you are a reasonably strong walker you will go cross country, over Hazel Gill Knot and Cobles to put in Fell Head next, the other end of the V. All this is trackless and, for the Howgills, rather rough going. Then retrace your steps to the shoulder overlooking Cobles and where the ground steepens take the right fork and continue to the Calf. From the Calf a well trodden track goes straight ahead to Bram Rigg Top and on to Calders where you bear well to the left and follow a faint track to the vague top of Great Dummacks. Continue to the edge of the cliff above the daunting hollow of Cautley Crag, turn left and you should find a good track that follows the edge - more or less - of the crag down into the valley below and in sight of the Cross Keys.

If you can't face the across the grain stuff, then follow the valley upstream for about a mile when you will see a good track on the right climbing quite steeply up the fellside. Follow this, traversing below the Calf and take the first track on the right, for the main track descends to Four Lane Ends on the west side of the Howgills. Continue over Busk How to Fell Head and on return retrace your steps keeping straight on to the top of the Calf, easily identified by its tall trig point. Now continue as above.

8.8 Carlin Gill, Black Force and Fell Head

This walk starts at Fairmile Gate about 4 miles out of Sedbergh on the minor road to Tebay. To find it, leave the town along Howgill Lane and follow this road. The whole length is single width with passing places and must be driven with considerable caution. As soon as the unfenced portion starts there is a large parking space in very pleasant surroundings at the foot of the fells.

Two versions of this walk are give, both visiting Black Force, but one much shorter than the other. Both are Category B. Map: 1:50,000 sheet No. 97, or Pathfinder 617 sheet SD 69/79. Time for the shorter walk: $2^{1}/_{2}$hrs; for the longer one: $3^{1}/_{2}$hrs.

Walk along the road to Carlingill Bridge, it has grass verges and good views, so is no hardship. Cross the bridge and then turn right following the stream on its north side to start with. You will soon be forced to cross it to the south side, and will no doubt cross and recross quite a few times seeking the best line, for there are little paths all over the place. Eventually you will be forced quite high on the fell whichever side you choose - unless you fancy a splash direct up the stream in a heat wave. It doesn't matter, for all the paths lead to Rome, the foot of Black Spout, a great black ravine of contorted rocks with a stream cascading down. It's not so scenic as Cautley Spout (Walking 8.5), nor so impressive, but rather a grand, grim sort of place. From the foot of the ravine a bit of a path leads up the left-hand grassy flank, zigzagging about a bit avoiding most of the broken rocky crest, but visiting it from time to time to view the drop beneath. Eventually this flank becomes an arête, and well up it, past the rocky bit, the path forks. This is where the short route parts company. (See Note A.)

Otherwise keep straight on up the arête to where it runs out onto the fell, then still keeping in the same direction continue to the skyline ridge. There is no path to speak of. Bear right, passing a pole, and keep going right to find the summit of Fell Head, the most westerly of the

2,000-footers and having splendid views extending from the Kent Estuary, the Lune gorge, to the Eastern Lakes, seen up Borrowdale no, not *the* Borrowdale, but a major tributary of the Lune. From Fell Head either of the westward running ridges will return you very easily and directly to your car, no walls, no stiles to worry about. If you choose to continue to The Calf it is better to do this before going up Fell Head as the main ridge continues in a south-easterly direction, and to go over Fell Head on your return.

In that case take care to take the left hand path at a Y-junction at the top of the first rise and follow it to the Calf. On returning take the second left off the main path to locate this track.

Note A

At the fork of the path take the right-hand one which traverses the earthy gully at the top of the ravine towards a rowan tree. Cross the stream as soon as you can and look for a path that doubles back on the ravine and climbs upwards. Its start is vague but it is only about 100 yards past the rowan tree. It soon becomes quite clear and takes you very easily to the little col between Fell Head and Far White Stones. The quickest way back to the car is from here, bearing right a little until you can see it, but if you do that you will miss the very fine views from the hill ahead. It only takes another 10 minutes, and the views are as good as from Fell head. You can't see your car from the top, indeed, there is no cairn to mark it, but keep going until the ground starts to drop markedly, bear left, and you'll soon pick up a good path to take you back direct to your car.

8.9 The northern side of the Howgills

The northern side of the Howgills is drained by five long valleys, the finest of them being Langdale, or Longdale, as it is sometimes spelled. This walk makes a circuit of that valley, reaching the highest point of the Howgills, the Calf, in doing so. Langdale is both long and many-branched giving the approach an air of complexity. In addition these outlying fells are almost trackless and not quite so straightforward as the map suggests, so this walk should not be attempted except on a clear day with a good forecast. The start and finish in Langdale use farm tracks that are not rights of way, nor are they shown on the map. I acknowledge A.W.Wainright as the source of this information. Category A. Time about 7 hours. Maps: 1:50,000 Landranger Series 91 or 98.

Park by the old school in Longdale, best reached from the M6 leaving it at junction 38 for the Kirkby Stephen road, A685. Leave this after a couple of miles turning right into the road to Longdale. Turn left at the T-junction then right through a gate after crossing the bridge.

Continue up the road which quickly becomes a farm track. After about 100 yards turn right then cross the beck by a fine arched stone bridge. Continue up the green rake into the field and then make for the farm buildings of Long Gills joining their access track on the right. Turn left on it and continue up the fell until the track starts to peter out. At this point keep by the wall to pick up another track dropping down into Uldale Beck and continue upstream to its source at the foot of a fluted gully on the left. (A mistake here, easily made in poor visibility, will see you dropping down into Carlin Gill.) Climb steeply up the left-hand side of the gully to reach the top of Docker Knott, the first top of the day.

Continue to an unnamed but higher top which, if the day be clear, has a magnificent unbroken panorama of the whole of the southern Lake District, from the rounded top of Black Combe in the west to the long level ridge of High Street in the east. Climb steadily to Breaks Head where a track appears on the right. This will take you up to the top of Fell Head, a 2,000-foot top and an optional extra. (If you do this, take the right-hand fork as you return from the top to join the main walk below Busk Howe.) Otherwise keep on in the same direction dropping down into the gap between Fell Head and the start of the climb up Busk Howe and the Calf. Here a good path awaits you. At the start of the next steepening of the ground the path forks - take the right-hand one and follow it to the top of the Calf, easily identified by its tall trig point. Here the Lakeland panorama, seen so well earlier in the day, has lost something of its quality, but as compensation, Ingleborough, Whernside and Pen-y-ghent (from right to left) come into view.

Take care on leaving the top. Facing the way you came, go off diagonally right on a wide well marked path that eventually goes down to Bowderdale. Having passed a tiny pool, often dry in summer, look out for a narrow track which goes off on the left and is the start of the path that leads to Hazelgill Knott. *Take great care to avoid the subsidiary ridge of Grains by bearing right,* but once the true ridge is reached it is fairly plain sailing, though there are a couple of distinct kinks in the ridge and a slight one after leaving the Knott. Hereabouts there is a fairly distinct track so there should not be any problems. Continue to West Fell, another 1½ miles, and shortly after leaving the top go well to the left to reach Langdale Knott. Continue down its easy angled north-west ridge to the intake wall and follow that down to the stream, Langdale Beck itself.

Cross an awkward stile and start the two mile descent of this charming valley, at first through rough pastures dotted with trees, later hugging the banks of the beck, now a sizeable stream, to keep out of the intake fields. Follow a rough cart track along the bank of the stream past the bridge that leads to the ruins of High Shaw, and when this track climbs out of the valley on the right, continue along the beckside through a succession of roughish fields until you come to a wall and gate with an air of finality about them. From here you continue along the very edge of the beck. The place is identified by the trunk of a large fallen ash tree close to the beck on which an old gate has been superimposed. Climb over them easily and continue, with some difficulty in places, until you reach the stone bridge you crossed on your outward walk, then retrace your steps to your car.

9: LOWER WENSLEYDALE
West Witton to Aysgarth

Around Aysgarth

9.1   A visit to Aysgarth Falls. Category C 241
9.2   The best of the River Ure: Aysgarth to West Witton.
      Category B 242
9.3   Aysgarth to Castle Bolton. Category C 244
9.4   Carperby to Castle Bolton. Category C 246
9.5   Aysgarth to Woodhall via Carperby. Category C 247
9.6   Castle Bolton to Low Row via Apedale. Category B 248

Waldendale and Coverdale

9.7   A walk round West Burton. Category C 250
9.8   A walk up Waldendale. Category B 250
9.9   From West Burton to Coverdale. Category B+ 252
9.10 From West Scrafton to Great Haw. Category B 255

Around Askrigg

9.11 A walk to Mill Gill and Whitfield Ford. Category C 257
9.12 Askrigg's river and high pastures, returning by
      Whitefield Gill. Category C 259

Wensleydale is the only one of the dales that takes its name from a village not its river, though formerly it was known as Yoredale from which the present river name, the Ure, is derived. Today Wensley is a small village and it is difficult to visualise it as the market town of the dale right up to Elizabethan times when Askrigg became more important. At that time Hawes was barely in existence. Wensley, Leyburn and Middleton are the three villages of the lower dale, but all are outside the National Park area.

Wensleydale is a whole family of dales comprising Coverdale, Waldendale, Bishopdale, Somerdale, Widdale, Mossdale and Cotterdale, and apart from the fells at the valley head these side valleys have the best of the walking. The valley floor below Aysgarth has some lovely park-like stretches, but between Asygarth and Hawes most of it is plain, dull and lumpy. The redeeming feature is some good walking

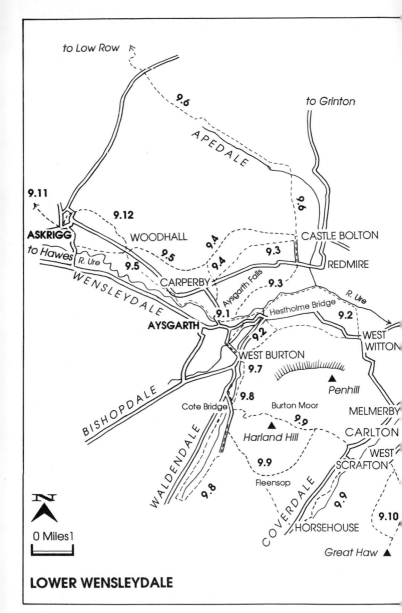

LOWER WENSLEYDALE

on the high pastures on the north side.

9.1 A visit to Aysgarth Falls

Everybody who visits Wensleydale visits Aysgarth Falls. The Y.D.N.P. car park stands squarely in the middle of them, so two walks are needed. The lower ones are undoubtedly the finest and lie below the road bridge, out of sight. The upper ones can be seen quite well from the road side opposite the Carriage Museum, but it is better to walk the curve of the river bank, leaving the car park by its far corner and following the obvious path.

The best time to visit the Middle and Lower Falls is in early spring, when the woods are carpeted with wood anemone, the trees not yet in leaf and the falls are seen through a lacework of branches. In full summer they are hidden. Time: anything from 30 minutes to an hour. Category C but it can be muddy.

Leave the car park by the footpath at the entrance: it takes you safely down the road to the start of the path into the woods. A fine new crushed stone path suitable for shoes in almost any weather leads you forwards into the woods, thick with starry wood anemone and bluebells in springtime. Soon you will see a path signposted to the Middle Falls. In just a few yards this takes you to a real grandstand of a viewpoint for them. Retrace your steps and continue to the Lower Falls, passing the return path from them. You will find another sign to the falls and if you want to climb down to the river bed - for the agile only - keep left and then turn right at the fence. This path takes you down a rocky cleft in the rocks to the river bed. It is quite some distance from the Lower Falls and you can walk almost to their foot along the limestone pavement of the river bed. Then retrace your steps to that cleft in the barrier of cliffs. Continue back to the fork and keep left there to find the fine viewpoint of the Lower Falls. Retrace your steps to the fork, turn right and emerge by the return path, your circuit complete.

The geology of the falls

There is a model with a very clear explanation of the formation of the falls in the information office on the car park and these notes are based on it. At the end of the last Ice Age, some 8,000 years ago, the retreating glacier in the dale deposited the clayey, stony debris it was carrying as a barrier across the valley at this point. Above it was penned a lake of the melt waters which gradually spilled over the top and started to erode it away. Eventually the river reached the Yoredale series of rocks beneath the glacial deposit and then cut right through these to reach the hard Great Scar limestone below and this rock forms the river bed today. Close beneath it is a layer of shale which is so easily eroded that the limestone is undercut. In due course this lip of limestone breaks off, as can be seen so well at the Lower Falls. Because of the repetitive nature of the Yoredale series of rocks there are a whole series of falls along the length of the river, not just at Aysgarth, but here they are well developed because of the power of the glacial stream. Even today the process continues and slowly, geologically speaking, the falls are travelling upstream.

9.2 The best of the River Ure - Aysgarth to West Witton

Wensleydale is not noted for the quality of its riverside walking, but here is a stretch fully up to Wharfedale's high standards. Best done in early spring for good views of the river. Time: 5 hours, Category B. Map: 1:25,000 Outdoor Leisure Map No. 30, Northern and Central Areas. Park in the Y.D.N.P. car park at Aysgarth.

Note: A shorter version of this walk starts at Hestholme Bridge and takes $3^1/2$-4 hours. Park on the small lay-by on the Witton side of the bridge.

Leave the car park by the lower corner, cross the river bridge and go up to the church by the passage by the Carriage Museum.[1] Turn left in the wood opposite then bear left to pick up a path on the top side of the wall. It gives fine glimpses of the river below. It is well way-marked and brings you onto the road at Hestholme Bridge. Turn left on the road, cross the bridge and look for a slit stile by a gate just beyond the lay-by. There's no path here but go past the barn on its right to find the next two stiles. Pass a farm on its right and then bear left to find the stile. The path now follows the river bank for a while then climbs up through a wood. Turn left at the top of it and go towards a fence ahead. Follow it to find the next stile into a long pathless field. Keep above the wall then climb to the stile 50 yards higher than the obvious gate. The next field is quite short, but the ladder stile is not easily seen. Do not go through the swing gate. The ladder stile leads to some newly built steps down to a superb stretch of river - the water coursing down limestone slabs or idling in deep green-brown pools, all overhung by stately beech trees. All too soon you leave this beauty and a finger post directs you to a stile into an exceptionally long field full of humps and hollows (drumlins) but scattered with trees and still part of the park-like landscape. There's no path, but keep near the river bank and you will find the gate at the end. The path goes past a house above the field but keeps near the bank although there are no more waymarks at the gates. Eventually you will enter a long, narrow, triangular field. At the same time the river scenery suddenly deteriorates. When you reach this point look for tractor marks coming in on your right, and turn on to them as soon as you can. Follow them to a farmyard and then past other farms when the tractor tracks become a tarmac lane, Back Lane, that leads to West Witton.

Turn right on the road, pass the pub, then take the lane on the left. It climbs steadily up the hill for some time and just where it swings left into the Chantry Caravan Site there is a walled, partly green cart track with a gate on the right. Follow this very pleasant lane, Langthwaite Lane, until it ends quite abruptly. 'Where now?', you'll say. The stile is on the right. Turn left and follow the wall to the next, then go through the right-hand of two gates. It brings you onto a bit of concrete road which you go down for 50 yards to a sharp right bend. Leave it here and go straight on, dropping down to a gate at the corner of the wood. At the bottom of this field you will see a ruin ringed by a fence.[2] Go through the stile on its left into the top of a stony lane. Here, if you are returning to Hestholme Bridge, see Note A. Otherwise, go through the little gate opposite into the long field on the top side of the wood. In due course drop down a little field to find the gate into the next field at the end of which there is a small sheepfold and a gate onto the Morpeth Lane. There are fine views up the dale. Turn right on the lane and follow it easily down to West Burton. Follow the Aysgarth road as far as Eshington Bridge. Go through the gate in the opposite corner, climb up the little hill and follow the line of stiles to the main road. Go straight across the road to the church and from the church back to the car park as you came.

Note A

Continue down the wood by the rough stony lane, turn right in the field at the bottom and follow the wall to the road. Turn left and 10 minutes' walk will see you back to your car.

Things of Interest

1. The Carriage Museum is a modern use for an old building. The original building was for cotton spinning, built in 1784, the early years of the industry. It was probably ahead of its time for these parts, for it failed and fell into ruin. It was rebuilt following a fire in 1852 and spun wool for which there was a big demand at the time, due to the Crimean war. Both these mills were powered by a large water-wheel taking its water from the River Ure by a sluice that goes under the road and behind the buildings. You cross the sluice as you go down the path from the church. Later still the mill was converted into a flour mill - the ugly red rusty ventilators proclaim that fact.

2. The ruin was the chapel of the Penhill Preceptory of the Knights Templar, built in the thirteenth century. It contains some tiny stone coffins and was part of a bigger establishment which has not been excavated.

9.3 Aysgarth to Castle Bolton

There is a network of paths between Aysgarth, Carperby, Castle Bolton and Woodhall. Here they have been divided into fairly short walks but the outward and return routes between the first three places are interchangeable and it is easy to extend to Woodhall. Time: 3 hours. Category C. Map: Aysgarth Footpath map or 1:25,000 Outdoor Leisure Map No. 30, Northern and Central Areas. Park at the Y.D.N.P. car park at Aysgarth.

Start as if you were going to visit the falls (Walk 9.1) and when you come to the signpost to Castle Bolton follow the path indicated.

Now the path is much less well marked, but it is easy to follow to Hollin House where you go through the gate below the buildings. Here you are on a good cart track. Take the right-hand branch that leads you to a slit stile and from that you make diagonally to a metal gate. Go through two more metal gates then keep along the wall side aiming at a walled lane Thorsby Lane,[1] ahead. There's one wet and muddy spot on it but pleasant walking to Low Thorsby Farm and the tarmac. Follow it for about 100 yards until a little footbridge on the left leads you to a stile and in a few yards to the left, another one. Turn right here and follow the wall up two longish fields to a stile on the road opposite the lane that leads to the castle.[2] Trudge up the road to it.

Leave the castle by the short lane passing the car park (toilets) and

Castle Bolton

as soon as you are through the gate bear left to a slit stile half hidden in nettles. Another opposite takes you into a large field. Go diagonally left down this field[3] to the left-hand one of two gates and go across this large field more or less at this level to pick up the line of electricity poles which will take you to the next stile. Now go down left to cross Belden Beck by a footbridge and after the next stile follow the fence to West Bolton Farm. Keep to the left of the house and buildings to find the stile beyond. Climb up past the wood, cross a tiny stream to the left to the stile by the barn. Then you will come to a tractor track wired off by an electric fence. You follow this to the farm and then go sharp left to find the stile onto the road at Carperby.[4] Turn right on the road and left through a wooden gate with a discreet yellow waymark on it, next to a new stone bungalow. Then go through the first gateway on your right, immediately turn left and go straight down the fields to a lane. Turn right here and left when you come to the road. Barely 50 yards away on the opposite side of the road is a slit stile. Go through, follow the wall and when you've crossed a driveway, bear right a little to pass a clump of trees on top of a knoll. You will see the stile in a wire fence and another below. A couple of swing gates takes you over the railway[5] and down to the car park.

Things of Interest

1. Thorsby Lane is of very ancient origin, being connected with the deserted medieval village of Thorsby which lies between it and the river. There are many deserted medieval villages in the Midlands, but

few in the Dales. Many of them were deserted as a result of the Black Death, 1346-8, which killed about one third of England's population. Plough lands could no longer be worked so the fields were grassed over and this has preserved the characteristic pattern of lynchets.

2.   Bolton Castle is not the remains of a Norman castle as are Middleham and Skipton, but a fortified manor house. In 1379 Richard Scope, who became Lord Scope, Chancellor of England, obtained a licence to crenellate his manor house and by degrees its structure was so altered and enlarged that the manor house became a castle, though its position is not easily defended. Its main claim to fame is that Mary Queen of Scots was imprisoned there from 1568-9 though there seems to be some doubt as to which rooms she occupied. It is open to the public and is a vast, gloomy, crumbling maze of rooms.

3.   You may notice you go down a whole series of quite large terraces in this field. They are lynchets, part of the medieval field system of Castle Bolton.

4.   Carperby is a village of character in a dale richer, perhaps, in interesting villages than any other. It lies on a terrace well above the valley floor backed by lynchets that indicate its ancient origin. The -by ending of its name suggests a Danish settlement. It was a market town in the Middle Ages and has kept its early form, a single street, as well as its seventeenth-century market cross. It has a large Quaker Meeting House.

5.   The railway, a branch of the main London and Eastern line at Northallerton, came to Leyburn as early as 1856 and was completed to Hawes in 1878. Later the Midland Railway, which owned the famous Settle-Carlisle line, built a spur to Hawes from Garsdale. The whole line was closed in 1954.

9.4 Carperby to Castle Bolton

This walk goes to Castle Bolton by the return route of the last walk. It is a better route than the Aysgarth route, having no road walking and making its height steadily. Time: $2^{1}/_{2}$ hours. Category C. Map: Aysgarth Footpath Map. Park in Carperby - not easy, but there is a small lay-by at the Leyburn end of the village, just beyond the start of the walk. Alternatively park at Aysgarth Falls and walk. See the next walk for guidance.

The first stile close to a farm is signposted Castle Bolton and the route is well waymarked throughout. Turn right onto a cart track where there may be problems with an electric fence, but these are temporary devices. Where this cart track swings left go straight ahead to find the next waymarked stile with a barn beyond. The way to West Bolton Farm is now clear. Go past the farm and buildings on the right and make for the gate beyond. Now you cross Beldon Beck by a footbridge and climb up to the electricity poles beyond to find the next stile. The castle is now seen very well and the way to it clearly marked.

When you are ready to leave the castle follow the track from the car park through a gate by the wood and from here follow a very well made bridle track through a number of fields to its end, something like 30 minutes, walking. It has gates all the way and has splendid views up Waldendale and Bishopdale. At the end of the bridleway turn left to follow the line of the wall and it will reappear shortly as a green grassy track giving delightful going. When you've crossed the second tiny stream you will enter a large rough field dotted with hawthorn bushes. As soon as you've entered the next field look out for a fork on the path and take the left-hand one to return to Carperby. The one straight ahead goes to Disher Force and Woodhall and is part of the next walk which may be continued here instead of returning to Carperby. The way to Carperby is obvious: take the left-hand fork in the walled lane for the shortest return.

Things of Interest
See the previous walk.

9.5 Aysgarth to Woodhall via Carperby

This walk has splendid views from the high-level tracks at the start and should be done this way round. The return is undistinguished. Time: 3 hours. Category C. Map: Aysgarth Footpath map or 1:25,000 Outdoor Leisure Map No. 30, Northern and Central Areas. Park in the Y.D.N.P. car park or at Carperby and start there.

Leave the car park by the main entrance, as signposted, and walk up the road for about 10 minutes to find a stile on the left. The path follows the road and joins it after about ½ mile. Turn left and then right into a lane and look for a stile a few minutes along it. This will bring you into Carperby. Turn right and go up the first lane on the left. Where it turns a walled cart track goes off to the fell. At the end follow the wall passing through several fields to enter a large field, Ox Close, at a gate in the middle of a long wall. There are glorious views ahead: first Addleborough comes into sight, then Widdale Fell, and East Baugh Fell at the very head of the valley. The track is well marked in this field and drops down to cross Disher Force, a sparkling little fall down a mossy cleft. Soon after it goes down left through a gate and winds down the hill to Woodhall. Here cross the road and go down the hill about 100 yards to the first lane on the left. Go to the left of the house and follow the wall at the foot of a wooded bank into some damp fields between a hillock - a huge tree-crowned drumlin - and the road. Go to the right of a barn, and follow the wall to find a couple of stiles that bring you onto the Carperby road beyond the house.

Turn right and turn right again down the next lane and when you come to the old railway embankment you will find a stile leading onto it. Walk along this track, dry firm going and with surprisingly good views until it swings left to end at a gate. Go through the stile by the gate plus two more in quick succession then straight ahead by the wood following the waymarks round the farm buildings to a gap in the old railway track. Then turn left and follow the green track back to the road bridge and up to the car park.

9.6 Castle Bolton to Low Row via Apedale

Most of the former tracks crossing from Wensleydale to Swaledale are now metalled roads. This is one of the few that is not, but you need a transport manager. Apedale alone is worth a visit. Time: about 4 hours. Category B. Map: 1:25,000 Outdoor Leisure Series No. 30, Northern and Central Areas. Park in the car park at Castle Bolton (fee) for the start, it is more difficult at Low Row, or to shorten the walk there is convenient parking on the Askrigg-Grinton road close to where the path crosses the road.

Pass the church and the Post Office and take the walled lane on the left between two blocks of houses. It is apt to be muddy. When it emerges on the rough field take the tractor marks to the left, and follow the general line of the wall up to the moor. You will find a stile in the cross-wall and a cart track takes you down to Apedale[1] by some shooting huts. Just beyond them is a sort of cross road. Take the left-hand one and follow it up the little dale, climbing steeply[2] out of it onto the moor above. As you approach the fence turn sharp left towards a fenced shaft[3] to find the gate and continuation of the path. First have a look at the views up Swaledale. More or less straight ahead is Gunnerside Gill, identified by the wide rough road running up the side of it almost to the top of Rogan's Seat. The village of Gunnerside, like all the other villages, is out of sight. The fell close at hand with the dark cap is Blea Barf, behind it to the left is Lovely Seat 2,213 feet (675 metres) and to its right is Great Shunner Fell, 2,340 feet (716 metres). Continuing from the gate the way leads through even more mine workings. You take the left fork soon after leaving the top and go left across the stream when you are quite well down towards the road.

If you are going on to Low Row go almost across the road to the farm below. Go between the farmhouse and its buildings and follow the road to the farm below as far as its sharp bend. Here turn left up the hill a little and turn right in front of the first building ahead. Go straight down the field to a gate and pass a barn making leftwards towards the stream to find the stile that puts you on the road. Then 10 minutes walk to the right sees you to Low Row.

Things of Interest

1. Apedale's name has nothing to do with the primates. It is believed to originate from a Norse name, Api's dale. It is a pleasant green valley between dark heather moors, filled with bird-song in springtime. It was the scene of much lead mining activity over a century ago. All the way up it there are spoil heaps and bell pit rings. The biggest and probably the most recent remains are the first ones you come to. Here there is the wheel pit of a small water-wheel and its leat can still be seen running up the valley towards the stream. The part below the heather patch is culverted in stone and its emergent height is such that it must have crossed the stream on a wooden flume to take its water from the little stone-built reservoir on the opposite bank. Here the beck has very little water in it, insufficient to work a wheel in a dry spell, but the reservoir is fed by streams from the moor and can supply much more water, and very importantly, at the right height.

2. As you start the steep climb out of the dale there is a mining level just to the right. It was probably a drainage adit for the many workings above.

3. There are some interesting plants to be seen in the higher spoil heaps in June: spring sandwort, scurvy grass and rather surprisingly, for it is not common, mossy saxifrage which bears a large white flower with rounded petals on a delicate stalk.

WALDENDALE AND COVERDALE

The first of these two scenic and little visited valleys leaves Wensleydale just below Aysgarth, the second some miles to the east. Both run to the back of the Wharfedale fells and offer some unfamiliar views of them. Although the Y.D.N.P. map displayed at Horsehouse and Carlton shows a wealth of right of way tracks in the valleys, many stiles have been lost or closed, and at the moment much of the valley walking is not feasible. There are one or two routes to the high ground and a very good double crossing of the moor between Coverdale and Waldendale.

9.7 A walk round West Burton

A little gem of a walk - a good waterfall in a woodland dell and fine views. Time: ³/₄ hr. Category C. Map: Aysgarth footpath map or 1:25,000 Outdoor Leisure 30, Yorkshire Dales Northern and Central Areas.

Starts at the bottom end of the row of houses on the 'up' road into West Burton. It is signposted to the waterfall and a minute or two takes you to the footbridge just below it. Cross this bridge and turn right at the stile above and follow the faint path round the corner of the wall to the right. Follow a line of stiles whilst climbing gently, and as you top the rise a fine view of Waldendale awaits you. The next stile is a little to the left and then the path goes down to the river bridge. After crossing turn right and climb up the hill following the line of trees. The stile onto the road is a bit further on than you would expect. Turn right on the road and a few minutes walk sees you in West Burton.

West Burton is a delightful and spacious village built around a triangular green and is more like the villages of Wharfedale than those of Wensleydale. It has no great air of antiquity, but one of trimness and being cared for, with a variety of architectural styles.

9.8 A walk up Waldendale

A delightful walk up and down the pastures of the dale, barely trodden. Time: 3-4¹/₂ hours. Category B. Map: 1:25,000 Outdoor Leisure 30, Yorkshire Dales Northern and Central Areas. Park at Cote Bridge on the Waldendale road.

Go back up the road towards West Burton and pass two iron gates

West Burton

to find a slit stile on the left on the brow of the hill. Turn left and follow the wall to another stile less than 100 yards along, turn right and look for another in the middle of the wall ahead. Now you are on the line of stiles and they pop up with satisfying regularity in every wall while you enjoy the unfolding scene of Waldendale. Mind you, the stiles are of the awkward sheep-stopping type and there's a lot of them. In due course you will pass two metal gates side by side and go through a long field of bracken, to a broken wooden stile at the left-hand end of the wall. Then make gradually towards a wall on your right, cross a broken-down wall at a well-used gap and aim for a fence that appears to meet the trees in a biggish gill ahead. Turn right up the gill staying just above the trees and you will find a tiny bridge crossing it to the house opposite and the stile is ahead. Cross the driveway leading to this house and make for a slit stile out of sight in the wall ahead. More stiles will lead you to Hargill House. Go to the gate on the right of the buildings, pass the farmhouse and the stile is ahead on the right. Continue in the same general line until Bridgend Farm comes into sight on the left. Go past the farm on its right and then turn back to cross the bridge. Immediately on the left is a well-built stile and a wooden one over the fence ahead. Then climb up right to a gate, go through it and follow the wall towards a barn. Pass below it and continue to another ruined building. Stay above this and above the wall to find a little wicket gate. Opposite is a metal gate and beyond a slit stile hidden by bushes. Not so easy to find, that last bit, but now you are on a line of stiles again and soon you will see another barn which is not far from Whiterow Farm and the tarmac road. There's no help for it, the way back to the car is along the road for some 25-30 minutes, but there's no traffic and it gives good views across Wensleydale.

9.9 West Burton to Coverdale

This walk makes a double crossing of the moors between Waldendale and Coverdale. The short version that takes about $4\frac{1}{2}$ hours does not go down to the valley floor of Coverdale, whilst the longer one taking around $6\frac{1}{2}$ hours goes through the hay meadows of the valley from Carlton to Horsehouse. It is quite possible to start at Horsehouse but the West Burton start is preferable not least because modest refreshments are available in Horsehouse. Category B+, Map: 1:25,000 Outdoor Leisure 30, Northern and Central Areas.

A couple of hundred yards beyond the bridge a bridle track to Carlton goes up the hill to the left. Its start is marked by a squat chimney.[1] It is steep and stony to start with, climbing up the side of the gill and keeping high above it. It makes a big zig-zag - take the lower track at the top of the zag. It is well marked all the way to the gate in the wall that runs across the gap between Penhill and Harland Hill. Through the wall bear right and follow the wall a litle way, then drop down quite clearly to Howden Lodge,[2] being restored in 1990. Here the track forks and you must choose between the longer and shorter routes.

The longer route

Follow the obvious rough cart track to the left. After a short stretch of open ground follow the left-hand side of the wall to enter a grassy walled lane that brings you down to the road at Carlton. Turn left when you first meet tarmac, then right on the 'main' road. Follow it to the first bend and go through the stile signposted Cover Lane. Go straight down the field, through the slit stile, then bear right going through another slit stile into the field above the barn. Carry straight on to reach the road. Turn left and at the first bend go over a wooden step stile on the right. After crossing a tiny stream you enter a biggish field. Leave it by the lower of two gates (not obvious), and continue straight ahead to cross a footbridge into an unmetalled overgrown lane. This brings you to the road at Gammersgill, a very attractive hamlet. Turn left on the road and go through the hamlet to a wide farm road signposted to Horsehouse. Follow it to its end then go gently down the fields towards the river. Shortly the river swings to the left and just after this place look out for

Cote, Waldendale, with the track winding over Burton Moor

an easy place to cross the fence on your left onto a well trodden path that leads into a long, fairly narrow field by the river. (This is not the right of way route but two or even three stiles are missing from it and most people go this way.) Follow the edge of the field - it is a hay meadow - cross the road leading to the bridge and continue over the fence; again there's no stile. The path follows the river as far as a wooden footbridge then goes diagonally right across the next two fields towards Horsehouse.[3] A sign then directs you straight up the next field into a little lane behind the pub. Turn left then right to find it, or if you prefer ice cream, keep straight on for 50 yards.

Whatever your choice in refreshments, turn right and at the end of the houses turn left up a tarmac lane that quickly becomes a steep rough bridleway climbing up the side of High Gill. At the top of the gill it becomes pleasantly grassy and continues unmistakably to a gate in the wall (the shorter route joins here). Turn left through the gate and follow the wall for about half a mile when the track swings to the right to another gate where it meets a stony cart track, the bridleway from Braidley to West Burton. Turn right and follow it across the head of Elm Gill where you bear left at the fork. The track continues as a very pleasant grassy cart track most of the way back to the tarmac in Waldendale when 20-25 minutes walk will see you back to your car.

The shorter route

Follow the same rough cart track as used by the longer walk but when you come to the sharp corner of the wall in less than 100 yards turn right and follow it until you join the new access track to the lodge. Follow this down the moor then through the fields to a walled lane which you follow to a sharp left-hand bend.[4] Here you turn right through the gate and follow the road past the farmhouse into the fields. Where it turns squarely left to another house, you keep straight on through the gate. Follow the tractor marks by the wall through a gate on the left. As soon as you're through the gate follow the wall and from its end drop slightly to find the gate in the wall opposite. Go straight ahead to the stream, Fleimis Gill, and cross it easily. A cart track climbs out but disappears in rough grass. Follow the stream for some time, until you can see a gate well to the right of a plantation of conifers. Go through this gate into a rough tussocky field and keep a look-out for a ladder stile ahead. Cross this and the dry valley beyond to the wall and follow the wall up the field to the first gate on the left. Go through this and follow the wall round to the first gate on the right and from here go down to the farm buildings below. Here you will come onto a rough road that leads you to Fleensop. Stay on it until you reach tarmac, then turn left and go through the gate you can see about 200 yards away. Here strike fairly well up the hill, aiming for the top right-hand side of a conifer plantation where you will find a stile onto the moor. Follow the wall to the corner, turn right and you will find a good track at the gate a little way along where you join the longer walk.

Things of Interest

1.   This little chimney and its flue is all that remains of a former lead smelting mill, a very much smaller one than many in the Dales. Lead was mined not far away in times long past. Half a mile up the road, across but quite close to the river is a long line of small irregular depressions. This is all that remains of some early workings on a vein. (See the chapter on lead mining and smelting in the Dales for more information.)

2.   Howden Lodge is a rather quaint building. Near the door is a stone inscribed 'Miss Lumley, Ripon 1826'. Presumably, it was built as a recreational facility for the lady. From it there are wide views of the hills on the other side of Coverdale: Roova, Little and Great Haw and Little Whernside.

3.   Horsehouse takes its name from the fact that it stands at the cross roads of two formerly important packhorse routes, that from Waldendale

View across Wensleydale to Penhill

to Coverdale which passed Fleensop colliery and lead mines, and that which came over the fells to the west from the direction of Lancaster and continued to Middleham.

4. If you do this walk in early spring these green uplands resound with birdsong - curlew, lapwing, skylark, even from time to time the honk-honk of a pheasant. As you come down the well made cart track there is a damp place on the right with marsh marigolds, lesser spearwort, buttercup and brooklime that flower with the amusing Latin name, *Veronica beccabunga;* it does, too.

9.10 From West Scrafton to Great Haw, 178 feet (544 metres)

Great Haw is almost the highest point of the modest fells that form Coverdale's south-east edge. Little Whernside is the true head of the dale and is 1,984 feet (605 metres) but it is an awful long slog from West Scrafton. This walk uses an old bridleway to Colsterdale which is still in good order as far as the coal pits on the top of Little Haw. The walk is not recommended in reverse. Time: 3½-4 hours, Category B. Map: 1:50,000 Aysgarth, Sheet 99. Park on the wide grass verge as you enter West Scrafton from Coverham.

Go towards the village, and the bridlepath leaves on the left just before the road crosses the stream. It winds its way stonily up the hill behind the house, follows the wall and then strikes across some wet ground on a sort of causeway to slant up the hill towards some prominent spoil heaps.[1] Keep to the left of these and continue over the moor to the biggest of all, ringed around by a wire fence. Make towards the fence and you will find much better going than you would expect. Follow the fence over the first rise, which is Little Haw to the second which is Great Haw. Here the fence you have been following meets another coming across.

If you had any thoughts of going onto Little Whernside follow the fence to the right until you can see the intervening ground. Unless you are a very strong walker the sight of it will deter you quite effectively.

The return uses another old track that has almost disappeared. Retrace your steps down the top bit of Great Haw for a good 5 minutes, then strike out at right angles to the fence, and with any luck you will soon pick it up. It will bring you to a tiny stream which you follow until you can see a large circular sheepfold below. There's a big bank of bracken between you and it, just probe for a way through. As you come nearer to the sheepfold you will see a row of stones on the near skyline. These are the parish boundary stones. Make for them because there you will find a little path. When the line of stones swings left, leave them and swing right crossing the stream just above a little waterfall. Assorted animal tracks will take you back to the bridle track you started on.

Things of Interest

1. Coal seams are found fairly frequently in the Yoredale series of rocks that are the basis of Wensleydale's scenery. Not all of them are thick enough or of good enough quality to be worked, even in the nineteenth century, and the best ones were on the high ground. The first spoil heaps you pass are from a seam that was worked as a series of levels where it outcropped, and is best seen when you pass below them on your return. The shaft on the top seems to have been a much bigger affair and was worked until the early years of this century. The changes in the rock strata can be seen here quite well - first a layer of peat, then some glacial drift full of pale stones, then a rather friable sandstone below which is a more solid layer through which the shaft was carved. It would have been lined with stone which has now collapsed. Coal from all these pits was used for lead smelting, lime burning and for domestic use. A point for the botanically mined, crowberry grows in the better drained spoil heaps; it is a typical plant of loose ground, whilst all around the moor is white with hare's tail cotton grass in June.

AROUND ASKRIGG

9.11 A Walk to Mill Gill Force and Whitfield Gill Force, Askrigg

A whole network of field paths and stiles fans out from Askrigg, an ancient village, much older than Hawes. The church was built in 1175 though little of the original work remains. In Elizabethan times it became the centre of trade in the upper dale and later developed a considerable amount of industry - cotton and wool spinning, hand-knitting and lead mining. The main street, close packed with three storey-houses, has an air of industry rather than one of rural uses. It is usually possible to park near the church except on Sundays.

Since the 1984 edition of this book the path of the gill has been made more direct and extended to Whitfield Gill Force giving a delightful walk, worth coming specially to Askrigg for in springtime. Time: for a stroll to Mill Gill Force and back, ¾ hour; for a slightly longer walk returning through the fields direct to Askrigg, 1½ hours; for the walk up to Whitfield Gill Force and returning through the fields, 2½ hours. Map: 1:25,000 Outdoor Leisure Map No. 30, Northern and Central Areas, though that does not show the new route up the gill nor the extension to Whitfield Gill Force. Category C.

The start of the route by the church is signposted 'To Mill Gill Force'. At the end of the road there is a stile on the right and a well marked footpath leads to a little bridge over Mill Gill.[1] The path now enters the wood and climbs high above the stream, only glimpses of it below are visible in high summer. You will come to a signpost directing you to the force, and having been suitably impressed by the waterfall, retrace your steps to the signpost. This is the return point for the stroll to the force, otherwise continue up the gill as indicated until you come to a footbridge, where a signpost gives you the choice of continuing to Whitfield Gill Force or returning to Askrigg. If you are returning to Askrigg, cross the stream, climb steeply up the hill opposite and join a stony cart track. Turn left and follow it up the hill until you join a walled lane, Low Straits Lane. Turn right here and a good hundred yards after crossing a stream turn right through a stile beneath an ash tree*. Go straight down a long field to a stile beside a gate, cross the little bridge ahead and then turn left. Go through the stile on your right at the end of the field and climb over the hill. When you reach the next wall and hedge follow them to the right down to some new houses and

Askrigg Church,
Cross and old pump

turn left through a little gate by the first one to get onto the road close to where you started.

Extension to Whitfield Gill Force

Continue upstream from the signpost, sometimes leaving the woods for a field's length or two, then popping back inside, always by well trodden paths. In due course you will come to a finger post offering you the choice of paths to a viewpoint for the Whitfield Gill Force or to continue to Low Straits Lane by the footbridge. Forget the path to the view point; you get a better view of the waterfall - provided there are not too many leaves on the trees - from the Low Straits Lane path. Follow this path right up the side of the wood perched on top of the gorge below until you meet Low Straits Lane. Then turn right and follow it for a good half mile until you have crossed the stream and found the stile* by the ash tree. Then return as for the shorter walk.

Things of Interest

1.   The waters of Mill Gill were harnessed to provide power for a cotton spinning mill built in Askrigg about 1785. Much more recently the water has been used to power a water-wheel housed in the building on the left. The galvanised overhead trough supplied it with water. You pass the dam later on. For the geologically minded the great variety of

the Yoredale series can be seen as you walk up the gill. It is one of the best exposures of them in the Dales.

9.12 Askrigg's river and high pastures, returning by Whitfield Gill

This walk gives varied walking with good views from its higher parts. There is a stretch of good river scenery, a length of old railway and some lead mine remains, as well as a return by a fine wooded gill. Time: 3½ hours. Category C. Map 1:25,000 Outdoor Leisure Map No. 30, Northern and Central Areas, but note that it does not show the path down the gill correctly. Park at Worton Bridge.

The walk starts at a stile in the bend of the Askrigg road and follows the river downstream as far as Nappa House. Here a building is being erected that may obstruct the gate onto the road, so look for the alternative. Turn left on the farm road and where it bends sharp left go through the stile ahead and turn right. At the end of the field a swing gate puts you onto the old railway track. Between 100 and 200 yards after you have gone under an old blackened railway bridge a fence bars your way. There is a swing gate on your right and you stay in the field just below the track until you come to a cart track. Turn left and follow this up through the scattered hamlet of Woodhall to the Askrigg-Carperby road. Go straight across the road between a bungalow and a barn and follow a stony cart track as it winds its way up the hill. Keep left as it approaches the wall and gate ahead and leave the field much further on. Follow the cart track through a short field, then go into one full of grassy mounds, old lead mine workings. Aim for a gate above some trees then roughly follow the wall until you come to a stone barn by some trees, passing through a little upland valley below a limestone scar. This brings you onto a lane. A little way along it is joined by another one on the left. One field's length after this junction a stile on the left takes you into the fields. The next stile is diagonally across, then go straight down into the wood to find a good path to the farm buildings below. Go to the right of them and pick up a line of stiles that takes you right into Newbiggin by a white gate. Straight ahead a walled lane leads to some barns.

(Direct finish to Askrigg: Opposite the last one you will find a stile. Make diagonally right and again follow a line of stiles down to the Muker road at the top of Askrigg. In the last field keep just below to find

a gate. Go down the road through the village to the church.)

Otherwise continue to the end of this little lane to the stile there. Follow the wall to the next one, turn right and then left to reach the Muker road. Turn right on it and climb rather steeply up the hill for about ¼ mile to the end of a rough walled lane on the left. Turn into it and follow it to the wood. There you will find the stile into the head of Whitfield Gill. Simply follow the well trodden path down the gill to the road where you turn left and continue to the church.

Opposite the market cross there is a narrow lane between houses. At the end of this to the left of a gate is a slit stile into the field and a very well marked path first crosses the old railway - hardly recognisable here - and then goes direct to the bridge where you are parked.

10: UPPER WENSLEYDALE AND MALLERSTANG

Walks around Semerdale

10.1   A walk to Semer Water from Bainbridge. Category C 263
10.2   A walk round Semer Water. Category C 264
10.3   Drumaldrace from Marsett, returning by Bardale.
        Category B 265

Walks around Hawes

10.4   A walk to Hardraw Force, Simon Stone and Sedbusk.
        Category C 267
10.5   Great Shunner Fell and Cotterdale. Category B 269
10.6   Great Shunner Fell and Hugh Seat from Hardraw.
        Category A 272
10.7   Dodd Fell to Horton-in-Ribblesdale. Category A 272
10.8   Drumaldrace to Bainbridge, returning via Sedbusk.
        Category B 274

Mallerstang

10.9   A walk to Hell Gill via Mossdale, returning by Cotter End.
        Category B+ 277
10.10   Wild Boar Fell, Swarth Fell, Hugh Seat, High Seat.
        Category A 280

HAWES

The Yorkshire Dales National Park has an information centre and car park in the former station yard close to the Muker road. Here, too, is the Upper Dales Folk Museum, by far the best of its kind in the Dales. It is no mere collection of articles from your grannie's parlour, but a well thought-out display of kitchen and farm implements that illustrate the old ways of life in the Dales up to the First World War, before the arrival of electricity and the tractor. Wall-sized photographs made from old newspaper cuttings show typical activities - haymaking and peat cutting for example. Every display is extremely well documented. The visitor does not need to guess the purpose of some unusual item, and

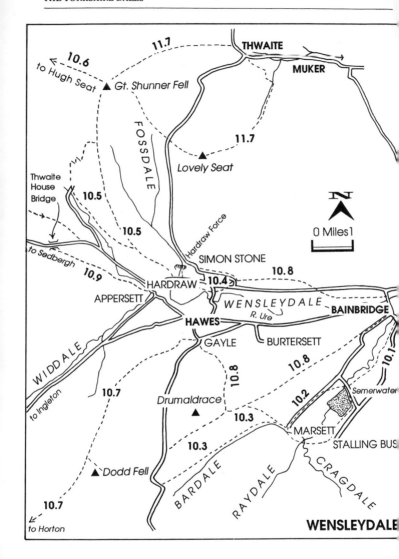

he will leave feeling the museum does provide a glimpse of how dalesfolk used to live. Open every day, Easter to the end of October, occasional weekends in winter, 10am to 5pm.

Because the fell walking is concentrated in the upper dale this chapter starts rather arbitrarily at Bainbridge. Hawes is the 'capital', a small town made important by the railway which linked it first to Northallerton in 1877 and a little later to Garsdale. Hawes is not of ancient origin like the other villages of the dale. It is not found in the Domesday book and only received its market charter in 1700, a sign of its late growth. Formerly coal mining and quarrying were important, there was a worsted spinning mill associated with the hand-knitting industry of the dales and today there is a cheese factory. Hawes' property has always been linked with agriculture, for Wensleydale is famed for its rich pasture.

10.1 A Walk to Semer Water from Bainbridge

An excellent walk, but unfortunately you return as you came. Time: 2½ hours. Category C. Map: Hawes footpath map or 1:25,000 Outdoor Leisure 30, Yorkshire Dales Northern and Central Areas. Park in Bainbridge near the Green.

The starting stile is on the right on the big bend at the start of the road to Stalling Busk. The path follows the wall at first and passes a small field on its left. Climbing steadily all the time it takes the right-hand of two stiles in the first cross-wall. Soon you are over the top of the hill and Semer Water lies before you with Bardale and Cragdale at its head.

After you've dropped down the hillside turn right at the stile to join

Bainbridge

Addleborough and Semerwater

the riverside path and follow it unmistakably to the bridge on the road where the next walk starts. This relatively new footpath diversion is a great deal more enjoyable than the old route that wandered across the fields, having the interest of the stream.

10.2 A walk round Semer Water

This walk has a fair bit of road walking in it, though it is pleasant enough. There are good views of the lake for birdwatchers. Time: about 2 hours. Category C, but it can be muddy. Map: Hawes footpath map or 1:25,000 Outdoor Leisure 30, Yorkshire Dales Northern and Central Areas. Park on the shore by the bridge, or at Marsett by the bridge as the walk can be done equally well from there. Note that there is a fee to park on the shore.

Walk along the shore of the lake for half a mile or so. After the second stream running into it there is a finger post and slit stile on the right. The stiles continue to the right of a barn and then the path becomes very clear if somewhat muddy. Follow it easily to the ruins of Stalling Busk church. Here the way forks and if you want to go to Stalling Busk itself, follow the signpost and the stream up to the left, but if you want to go direct to Marsett across the fields, find the stile in the bottom corner beyond this signpost. There is now a whole line of stiles crossing small fields and the way is easily found. At the last one you find yourself on the rough lane that links Stalling Busk with

Marsett. Turn right and follow it to Marsett. If there has been recent heavy rain you may have trouble at a ford. If so, retrace your steps to between the last two barns you've passed where, if you look left, you will see a ladder stile. This will take you to a fine metal bridge that sees you high and dry across the water. In Marsett follow the road past the caravan site and down the hill on the other side. A long, long, hill faces you, but cheer up, your path leaves at a stile at the bottom of it on the right. From it go down the hill leftwards towards a little stream to find a gate hidden by trees. Continue leftwards and downwards towards more trees to find a path that puts you on the road by the bridge not far from your car.

Things of Interest

Semer Water is all that is left of a larger lake formed in the immediate post glacial period some 8,000 years ago. The melt waters from the glaciers in the higher part of the valley were impounded by the bank of clayey debris formed by the bigger glacier flowing down the main valley of the Ure. As Semer Water is one of the few lakes in the Dales and is its largest natural sheet of water, it is in considerable demand for water sports. These activities are controlled by the Semer Water Sports Association which allows power boating only by its members, but allows the general public to sail or canoe on payment of a small fee. Stalling Busk church, like the disused barns all around it, is a relic of changed agricultural practices and a declining rural population. This church was built in 1722 in a style far more domestic than that of most Dales churches; a reflection of the times when it was built. Gothic architecture had come to an end with the Reformation and its revival in Victorian times was still a long way off. Few churches were built anywhere in the country in this period. In 1909 a new church was built nearer to the hamlet but the graveyard continued to be used right up to World War II.

10.3 Drumaldrace from Marsett, returning by Bardale

This walk has some of the best views in the whole of upper Wensleydale - so choose a good day and go this way round, for there is a fine finish. Time: $3^{1}/_{2}$-4 hours. Category B. Map: 1:50,000 Wensleydale and Whafedale Sheet 98 or 1:25,000 Outdoor Leisure 30, Yorkshire Dales Northern and Central Areas. Drive to Marsett from Bainbridge and park near the bridge.

Turn back along the road you have just come along and go left up a stony lane towards Knight Close. As you turn through a gate into the farm start to climb up to a little gate just above it. Go through it and the stile straight across the field, then very steeply indeed up a long field to find the stile slightly to the left. Continue in the same general direction - there's no path - until you come to a little ravine cut into the shale just below the top left-hand corner of the field. The stile lies across it. Now a little path leads you on but fails before the next stile just to the right of the corner of the field. Again, keep the same general direction and you will come to a wide tractor-grooved path. Turn left on it and follow it to its gate on the Cam High Road.[1] Soon it becomes grassy and gives very good walking below Wether fell, whose highest point, Drumaldrace, 2,015 feet (614 metres), can be reached in a few minutes if you leave the road a couple of hundred yards or so before it becomes fully walled again. The bulk of Dodd Fell now looms ahead filling the landscape. Follow the Cam High Road to its junction with the Hawes-Kettlewell road, from where there are good views behind you down to Hawes. Turn left on this road and follow it for about $^1/_2$ mile taking care to turn left at the Y-fork for Cam Houses.

Go through the first gate on the left, about 200 yards along. A tractor-marked track winds its way down the hill in big curves to the corner of a stone wall. Follow the stone wall to a gate just below a clump of small sycamore trees and go through it. This can be a good spot for lunch whilst admiring the fine views of Semer Water with Addleborough to its right. Now go down the middle of a tongue of land between the becks. The track is well marked and goes through gates or gateways all the way to the stream which it then crosses, but you do not. Stay on this side and follow the stream for some time. Much lower down you will see a small gate on the left. This is the true way and the way to go if the river is high. There are slit stiles all the way close to the river. If the river is low and you can cross and recross easily, you may prefer to do this for the sake of the views into the little limestone gorge with its clear deep pools below. Once at the gorge stay on that side and it will bring you onto the road at the back of the chapel. The usual way ends at the river bridge.

Things of Interest

1.   The Cam High Road was originally part of the Roman road from the fort at Bainbridge to Ribchester, built by Julius Agricola as part of

his campaign to subdue the Celtic tribes of Yorkshire. It is not now in its original form for it has seen much use and change throughout the centuries and was part of the 1751 Richmond to Lancaster turnpike road. Wether Fell is a favourite place for hang-gliding - easily reached by road and exposed to the wind.

WALKS ROUND HAWES

10.4 A walk to Hardraw Force, Simon Stone and Sedbusk

Waterfalls are two-a-penny in Wensleydale, but Hardraw Force could be described as the finest of them all. It is on private land and can be reached only by going through the Green Dragon Inn, Hardraw, and paying a small charge. 1:25,000 Outdoor Leisure 30, Yorkshire Dales Northern and Central Areas or the Hawes footpath map. Time: 3-4 hours depending on how long you linger. Park in the Y.D.N.P. car park in Muker road, Hawes. Category C.

Turn right on the road on leaving the car park and after about 100 yards turn left into the fields on a paved path. It joins the road a little further on, and after crossing the River Ure, again turn left and follow the paved path to Hardraw where it arrives opposite the Green Dragon.

Walk up one side of the falls and if you are a bit daring, or prepared to get slightly wet, walk under the cliff behind the waterfall - quite an experience passing under the great jet of water that shoots over your head. Walk back down that side and cross the stream by a good footbridge.

About the Falls

Hardraw Falls are reputed to be the highest single drop in England. 92 feet (30 metres) and lie at the head of a sizeable gorge. The topmost rock strata is a hard limestone and the softer shales and sandstones beneath have been cut back selectively by the swirling action of the stream. In severe floods this top strata may collapse - it happened at the end of the last century - and thus the gorge is formed. At one time there was a good path on the left-hand side of the stream leading to the top of the falls. At present it is in a poor state of repair and is not recommended. These paths were laid out in Victorian times so that ladies in the cumbersome dresses of the time could enjoy the scene, for Hardraw was one of the attractions of the Dales complete with bandstand and its rows of stone seats. At the turn of the century brass band contests were held here,

Hardraw Force

taking advantage of the fine acoustics. The author believes her grandfather, who lived at Barnoldswick, came here to enjoy them, travelling partly by train and then by wagonette. The contests have been revived recently.

The Woodland Dell above the Falls

Whilst at Hardraw it would be a pity not to visit this dell, for it is of a rare quality. Unfortunately it is not possible to enter it from the falls themselves, only from the road at Simon Stone.

Next to the Green Dragon but separated from it by the entrance to its holiday flats is a cottage through whose backyard the field path to Simon Stone starts. It looks a bit improbable, but this is the start. Go through the wicket gate and steeply up the hill to a stile. Beyond the house at the top of the hill turn sharp right and follow the well marked path to the road. Turn left and follow it to the first big right-hand bend, when on the left you will see a narrow walled footpath leading down quite quickly to the stream and footbridge. There is a path on both sides of the stream and a bridge at the top. Make the circuit as you please and return as you came. Enjoy the many little waterfalls with deep green pools below, the banks of bluebells and wild garlic, the air of peace and harmony.

Once you have returned to the road continue along it to the hamlet of Simon Stone. On a bend of the road there is a farm gate on the left and a yard or two away a stile. From this gate follow the concrete cart track to the barns until it ends. Then you will find a line of stiles on the left passing more barns; indeed, every field on this 'shelf' high above the river has a barn. Soon the stiles change sides as it were, and are on the right-hand side of the barns, then the fields become very narrow, but always the stiles are in line and lead you into Sedbusk. Turn right down the village street, and as you pass the last building keep a look out for a slit stile on the right, not easy to see. Go down the field below the clump of trees then go right to find the next stile. The one after that is right of the gate and brings you onto the road opposite the next one. From here a well trodden path goes diagonally right down the field passing left of a house to another stile. The same direction takes you to a hump backed bridge over a little stream and the road. Turn right on the road and go up the hill a little way. Just past a clump of trees on the left there is a stile at the top of some steps and from it a flagged footpath leads you back to Hardraw opposite the pub.

Things of Interest

Sedbusk, like Burtersett, is a Norse settlement on a shelf above the valley floor, a characteristic of the Yoredale strata of Wensleydale. Like the 'shelf' across the valley it is dotted with hay barns belonging to an agricultural way of life no longer practised. The line of stiles was, in effect, the service road to these barns in the days before the ubiquitous tractor.

10.5 Great Shunner Fell, (234 feet) 716 metres and Cotterdale

The ascent of Great Shunner from Hardraw is easy and rightly popular, being almost free from the peat groughs and bog of the Swaledale side. Too short to make a day's outing, but it is well worth returning via Cotterdale instead of retracing your steps all the way. From the hamlet of Cotterdale the route goes through the fields and climbs gently to regain the Pennine Way track on Great Shunner just above the walled section. It requires care with the route finding but has excellent views and most pleasant surroundings. Time: 4½ hours. Category B. There is limited roadside parking at Hardraw just beyond the former school on the Appersett road. Map: 1:25,000 Outdoor Leisure 30, Yorkshire Dales Northern and Central Areas (both sides!).

The path starts as a walled lane beside the former school. A wide stony cart track takes you a long way up the fell; avoid the branch on the right at the end of the walled part and take care to follow the Pennine Way sign at the top of the first steep step. When you get to the top admire the view then retrace your steps for about 30 minutes to a large cairn on a stony edge. Look to the right and you will see two dark conical mounds well below you, the spoil heaps of former collieries. The track to Cotterdale starts there but it is roughish going to that point. Turn left at the spoil heaps and follow the track, rather boggy in places, which approaches the top of the afforestation in Cotterdale. Keep a sharp look-out for a gate into it, for this is where you go down to the valley. (Failure to find it is no disaster: the track you are on is well marked and joins the Pennine Way track higher on the fell than the one from Cotterdale.

When you meet the forest road turn left and after a short half mile look out for a little track on the right that goes down to the river, crossing it by a footbridge to bring you right into the hamlet of Cotterdale. Failure to find it means you will have to ford the stream lower down which will be difficult. Just beyond the houses there is a white footbridge on the left, the start of the route back.

The first three slit stiles are all in line with the bridge. The third one bears a notice "Beware of the Bull", but do not be deterred. He will almost certainly be with a herd of cows and calves and be far more interested in them than in you. Move gently and do not disturb them, and I would be surprised if His Lordship did more than cast a glance at you. A solitary bull is another matter. Next you will come to a wall with a gap in it and from it a slight ramp leads up the field to a small gate hidden above the trees. It is important to find this. Turn right above the wall and continue on vague tracks past three barns. At the third one climb up a little to find the slit stile above the power lines. You find yourself on a broad green path that continues through a huge field to a gateway with a reassuring yellow dot. Continuing above the wall, the path gradually dwindles and starts to subdivide, but try to keep your height. You will come to a long cross-wall more or less opposite a gateway and you now bear left up a steepish ramp to a fence post with

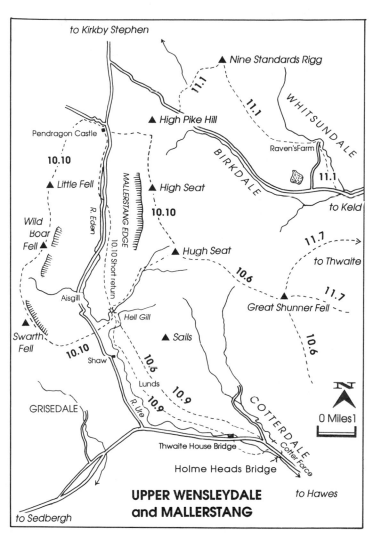

a yellow dot. Beyond it, a little path takes you to a gap in the next wall and then quite shortly the cart track just above the walled section. Ten minutes walk sees you down to Hardraw.

Things of Interest

The well-made lane now used by the Pennine Way was once the approach lane to the colliery on the flanks of Cotterdale. The left-hand branch goes to it.

10.6 Great Shunner and Hugh Seat, (2,257 feet) 688 metres from Hardraw

To make a real day of Great Shunner this extension is recommended. Time: 7 hours. Category A. Park as for the previous walk. 1:50,000 Landranger map, Sheet 98 is needed to cover Hugh Seat.

See the previous walk for details of climbing Great Shunner. Identify Hugh Seat and then set off directly for it. Little height is lost and the going is not bad for most of the way which follows the new fence. The way from Hugh Seat lies down Hell Gill Beck. It is probably best to go right down the nose between the two main tributaries of the stream and then cross over to the true right bank, but none of it is good going. At Hell Gill Bridge you join the track used in Walk No. 10.9 and follow that walk to the road. When you reach the road there is a good mile or more of it between you and Hardraw.

10.7 Dodd Fell, continuing to Horton-in-Ribblesdale

A good way to do Dodd Fell if you have a transport manager is to traverse it by the Pennine Way path and be picked up on the road near Gearstones. Even better is to continue to Horton-in-Ribblesdale and this can be done using a Sunday excursion train on the Settle-Carlisle line that has a connecting minibus at Garsdale station to Hawes. Check by ringing J.Woof, the operator, Sedbergh 20414. On 1990's train timetable this allows you about 7 hours for the walk. No place for dawdlers! The walk starts by the Pennine Way which it follows to Old Ing, Upper Ribblesdale, where it transfers to the Dales Way which is considered to be slightly quicker and certainly much pleasanter under foot. The shorter version takes only about 4 hours. Map: 1:25,000 Outdoor Leisure Map. No. 2, Yorkshire Dales Western Area. Category A. B, for the short version.

Pick up the Pennine Way in Hawes on the upper road at a ginnel close to the western end of the churchyard. It is signposted Pennine Way. A line of stiles and a well marked track take you to Gayle.[1] Now forget about P.W. signs, they're misleading. The simplest way is to walk straight up the main street to the cross roads, turn right and almost at once turn left up a ginnel by the side of the Methodist chapel. This takes you onto a road. Turn right and opposite the last house you will see a swing gate up steps leading into the field. From here the path is well trodden with stiles onto the next road. Turn right here and in 50 yards go left along a farm road. Just before the last gate to the farm turn left into the field. The path now climbs easily and clearly right up to Ten End and then moves onto its Widdale Flank.[2] Here it acts as a splendid balcony giving fine views into the valley of Snaizeholme, of the fell of the same name and further still, the top part of Widdale Fell. In due course you will see Dodd Fell ahead. The Pennine Way path continues to traverse below it, and if you want to visit the summit, a fine viewpoint but otherwise quite indistinguished, make for it from this point. It is hardly worth the very considerable effort as there's much rough ground and no path. Add on ¾ hour if you do this. Otherwise continue along the excellent track until you reach a P.W. signpost on a short stretch of tarmac road.

Follow the tarmac to a gate, go through it and continue on it until it swings left to Camhouse Farm. You now keep straight down the good track ahead for almost a couple of miles until you come to a junction with a small cairn.

If you are doing the shorter version take the right-hand branch. It goes down the hill, crosses Gayle Beck by a footbridge and climbs up to the road a few minutes away. There is a small parking space a little way to the left.

If you are continuing to Horton-in-Ribblesdale take the left-hand branch. It winds its way into the head of Ling Gill, a national nature reserve, and then follows its left bank continuing all the way to Old Ing where you transfer to the Ribble Way. Only go 200 yards or so down its road, as far as a junction with a cart track on the left, then follow this track to a gate. Beyond the gate leave it almost at once on the right and skirt across the top of the plantation to drop down into a steep-sided gill. There's a little footbridge in the bottom and once up the precipitous side facing you, it is only a matter of following the line of ladder stiles through the pastures to Sell Gill Barn. Then follow the rough lane down to Horton at the Crown. Go straight ahead over the bridge to reach the station in 5 minutes. If you have time in hand, the Pen-y-ghent cafe is 5 minutes along the road in the other direction.

NOTE: If you are short of time, a few minutes could be saved by resorting to the road from High Birkwith. If you want to take this soft but safer option simply continue down the rough road from Old Ing to reach the tarmac at High Birkwith. This will bring you to the river bridge at Horton where you turn right and reach the station in 5 minutes.

Things of Interest

1.   Gayle now looks a little like a suburb of Hawes but at one time had its own industry - spinning. The mill, built in 1784 to take advantage of the water power of the beck, still stands and can be seen shortly after joining the road.

2.   The Cam High Road is the name given centuries ago to the Roman road that ran from Bainbridge to Ingleton direct, as Roman roads did, over the fell. It is probably the best preserved and authenticated length of Roman road in the Dales. In the middle of the eighteenth century it was improved to become the turnpike road linking Richmond with Lancaster, two unlikely sounding bed fellows. In those days Richmond was not only an important market centre from which lead was sent to the east coast ports but the seat of the Court of Archdeaconry whose jurisdiction extended over a large area including part of Lancashire. Lancaster was then an up-and-coming port with a substantial trade to the West Indies, importing such desirable commodities as mahogany, cotton and molasses. The turnpike road went up the dale via Askrigg to Bainbridge then followed the line of the Roman Road from Bainbridge over the flank of Dodd Fell, dropping down to cross Gayle Beck. It then continued over Newby Head and went onto the northern side of the dale to reach Ingleton by a steep descent between the rivers Doe and Twiss. Little is known about the onward route to Lancaster.

10.8   Drumaldrace to Bainbridge, returning via Sedbusk

There are two possible return routes. The first, by Bainbridge and Sedbusk gives a particularly fine and varied walk, but if this seems a bit long at 6½ hours, there is a much shorter one by Burtersett, 3½-4 hours. Both are Category B and need map1:25,000 Outdoor Leisure No. 30, Yorkshire Dales Northern and Central Areas. Park in the Yorkshire Dales National Park car park at the old station in Hawes.

Walk to Gayle by the Pennine Way path (see Walk 10.7), then follow the Kettlewell road over the bridge, turn left onto the Burtersett road and you will find the first stile after the first house on the right.

Take a diagonal line upwards across the first four fields, finding slit stiles easily right up to a barn. The next stile is straight up the field from the barn and is not easily seen. The next couple are fairly obvious and bring you into a long field with a stream in it. Follow the stream for a while, cross it when convenient and make for a gap in the wall well left of the wood. Go very steeply upwards bearing left at the top into the next field to find a small gate. Continue upwards and leftwards to a gate, but use the stile just above it. Turn right and follow the wall to join the green bridleway from Burtersett. Now cut across to a gate with a hen hut (!) beside it. From this gate the bridleway climbs up to the right but does not go to the top of Drumaldrace. Go only as far as the first sharp bend to the right then keep straight ahead along a well marked little path that goes over the shoulder of the fell to meet the Cam High Road.[1] Turn right on the road and keep going for a good mile until you are within about 200 yards of it becoming enclosed in walls. Then 5 minutes walk up the hill on your right will see you at the cairn. Admire the wide views and retrace your steps to the Cam High Road. If you are returning via Burtersett, see Note A.

Otherwise turn left and follow the road all the way down to

Gayle Mill

275

Bainbridge.[2] It is inclined to become boring, it's so straight, but at least it has good views across the dale and enough grass to be fairly kind to the feet. In Bainbridge, which has a village shop and pub, take the Askrigg road and go through the stile as soon as you are across the River Ure. Make for the old railway line but instead of crossing it by a swing gate, go ahead to a slit stile, then cross the line by a pair of swing gates. Turn left in the field and follow the boundary fence through three fields when you can get back onto the old track. The track gives far better walking than might be expected, with good views up the valley.[3] There are wire fences here and there and they have stiles, but when you come to a very solid fence topped with barbed wire you are at the end, but not of all things. A swing gate puts you onto a tarmac lane. Follow it for about half a mile, go through a substantial gateway, but before it swings right into the farm buildings, go left to pick up some tractor marks which will take you up the hill to a gate onto the Hawes-Askrigg road. Go straight across the road and through another gate, then climb only a little: the stile is just below a hawthorn tree. Make across to a gate at the top of a wood, then follow the track to the tarmac lane that leads to the hamlet of Litherskew. If you wish, follow this to Sedbusk, but the field path is much more agreeable.[4] To find it, follow the tarmac into the hamlet, go past the house on the right and the first one on the left. Then, and not before, turn left between the house and the farm buildings. You will find a stile by the gate and a whole line of them leads you to the road at Sedbusk.

Turn left on the road and in less than 50 yards look out on the right for a stile near a gate; it is not easy to see. Go down the field passing below the trees and onto the next field by a stile half-way down. Still keep to the same line and you will find a stile onto the road beyond the gate. Almost opposite is another stile and a very well marked track leads you down the hill across a stream by a hump-backed bridge onto the road. Continue along the road to Hawes, using the Pennine Way footpath to cut the corner.

Note A

Retrace your steps to the green bridleway and simply follow it all the way down to Burtersett. As soon as you come to the tarmac turn right and then left into the village. Part of the way down the road on the left is the Methodist chapel and the path to Hawes starts just past it. It is flagged and unmistakable all the way.

Things of Interest

1. The Cam High Road - see note after Walk 10.7.

2. Bainbridge is a very ancient village and was a Roman fort built to subdue the local Celtic tribes. The fort was on the hillock (a drumlin) just off the main road. There is access to it from a stile a little way along the Aysgarth road but little to be seen.

3. Removal of the fences has restored the field to the shape it was before the railway was built in 1879. If you do this walk in early summer when the hayfields around are coming into flower you may notice that these flowers have not spread onto the former line to any degree. The track is being colonised by plants that tolerate drier conditions than the rich moist soils the hayfields offer - hawksbit, hawksweeds, black knapweed, which are not seen in the fields where buttercups, crosswort, speedwell, meadow cranesbill and many others are found, though not in quite such glorious profusion as in Swaledale.

4. Between Litherskew and Sedbusk there is a fine example of what happens when an old meadow is reseeded - not a flower in sight!

10.9   A walk to Hell Gill via Mossdale, returning by Cotter End

This long but easy walk takes you through the rough pastures of the uppermost parts of Wensleydale onto an old highway, now a green track, which crosses Hell Gill before descending to the Eden valley. Hell Gill[1] is a quite remarkable chasm on the boundary of the Park. There are magnificent views of Wild Boar Fell on the outward leg. Though the walking is easy the route finding can be tricky in places and eagle eyes are needed to spot the slit stiles. The 1:50,000 Wensleydale and Wharfedale map covers the entire walk but the use of the 1:25,000 Pathfinder Map sheet 617 together with the Outdoor Leisure Map 2 gives almost complete coverage and this pair is recommended. Allow 5½ hours plus stops. Category B+. Limited roadside parking is possible near Holme Heads Bridge on the A684 Hawes to Garsdale road where the walk starts. A quick trip to see Cotter Force is well worth while. The path starts by the bridge and it will take you 15-20 minutes return.

Continue up the road for about 200 yards then take the access road on the left to Birkrigg Farm. As you approach the farm continue along the cart track below the farm. It runs up the flank of the valley then turns left to reach Mid Mossdale. At the sharp bend below the last climb up to the house, a finger post directs you to the right. The path soon disappears but follow a line of gates fairly close to the river - but do not cross it - to Mossdale head and go through the farm buildings. Beyond them a fine view of the triple-arched Mossdale viaduct[2] spanning the gill above a series of little waterfalls awaits you. Then continue straight ahead up a rough cart track. Turn right after the wall and follow it down to a stile onto the road opposite Thwaite Bridge House.

Cross to the house and go left to find a gate and finger post to Garsdale Y.H. The path is fairly well marked as far as Yore House, passing just above two short lengths of woodland and beneath a third one. Then aim at the viaduct in the distance and you will pick up a cart track that brings you to the back of Yore House where you will find yet another finger post, this time to Lunds Church. There's no track to guide you here, but when you see the plantation keep left to spot the slit stile. Beyond it an access track takes you into the hamlet of Blades. From Yore House onwards a magnificent view slowly develops. First, the whale back of Baugh Fell comes into view, then Swarth Fell, and only some time later does the whole of Wild Boar Fell, King of Mallerstang, appear. Go through the hamlet and out of the gate on the right, then immediately turn left through another gate. The right of way path now goes down to a bridge over the river and then comes back to the gate you want, but it is much simpler just to follow the fence through this trackless, rush-grown field to the gate you want on the right of a corner. Opposite is another small gate then you turn left and follow a line of slit stiles over the hill to spot the tiny barn-like Lunds Church[3] with its long disused graveyard. Keep to the right of the church to reach the lane at Beck Side.

Go straight across the lane into another one and at its end go through the slit stile. The ground is untracked as far as the distant barn of Low End but a line of slit stiles takes you there without difficulty, passing to the right of an intermediate barn. At Low End go straight across the lane and through the stockyard, bearing left across the stream then following the wall to a gate beyond which you join a bold cart track that runs gently up the fellside to Hell Gill Bridge, identified from a distance by its guardian ash trees. When you get there look over the parapet of the bridge on the right-hand side. You'll be amazed at the drop below! Have a look around though not surprisingly there is no way into the gill.

If this outward part of the walk has seemed unduly long, take heart. Although you have not finished with gentle uphill, the return is much more direct and far less time-consuming. Retrace your steps only for about 150 yards. A relatively unobtrusive path leaves on the left amongst some limestone slabs and this is where you go. It meets a wall and continues crossing two deep-cut gills and passing the ruins of High Hall at the second one. The track used to be a good grassy one, but unhappily has been mangled in many places by motorbike traffic which is deplorable. However, there are fine views into Garsdale and the tops of Whernside and Ingleborough come into view as you make progress to Cotter End from where Great Shunner Fell is visible on the left. The path now drops steeply down, then goes through the left-hand one of two gates and continues to follow the wall for quite a time. It then swings left to go over a hillock and continues down to the Cotterdale road junction where a sign post informs you that you have just descended Lady Anne Clifford's Highway.[4] Turn left on the main road and continue a good $^1/_2$ mile down the road to your car.

Things of Interest

1. The extremely deep chasm of Hell Gill is not a collapsed cave but a fault opened up by the erosive action of the stream. Its waters flow westwards into the River Eden and the Irish Sea.

2. The Mossdale viaduct was on the branch line from Garsdale to Hawes, built in 1877.

3. Lunds Church, a tiny barn-like building, was established as a chapel of case when Aysgarth parish, which covered the whole of the upper dale in medieval times, was divided into more convenient parts.

4. Lady Anne Clifford was a redoubtable traveller of the mid-seventeenth century. She owned many scattered properties in the Dales and Cumbria (Westmorland as it was then) and visited them from time to time keeping a diary which gives her route. Most fortunately this has survived. Her principal home was Skipton Castle and from it she travelled into Wharfedale and over Kidstones into Wensleydale. From Askrigg the route followed an old road as far as Simonstone, then presumably down to Hardraw and across the valley to climb Cotter End, a very steep and difficult route. It then ran along the moor on a limestone terrace for three miles, crossed Hell Gill and descended into the Eden valley, continuing along the valley floor to Pendragon Castle and Kirkby Stephen. This route became known as Lady Anne Clifford's road. It sounds a bit more romantic when called a highway. Hell Gill Bridge is not, however, of that early vintage. It was built in 1825 when the road from Hawes to Kirkby Stephen was being improved. This new

road did not climb up Cotter End but took an easier line from Shaw Paddock to Hell Gill Bridge and is the last bit of green track used by this walk up to the bridge. For a bit more about Lady Anne Clifford see the notes to Walk 1.4.

MALLERSTANG

10.10   Wild Boar Fell, Swarth Fell, Hugh Seat and High Seat

This grand walk is really a circuit of the fells round the head of the valley of the River Eden. Wild Boar Fell itself, 2,324 feet (708 metres) is not in the National Park Area though. The rest of the walk follows the park boundary.

A shorter version is given, doing Wild Boar and Swarth Fells only, returning to Pendragon Castle by valley paths. The valley paths can be walked in reverse to get to Hell Gill Bridge to do the second half as a separate day. If you do the latter, do not be deterred by the Private Ground notice on the cabin by the bridge. The ground is indeed private - as is most of the land in the Y.D.N.P.: a right of way path goes through it. Make sure you locate the wobbly stile mentioned in Note A. It is not very obvious and is to the right as soon as you have crossed the streamlet in the first field. See Note A. Maps: 1:50,000 Landranger Series Sheets 91 and 98. Category A+. Time: 8-9 hours including 1 hour for rests, 5 hours for the shorter walk.

This is a hard walk, not to be tried in poor weather unless the partly has considerable experience with a map and compass.

Some of it is trackless and hard going, especially the ascent of Hugh Seat, and finding the correct descent route from High Seat in thick weather is not easy. There is, however, a pleasant and easy return on that side of the valley from Hell Gill Bridge, so you are not totally committed. Start at Pendragon Castle[1] an unlikely sounding name in the Dales, four miles south of Kirkby Stephen on the B6259 road to Garsdale Head. It is possible to get a couple of cars off the road opposite the castle and there is a small lay-by 100 yards towards Kirkby Stephen.

Follow the fell road for Ravenstonedale that leaves the B6259 by the side of the castle for about ¾ mile to the point where it crosses the railway, here in a tunnel. The place can be identified by a clump of trees on the left. Cross the greensward on the left and move diagonally right to the flank of the moor. Here, with luck, you will find a tiny track that takes you across the first ½ mile or so of hard going. When you can see

Wild Boar Fell

the wall, aim for the top side of it, where the track improves and continues over the top of Little Fell and up the steep end of Wild Boar Fell[2] to a bold cairn spectacularly placed on the edge of the eastern escarpment. This is marked on the map as the Nab.[3] (Note: at the foot of the steep bit the path passes a wall corner that offers the last shelter before the wall on Swarth Fell.) An even bigger cairn lies straight ahead, in fact a collection of them, but the true top lies well over to the right on the north west edge. A well trodden path leads to it, a circular wall built around the trig point. Then it is well worth while cutting back to that collection of cairns to enjoy their fine position, and a faint track will lead you to them. Here a stile takes you over the fence onto an ever strengthening path that leads pleasantly down to the dip between Wild Boar and Swarth Fells. In thick weather it may be better to follow the fence to this dip. Aim to pass the little tarn there on its right and follow the track up the wall side to the top of Swarth Fell, 2,234 feet (681 metres). Follow the broad ridge to the second top and then turn left and go more or less straight down to the road by Aisgill Moor Cottages. There is a gate just to their right. Go straight across the road and follow the track over the railway[4] up to Hell Gill Farm. Keep on past the farm to Hell Gill bridge where you join a green track or lane. Be sure to look over the bridge. The stream is an astonishing depth below.

This is decision time: do you want to follow this track back to the road, the short walk (see Note A) or go boldly round the hard part which will take about 4 or more hours? Assuming you go on, follow the wall on the left-hand side of the gill. There are tractor marks to start with, but they wander about a bit. Keep on the edge of the gill and eventually a good sheep track starts to traverse into it, and reaches the stream at the point where the county and park boundaries meet. Continue upstream for some little way following the path until it climbs out of the stream and gets lost in the rough ground. The going now becomes arduous. It is probably better to continue upstream for some little way to a major stream junction and then make directly for the summit up the tongue between the two streams. From the cairn on Hugh Seat continue to the fence corner and follow the left-hand part to another corner where there is a little cairn. Now strike left to a tall slender cairn on the shoulder of an unnamed top, where a circular wall gives shelter should you need it. From it a faint path leads to the cairn on that top, continuing to High Seat, at 709 metres one metre higher than Wild Boar Fell, though not nearly as fine a summit. The descent path soon disappears leaving you to wander over the wide dip before the last top, High Pike Hill, 642 metres. Then retrace your steps to the flatter ground and keep to the right to find a wide ramp with an old track that leads you easily through the broken crags of the lower escarpment. Continue on the left of the stream to a barn above the intake wall from where you follow a wide walled track to the hamlet of Castlethwaite and the road at Pendragon Castle.

Note A

At Hell Gill bridge you are on Lady Anne's Highway (see Walk 10.9 for something about this old road). Turn left and follow it down to the road, about 2 miles distant. After the good green track leaves the wall side it becomes wet and rush-grown but is easy to follow. Cross the road and go through the first gate on the left onto a cart track. As soon as you have crossed the bridge turn right along the river bank and into the fields. Continue by the river to a collection of farm buildings, bearing left as soon as you have past the first one and right after the last one. Leave the track almost at once to cut across the field to a slit stile, then go down to the river bank which you follow towards the hamlet of Shoregill. Here turn right past the third set of houses, going through the upper gate. Then follow the wall to a gate, continue to a slit stile then go left across the corner of the field to a gate from where a cart track leads you up the field. Aim for an old metal ladder stile, keep below the ruined barn, then somewhat left to find the gate at the end of a long field. Now make for the next barn, go through the gate just beyond it, and hold your height through another long field until approaching the house. Then drop down to find a very wobbly stile and continue to the gate by the river bridge. Turn right on the road and 2 minutes walk sees you back.

Things of Interest

1. There is no access to Pendragon Castle but it can be seen quite well from the gate. It stands on a well-defined mound but any moat there may have been has disappeared. Not a lot is known about the castle but legend has it that King Arthur, son of Uther Pendragon, was born there, not in this building which is of Norman origin, but in some earlier one on the same site. The castle and its estates came into the hands of the Clifford family in the early thirteenth century and it has a chequered history of burning and pillage at the hands of Scots raiders. It was in ruins when the redoubtable Lady Anne Clifford inherited the estate and having done major repairs in 1660, she visited it from time to time in her travels around her properties in Westmorland and the Dales.

2. The last wild boar in Britain is reputed to have been killed here. More useful to today's walkers may be a little geological observation. The upper Eden valley is a typical Craven dale with limestone flanks, though this is Permian limestone not Carboniferous. It has well marked terraces beneath the Yoredale series of rocks and Wild Boar Fell has the usual gritstone cap. Major landslides took place forming the steep escarpment facing the valley during the freeze-thaw cycles that occurred at the end of the last Ice Age. Their crumpled remains can be seen below when looking down from the edge between the Nab and the cairns. At the northern end the broken mass flowed over the top of the limestone, where its boundaries are easily traced in summer by the changes in vegetation from the bright green of the limestone turf to the dull green-brown of the peat moor. There are a set of shallow pot holes, the Angerholme pots, in this limestone shelf and they can be seen from the Nab. Note that they have been covered by the landslide mass. Typical moorland vegetation is found: heath rush, bent grass, mat grass, a little cotton grass and sphagnum moss, and here and there in the sphagnum, sundew, more commonly found in the Lakes than the Dales.

3. There are the remains of a Bronze Age burial mound on the Nab, marked on the map as 'tumulus', and the best views are from here. Across the valley is the long ridge of Mallerstang Edge along which you are going. There is just a peep down Wensleydale, no more, before it is cut off by the foreground. To the west the Sedbergh Howgills stand up quite boldly, and beyond them, the long ridge of High Street then the

northern outliers of the Lake District. Then comes the fair Vale of Eden and to its right, the great masses of the northern Pennines:- Cross Fell, Little and Great Dun Fell and, further right, a long ridge which is Mickle Fell.

4.   As you come onto the road you will see a board on the side of the railway saying, 'Aisgill Summit, 1169ft.', the highest point of the Leeds to Carlise railway. This level bit of railway, road and moor is part of the main Pennine watershed. The River Eden flows westwards to the Irish Sea, the beck on the east becomes the River Ure flowing into the North Sea.

11: SWALEDALE

Walks at the head of the valley

11.1   The Nine Standards Rigg. Category B+ 287
11.2   Two walks around Kisdon Pike. Category B 290
11.3   Walking the banks of the River Swale from
       Keld to Reeth. Category B 293
11.4   Gunnerside Gill, Ivelet Moor and the River Swale.
       Category B+ 294
11.5   From Gunnerside to Healaugh by the River Swale.
       Category B+ 298
11.6   Hard Level Gill and Great Pinseat from Surrender Bridge.
       Category B 300
11.7   Great Shunner Fell and Lovely Seat from Thwaite.
       Category A 303

Walks round Reeth

11.8   From Reeth to Langthwaite and back. Category C 307
11.9   Round Slei Gill from Langthwaite. Category B 309
11.10   Cogden Gill and Grinton Smelt Mill. Category B 310
11.11   Apedale and Harkerside Moor. Category B 313

Swaledale is the most northerly of the dales within the Yorkshire Dales National Park and is probably the least visited. It has an air of being undiscovered, a lack of publicity, neglect almost, by the Park authorities. In spring 1990 they have neither Park Centre nor car park, though there are local information offices both in Reeth and Richmond. That in Reeth is housed in the Swaledale Folk Museum (second only to the Upper Dales Folk Museum in Hawes for the wealth of its exhibits, located in an alley behind and to the right of the post office). By far the best of the walking is in the upper valley above Reeth, below that there is little of consequence. Sadly, Richmond is not within the Park area which comes to an end a mile or two from the town. In some ways Richmond is to Swaledale for the people of the north-east what Skipton is to Wharfedale for the Lancastrians. Despite both towns having a castle and a fine parish church there the resemblance ends. The Industrial Revolution set its stamp on present day Skipton: it has

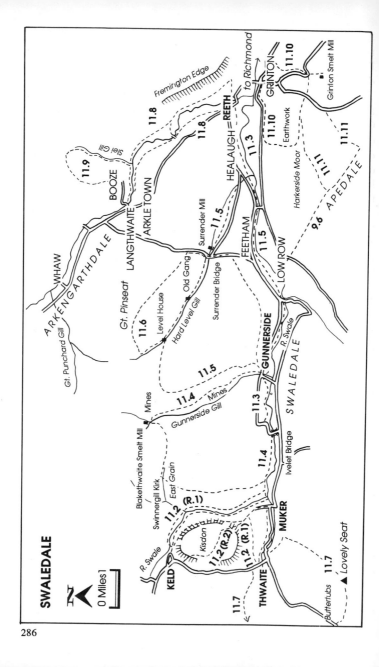

SWALEDALE

N

0 Miles 1

To Richmond

GRINTON 11.10

Grinton Smelt Mill

11.10

REETH

HEALAUGH 11.3

11.8

Fremington Edge

11.8

11.8

Stel Gill

11.9

BOOZE

LANGTHWAITE

ARKLE TOWN

WHAW

ARKENGARTHDALE

Gt. Punchard Gill

Gt. Pinseat

11.6

Level House

Old Gang

Hard Level Gill

Surrender Mill

11.5

Surrender Bridge

FEETHAM

11.5

LOW ROW

Earthwork

11.10

Harkerside Moor

11.11

11.11

APEDALE

9.6

11.11

11.5

GUNNERSIDE

SWALEDALE

R. Swale

11.3

Mines

11.4

Mines

Gunnerside Gill

Blakethwaite Smelt Mill

East Grain

Swinnergill Kirk

11.2 (R.1)

Kisdon

11.2 (R.2) 11.2 (R.1)

R. Swale

KELD

11.4

Ivelet Bridge

11.3

MUKER

THWAITE

Buttertubs

11.7

11.7

11.7

▲ Lovely Seat

286

nothing of the rich array of monuments and fine buildings that give Richmond a splendid air of antiquity. There is much for the visitor driven by rain from the upper dale to enjoy - the Castle, Georgian Theatre and Museum, the Richmondshire Museum of local exhibits and the Green Howards Museum housed in the former Holy Trinity Chruch. In fact, even if it is raining in Reeth it may easily be fine and dry in Richmond. In that case it is worth taking a walk to Easby Abbey or a stroll in the National Trust woods. They lie across the river bridge on the road to Catterick. Turn right as soon as you've crossed the bridge. As these woods are north-facing on the steep bank of the Swale they are inclined to be dank and unattractive in poor weather.

The former lead mining industry has left its mark upon Swaledale. It has contributed a good deal to the character of such villages as Reeth and Gunnerside and left a wealth of interesting remains on the moors. It's worth reading the chapter 'Leadmining and smelting in the Dales' before doing those walks that visit the many remains.

11.1   The Nine Standards Rigg, 2,170 feet

This 2,000-foot top is just outside the Y.D.N.P. by a mere $1/4$ mile, yet as its becks drain into the Swale it quite properly belongs to Swaledale. It can be climbed from Keld but this is a long drag. It is most easily climbed from the top of the Keld-Kirkby Stephen road from a starting point at 1,698 feet above sea level. Category B+. Time: $2^1/2$-3 hours. Map: 1:50,000 Sheet 92.

Note that this walk is not recommended for parties inexperienced in rough hill walking in less than perfect weather. Most tracks are faint, walls for guidance absent when you need them.

If you have a transport manager it makes a more satisfying walk to return to Keld or Muker or even Gunnerside.

Allow four hours to Keld, five to Muker, six or a little more to Gunnerside and add the 1:25,000 Outdoor Leisure Map No. 30, Northern and Central Areas if you return to any of these places.

Park on the roadside by the county boundary sign - there's plenty of space. Walk along for a few hundred yards until you come to a faint green cart track marked by a cairn. If you reach the finger post to Hartley Fell you've overshot - try again! There are a puzzling number of cart tracks or branches of cart tracks across the limestone area ahead. Once you have located a tiny pool (there are two of them actually), the important thing is to get to the right-hand side of the wall that curves down to the beck, visible from the pool. There you will find a well trodden path that grows fainter after it has crossed the stream. Follow it with care up a steep slope to a sheltering wall corner, once a little hut belonging to the coal mine higher up. A few yards beyond it you reach a good wide track leading to the spoil heap of the former mine where it ends. A thready track continues to the right, gets lost in the area of peat hags beyond, but reappears on the final slope up to the trig point which is pleasingly close. The nine cairns from which the fell takes its name are about ½ mile away to the north and a little path takes you there. The view is absolutely splendid on a good day. Just across the valley are the Mallerstang Edge tops, High Seat and Hugh Seat. Behind them is Wild Boar Fell, to its right the Howgills, right of them and far away are the Lakeland hills. Then comes the wide expanse of the Vale of Eden, and on its right lower edge the little conical hills of Dufton Pike and Knock Pike. Above them rise Cross Fell, best identified by its sharp left-hand escarpment. Great and Little Dun fells are not so well seen, being end on, and Mickle Fell, at some 2,500 feet (790 metres), the highest in Yorkshire, is the long whale-back to their right. Further right, the landscape consists of the somewhat featureless Bowes Moor and Stainmore Forest, with the head of Swaledale lost below you. A little further right it is backed by Rogan's Seat, and further right still Great Shunner Fell completes the circle.

Having drunk your fill of the view, you may retrace your steps all the way.

Return to Keld from the Nine Standards

The Trig Point to Ravenseat Farm

You joined the Coast to Coast Walk at the sheltering wall corner on the way up but though the way is fairly obvious most of the way down to Keld some guidance is no bad thing. Leave on a well-trodden path for White Mossy Hill (not named on the 1:50,000 map but shown as a single contour line) and cross another band of peat hags in the dip. Continue in much the same direction for about 1½ miles down Coldbergh Edge to another square-cut pile of stones that gives some shelter. From it a better track leads to a tall pillar of stone and continues rather more to the left to a most misleading Coast to Coast sign. It is the original sign and the route has now been changed. Take great care here, for many have gone astray - including the author on her first time of

passing! A well trodden path leads straight on, as signed - AVOID IT.
TURN RIGHT on to a much fainter track which is now the true route.
A few posts give guidance and shortly you will come to another sign
that confirms you are on the route. Now simply drop down onto the
Land Rover track that runs from the road to the shooting hut at the head
of Ney Gill. Turn left on it and five minutes walk sees you at the hut,
open and available for your use, a good place for lunch. It is private
property so please don't abuse it. Here you have arrived on the 1:25,000
map by a hair's breadth. Continue pleasantly down the gill to the road
at Ravenseat Farm.

Ravenseat Farm to Keld

Turn right at the bridge to pass through the first farm by the waymarked
gates and stiles, continue through two fields then, after passing a barn,
start to climb up the field, despite a well trodden path that keeps level.

This level path takes you to a viewpoint into the rugged gorge of
Whitsundale Beck, a well worthwhile variant even though the climb up
the hillside to regain the true route is so steep it requires the use of steps
kicked in the hillside. At the gate continue along the side of the wall on
a green cart track for about ½ mile to a fork where you take the right-
hand track and continue to Smithy Holme. Beyond another cluster of
buildings the track starts to drop more steeply. When you have reached
a gate at the end of a small wood look out for a minor track on the left
above a wall that continues along the top of Cotterby Scar. It leads you
onto the road into West Stonedale. Cross it and continue along the
private road and bridleway opposite to East Stonedale Farm. Turn right
in the yard and go through the bottom gate, descending steeply towards
the river. Turn right just before you cross East Gill to follow the
Pennine Way across the River Swale and, turning right, reach Keld in
a few minutes.

Continuation to Muker or Gunnerside

Turn left instead of right when you have crossed the river. Here you join
Walk 11.2, following either of the routes described, to Muker.

Things of Interest

The limestone pavement at the start are part of the Yoredale series of
rocks where drainage is good and soil fertile if shallow. The peaty
moorland, by contrast, is on the sandstones of the Yoredale series. Here

drainage is poor, soil infertile and peat accumulates. The origins of the nine standards or cairns from which the hill takes its name is not known. They can be found in groups like this in other parts of the Pennines, for example on Gragareth. Coal mining was carried out here in the early to mid-nineteenth century to supply limekilns and lead smelting mills.

11.2   Around Kisdon Pike (499 metres)

Kisdon Pike is almost an island formed by the River Swale and Straw Beck, no minor stream. The villages of Keld, Thwaite and Muker are placed strategically around it and are linked by several paths which all unite at Keld. The first route starts at Thwaite and uses the Pennine Way to Keld, returning by the cart track on the east side of the Swale to reach Muker and then by field paths to Thwaite. Alternatively return by the banks of the Swale on the west side, reversing Route 2. See Walk 11.3 for details. The second route starts in Muker and goes up the west side of the Swale to Keld and returns by the west side of Kisdon Pike by an old green road. There is no right of way path to the top, but the high point of this route is not far from it. The advantages in going this way round are the dramatic beauty of the gorge of the Swale and splendid views down Swaledale as you descend the lane into Muker. Both routes are Category B and both take about 4 hours. Map: 1:25,000 Outdoor Leisure Series No. 30, Northern and Central Areas.

Route 1. Thwaite to Keld by the Pennine Way

There is room to park at the junction of the Hawes road just outside Thwaite.

The starting stile is an insignificant corner 100 yards below Kearton's shop. Turn left at the P.W. sign and you will find the path is waymarked as it slants easily up the pike to the right. As you approach the farm go straight up the narrow field, through a gate and behind the farm fence to join a short section of walled lane. At the top of this bear right to a barn and then left. Where the tractor marks turn to the left, go straight ahead to a ladder stile. The path, at times very stony and quite rough, circuits the hill at this level until you are almost at Keld. There are splendid views across the Swale to Swinnergill Kirk and Rogan's Seat. After a number of ups and downs the path finally drops through a gap in the wall on the right and shortly afterwards you will find a Pennine Way finger post, a useful marker on Route 2. You now join a good path into Keld. There is a tap in the village square if you are

Kisdon

thirsty, but in 1990 that was all. There are toilets a little way along the road. Retrace your steps from the corner of the village square to the first Pennine Way post, turn left, and cross both the River Swale and East Gill and turn right onto a good cart track that runs down the east side of the river. It's all easy and straightforward to Ramps Holme Bridge, which you cross, then turn left at a stile at the top of a few steps and follow the well marked path to Muker. One thing to remember, take the lower track at the old lead mines or you'll find yourself in Swinnergill - not fatal, just longer. In Muker the field path to Thwaite starts at the end of the little lane which is on the right as you come out of the fields. It goes first to Usha Gap Farm and is paved to start with. It leads unmistakably to the farm. Turn right on the road and in a hundred yards or so the field path starts again in the corner before the bridge. The way is unmistakable and delightful.

Route 2. Muker to Keld by the banks of the Swale

Use the car park by the river. Turn right between the Literary Institute and the Farmers' Arms and continue bearing left a little to come face to face with the post office. Then turn right and you will see the sign to the path to Keld and Gunnerside. A well trodden field path takes you to Ramps Holme Bridge. As soon as you are over the wall at the bridge turn left, for if you cross the bridge you are on your way to Gunnerside. From the barn ahead a wide but vague grassy track leads along the riverside pastures with their hay barns for a mile or more, giving good views into the great cleft of Swinnergill Kirk. Then it starts to climb steadily and becomes better defined whilst giving dramatic views down to the river from time to time. In due course you will join the Pennine Way track. Simply continue along it to reach Keld in its tiny square.

Leave the square on the road and after passing the toilets take the left-hand branch. Turn left when you reach the road and in a few minutes turn left down a walled lane that crosses the little stream of Skeb Skeugh and climbs gently up the flanks of Kisdon Pike. The track loses its guiding walls but is well marked right over the shoulder of the hill. After you've descended a little way make a sharp turn to the right by a wall and shortly enter another length of walled lane which continues right down to the lane just above Kisdon. Then simply follow it down to Muker, soaking up the glorious views of Swaledale. In Muker simply keep more or less straight on to find the car park.

Things of Interest

Kisdon Pike, standing in the middle of the valley, was formed by the last Ice Age. Before it was formed the river ran on the other side of the Pike and that became the main drainage line.

Thwaite and Keld are typical Norse names. 'Thwaite' signifies a woodland clearing, indicating that at the time the Norsemen colonised this part of the dale, the landscape was still largely forest. The woodland of the Kidson Gorge is a descendant of that forest. Keld means a spring or stream.

Early in the spring the banks of the streams and woods abound with primroses and cowslips, but the hay meadows in June and early July are the chief glory of the walk. The most striking flower, in various shades of pinky purple is the meadow cranesbill, the feathery white one is pignut, and there's plenty of clover, buttercups and daisies. In one field there is a big patch of pink bistort, and the silver-gray leaf of the melancholy thistle appears in several fields. Quite noteworthy is the mossy saxifrage. That is found growing in the scree on the north flank of Kisdon Pike, where there's not so much sunshine. It is not common because of its special needs - shade, moisture and limestone. The woods of the Kisdon Gorge are typical of the area, mostly ash and hazel with some elm, birch and hawthorn and the occasional rowan. Alder is found in the wet ditches of the lower pastures. Oak is conspicuous by its absence, because it prefers acid soils and these are neutral or basic ones.

Lead mining remains can still be seen in several places across the valley. There was the Beldi Hill mining field, with its smelt mill, at the foot of Swinnergill. Higher up, just below the gorge, are the remains of a crushing and washing plant. In June, the characteristic spring sandwort covers the ground round the old spoil heaps with its starry white flowers. Crackpot Hall was abandoned about thirty years ago, partly because of subsidence and partly because of its distance from a road.

Swinner Gill Kirk takes its name from a cave near the waterfall where Nonconformists held services in the seventeenth century. At that time it was illegal to hold these services and participants where fined if caught.

11.3   Walking the banks of the River Swale from Keld to Reeth

The River Swale is formed by the confluence of Birkdale Beck and Great Sleddale Beck, both sizeable streams that rise at the back of Hugh Seat and High Seat. From Keld to Reeth, a distance of 13 or 14 miles, it gives riverside walking as good as the best that Wharfedale can offer, indeed, the Wharfe has nothing to compare with the Kisdon Gorge. There is just one major break in the footpath beyond Feetham where there simply isn't room between the road and the river for a path. Beyond Reeth, apart from a short half-mile near Grinton, there are no more riverside paths within the area covered by this book. The walk from Keld to Reeth can be done by using the morning bus from Richmond to Keld (Saturdays and Tuesdays only in 1990) if you haven't got a transport manager. The author, however, prefers some variety in her walks and therefore divides the best of the river into three walks, first from Keld to Gunnerside, then from Gunnerside along the riverside path to just beyond Feetham, returning over the moors. The remaining fragment is possibly best done from the car parking area about 1½ miles upstream from Reeth as a there-and-back evening stroll, but Walk 11.3 which follows puts this rather broken account together. Category B but only because of its length. It is all very easy walking. Map: 1:25,000 Outdoor Leisure Series No. 30, Northern and Central Areas.

Start in Keld's tiny square at the lowest point in the hamlet, going down a wide rack signposted to Muker. Go past the turning to the bridge where you join Walk 11.4 at * and follow it to Gunnerside. Here you start Walk 11.5 and when that walk leaves the road at the start of the field path to Healaugh, continue along the road until you find a wide parking place by the river, about a mile away. The footpath continues on the left and quickly reaches the riverside fields. Cross Barney Beck with a bit of neat footwork on the stones and after a short length of shingle regain the bank. The path continues through a delightful bit of riverside woodland then into open pasture. Some distance along the river swings towards the road making a steep enbankment. Here there is a gate and the right of way path leaves the river bank and climbs up to reach Reeth by a series of waymarked stiles. However, there is another waymarked stile at river level immediately after the gate, and this allows you to continue to the suspension bridge where you cross and walk through walled lanes to Reeth.

11.4   Gunnerside Gill, Ivelet Moor and the River Swale

A superb walk of great variety with much to be seen of the old lead mining remains. It will take 6-7 hours for the full version, about an hour less if you don't go up to the old dams and 3-4 hours for the short version. Start at Gunnerside where there is a little car park by the bridge. Category B+. The walk easily becomes A in poor weather. Map: 1:25,000 Outdoor Leisure Series No. 30, Northern and Central Areas.

The footpath starts at the other side of the bridge. After 100 yards or so turn right up some steps into the field. The path is now obvious enough, working its way up the side of the gill, here quite broad and full of trees. After some time you will emerge from the woods into pasture with the remains of some old buildings[1] and spoil heaps on the right. A well waymarked route takes you through the various walls to a stile on the right from which a fine green track climbs steadily out of the gill[2] and up to a higher track close to some old lead mine workings.[3]

Ahead and across the valley are some huge deeply cut gullies, now well grown over.[4] Continue through the old spoil heaps where the track is not so well marked, but keep upwards towards more fine greensward that runs right up the side of the valley for a good mile, only dropping down when well above the Blakethwaite Smelt Mill not named on the O.S. map but at the junction of Blind Gill with Gunnerside Gill.

Here you can take an optional extra to the former Blakethwaite dams. It is very much rougher walking, but here it is:

Follow a tiny track well above the stream towards the junction of the streams which is ahead. Cross to the walled enclosure and continue above it up the left-hand beck. The path is poor and a bit tricky in parts. Ahead is a waterfall and at the top of it are the remains of a dam[5] where the tiny track ends. Return as you came to the ruins by the stream.

Gunnerside Gill

Just below the wall nearest the stream it is usually easy to cross the stream and pick another faint track on that side which will bring you back to Blakethwaite Smelt Mill.[6] From the smelt mill a broad green track climbs gently up the hill on the right of the gill. Not far along it, by the first gully on the right, there is the start of a small track that runs up into Blind Gill. You do not use that track but at this point go straight up the fell for about 100 feet on the left-hand side of the gully until you come to a track that runs across the head of it, quite well marked. Turn left and follow it as it climbs leftwards up the moor to the side of North Hush, which you saw from the other side of Gunnerside Gill. At the top of the hush you will come to a newish wide stony road. Follow it up the moor until it bears left a little to run along the edge of the moor then leave it at a yellow-topped pole for a narrow wettish path on the right. This soon improves to a good stony track and takes you down into Swinner Gill. Continue well down the gill and when opposite the ruined mine buildings, cross the stream to pick up a tiny path that contours the hillside for almost a mile, eventually reaching a gate and stile in a long wall. Once over the wall you follow the path on a fairly intricate route round ridges of grass and across many rivulets which finally brings you onto a shelf of good green grass below a line of crags. Continue along this shelf, crossing another stream where care is required because of a minor land slip. Then drop steeply down to the

295

mine workings below, from where a fine grass track takes you down through the wood to the cart track by the Swale. Almost directly below but out of sight is the bridge* that leads to Muker and the riverside path starts besides it.

The rest of the walk is along the Swale and it takes about 1 ½ hours back to Gunnerside. The cart track rapidly becomes tarmac and is emphatically not a soft option. It has a distressing amount of uphill in it. The riverside path is delightful and easy to follow. Only one or two places need a mention. The path starts by the bridge and goes below the barn into the field. Fairly soon you will come to a signpost indicating Calvert Houses one way, Ivelet Bridge the other. Take the one to Ivelet Bridge. If at one stage you miss an uphill trend in the path and find yourself against a blank wall, just walk up the wall side for half a field's length to find the gate. At Ivelet Bridge[7] go left up the road until you come to the phone box. Here a signpost directs you to Gunnerside. Where this lane turns left into a farmyard you go straight ahead. You cross the Ivelet beck and climb steeply up its opposite bank to an obvious stile and the way to Gunnerside is now quite clear.

Things of Interest

1. These buildings are the remains of crushing and washing floors for the mines in the gill. The row of bunkers or bings as they were called at the back were used for storing each group of miners' ore. A little higher up on the other side of the stream you will see what looks like a rusty iron boiler near the remains of some buildings.

This is the compressed air tank used in the cutting of the Sir Francis Level between 1864 and 1869 and was named after the son of a local mining engineer, Sir George Denys. The level was driven in the direction of Blakethwaite and was designed to pass well below the Friarfold vein complex. It enabled more oreshoots to be reached and drained the whole of the network of veins in the vicinity. A great deal of ore was extracted from these veins and was crushed and dressed at the mouth of the level, then taken across the gill to the Bunton Level where it was despatched underground to emerge at the Hard Level just above Old Gang Smelt Mill, there to be smelted.

The Level went through very hard rock and to speed the work, rock drills worked by compressed air were introduced: new technology at that time. A water wheel worked the compressor and air pressure was built up in the iron tank you now see.

Ivelet Bridge over the Swale

2. As you look across the gill here you can see the waterfalls in Botcher Gill and more lead mine workings at its foot. On the right of the waterfall you can see very clearly two different sorts of rock: low down a sandstone and higher up a much thicker bed of limestone. These two types can be seen in many places in the gill and are part of the Yoredale series of rocks which makes up the greater part of Wensleydale and Swaledale.

3. These are the crushing and washing mills for the Bunton mines close by. The pit that housed the water wheel is just below the track as is a row of 15 or 16 bunkers for ore.

4. The deep gullies on both sides of the gill are hushes. (See the chapter on lead mining for an explanation of the term.)

5. The empty dams once held water for use at the smelt mill, as did those seen on Ivelet moor from the stony Land-Rover track.

6. Blakethwaite Smelt Mill is the only mill in Gunnerside Gill and was built in 1820 as a result of striking the rich Blakethwaite vein. The lowest building by the stream with four big arches was the peat store. Peat was cut by the women and children in early summer and brought here by pony to store until it dried out; hence the wide arches for ventilation. it is connected to the smelt mill by a large single slab bridge across the stream, the only bridge left in the gill. There's not much left of the furnace shop compared with what there is at either Grinton or Old Gang. The most striking feature is four cast iron pillars that supported the furnace arches. There were two reverberatory furnaces separated

by a wall now buried in the rubble. The wall and the pillars supported the three arches that made the front of each furnace. Behind the furnace room was the water-wheel and bellows, and on the other side of them, a roasting hearth. When R.T.Clough made his drawings in 1949 the furnace arches were still intact. The flue can be seen climbing the hillside, even scaling a little crag to do so, but the chimney has gone. The roundish construction in this little crag is a limekiln. Limestone was burnt on the spot for building use - today the limekiln gives good shelter for lunch on a poor day.

7.   Ivelet Bridge is a fine high single-span bridge of considerable age, best seen from the field opposite.

11.5   From Gunnerside to Healaugh by the River Swale

After a first rate length of river bank the path reaches the road leaving you with a good mile of tarmac so this walk returns through Healaugh, Barney Beck Wood, and Hard Level Bridge to reach Gunnerside Gill just above the village. Arguably it could be claimed to be the finest middle distance walk in Swaledale, having a something of all the finest characteristics of the dale. Time: 5½-6 hours plus time spent looking at the conserved remains of the old smelt mills. Category B+. Map 1:25,000 Outdoor Leisure Map No. 30, Northern and Central Areas. Park by the bridge in Gunnerside.

Cross the bridge and turn right in front of the King's Arms. The public toilets are now in view: turn left in front of the *Gents* then right immediately after crossing the stile. Follow the line of stiles down to the river bank then turn left and follow the river for about a mile until you have to leave the bank at a little gate. Climb steeply up to the road and at once turn right to regain the river bank. Continue through the riverside fields until another bit of broken ground forces you onto the road, though briefly. At its end go through the gate and cut across the field to a stile near the corner. Continue to the stile on the left, turn right, then half-way down the fence, turn left and cut straight across this big field. There's no path to start with but you may find it before you've gone all the way. Cross a wet patch by the trees then continue to a loop of the river, which is a flood channel of the main stream, and makes a little island. It is hardly possible to cross so turn left on the clear path above the river and follow it down to the road at Isles Bridge.

Go straight across the road then follow the top of the river's flood embankment through several fields. It becomes a stone wall - no ordinary stone wall for it is a couple of feet wide and smoothly flagged and you just keep along it, keeping your fingers crossed you don't meet anybody! At its end you walk a particularly pleasant stretch of river - sheep-cropped grass right up to the water's edge, neither fence nor hedge interposing to diminish your enjoyment of the waterside. Then again the character changes. The bank steepens and is wooded and another sign directs you to Reeth and the road - a mile or more of it if Reeth should be your destination.

After about 200 yards along the road to Reeth at the end of a cluster of houses, take the field path to Healaugh. At first it is faint then disappears altogether but the line is fairly direct. Keep below the barn in the last field to find the stile onto the road. Turn right and having crossed the bridge over Barney Back, take the bridleway on the left to Thiernswood Hall, an unpretentious Victorian house. Go past it into the wood and where the bridleway turns right, keep straight on through the stile. A well marked path takes you up the hill and through the wood. Where it emerges go through the stile on the left into the wood and turn right, following the path inside the wood, not outside it as shown on the OS map. Barney Beck is far below in the ravine screened by the trees and the ground is thick with bluebells in springtime. By degrees the wood thins out as you climb steadily and you get a view up the stream to the road near Surrender Bridge. You will come to the major side stream of Bleaberry Gill. Drop all the way down and climb all the way back up then continue pleasantly and easily along the top of the ravine to the ruins of Surrender Smelt Mill, now an ancient monument and in process of conservation in the spring of 1990. Having looked around it and noted the twin flues from the furnaces that join just above the buildings, the slag heaps by the door and the stream, and pondered what a hell hole of pollution this must have been 130 or so years ago, carry on across the road onto the gated track that runs to Hard Level Bridge.

After a short mile you will pass Old Gang Smelt Mill. Another of these historic ruins, built around 1830 on the site of an earlier mill. In its hey-day it was far bigger than Surrender, and, like it, is now an ancient monument in process of conservation. Not far beyond it some spoil heaps are being processed to recover the barytes in them. They do nothing whatever for the landscape. Barytes is used in making oil well drilling mud. Another half mile brings you to Hard Level Bridge, a finely arched specimen and a good spot for a break by the stream.

Here the track forks and you take the left-hand one that goes over the moor to Gunnerside Gill. It climbs steadily passing through an area once devastated by lead mining, now weathered and partly heather-grown. After passing a line of shooting butts at the top of the moor take the left fork where the track divides at a couple of large cairns. It soon becomes pleasantly grassy and zigzags down the slope then traverses the gill at quite a high level giving good views. The broad track dwindles as you cross a length of broken ground but you will find it again on the other side. It continues to drop and in due course approaches an area of small fields, barns and cottages. As you reach the first group of them on the right, drop down to their gateway, partly blocked by a large fallen tree, one of the group that shelters this little fold of buildings clustered around a tiny field. Pass to the right of the 'barn' with two chimneys and continue down two fields with very tight slit stiles to reach a ruined barn. Here turn left and pick up a well trodden grassy track that leads you down to the path in the bottom of the gill which you follow down to your car in about 15 minutes.

11.6 Hard Level Gill and Great Pinseat from Surrender Bridge

If you are interested in visiting some of the old lead mining areas yet do not feel up to the longer walk just described, you might like to try this one. It visits the ruins of both Surrender and Old Gang smelt mills and takes you over the moor to see some of the former workings. It is an easy walk on old lead mining tracks all the way, but somewhat open to the weather. Category B, Map 1:25,000 Outdoor Leisure Series No. 30, Northern and Central Areas. Park at Surrender Bridge which is on the Feetham-Langthwaite road. Time: about 2 hours.

Start up the bridleway by the stream, and after about 20 minutes you will come to the remains of the Old Gang Smelt Mill.[1] Further on the track climbs fairly steeply past old spoil heaps that are being reworked. When you come to Level House Bridge keep straight on, on the right-hand side of the stream. There's a good spot for lunch here. Higher up the track crosses and recrosses the steam amongst old spoil heaps and finally turns right through a gate and climbs gently up a hillside covered in little stones. When you are some little way up turn round and look across the valley and you will see on the opposite hillside a wide strip of ground that is just the same as the one you are on, a fine example of how the miners followed a vein across the moors.[2] The track tends to get lost here, so just aim for a pole that's stuck in a cairn on a prominent spoil heap. From here, if you want to go to the genuine summit of this gentle hill, Great Pinseat, 1,914 feet (583 metres) turn sharp left to the wall and follow it until you come to the trig point. If you're a six-footer you'll see it; it's about 300-400 yards along on the other side of the wall.[3] Rejoin your main track at the next pole-marked cairn and follow it down to a sheepfold where it turns right. Then simply follow it back to the tarmac road about $^1/_2$ mile from Surrender Bridge. Turn right and in 10 minutes you're back at your car.[4]

Note that the track you can see amongst the old workings ahead, when you are on top of Great Pinseat, does not connect with the one you are on. If you want to go that way it's rough stuff and a wall to climb. Not worth it!

Things of Interest

1.   The Old Gang Smelt Mill. There is quite a complex of buildings on this high and remote site. The most striking feature is a chimney, relatively rare these days, but it is not the chimney of the smelting furnaces, which is high on the moor out of sight. The chimney on the edge just above the mill is an old one, not used in the final lay-out of the mill. The long building nearest the road holds what remains of a row of four ore hearths. There's little left except the big well-cut stones from which the furnace arches sprung. The water-wheel that supplied the air blast was at the left-hand end of the building, but the wheel pit is filled in now. The flues above the building join some distance up the

Old Gang Smelt Mill

hill to make one main flue. To the right of this building is a separate building where the ore was roasted before smelting and it is this that retains the small prominent chimney. Across the track by the beck are the slag tips, a black crumbly material that hardly looks as if it had been melted. It hasn't. The idea was to melt just the lead, not the dross.

The mouth of Hard Level from which the gill takes its name is a few hundred yards above the mill just above the stream. It was driven in 1785 as the main entrance to the Friarfold vein complex from this gill and connects with the Bunton Level in Gunnerside Gill through a maze of levels. Hard Level is so named because it runs through very hard rock and was difficult to cut.

2.   The vast devastated area is the result of mining in the rich Friarfold Vein. There was a network of passages extending many miles underground and a man could go underground in Gunnerside Gill and emerge in Arkengarthdale.

3.   In the base of the wall just beyond the top of Great Pinseat is a huge boulder with this inscription carved in its north-east side: Whetshaw Head 3 Ap 1759. This gives an indication of the date of the nearby mines - possibly the bell pit only 100 yards away was dug that year.

4.   As you walk down the road you will see on the ridge the remains of a building which looks a bit like a house or a barn, but it is actually a part of the Surrender Smelt Mill's flue system. It was the Stokoe condenser: a device for trapping and recovering the lead from the flue gases. The flue itself cannot be seen from here.

Surrender Mill was built on the site of an earlier one about 1840 and is unusually compact for a large mill. It is being conserved by the Park Authorities who have cleared away much rubble and partially excavated the water wheel pit in the central room of the main part of the ruins. On either side of this room were two pairs of ore hearths placed back to back and each pair of hearths had a common flue which joined up 40 or 50 feet behind the mill. Part of one of the furnace arches is still there, and sufficient of the stonework of the flues to see that one went over the top of the other before they joined. The flue was roofed with flat slabs where it left the mill; higher on the moor it was arched over, well seen above the road. Below the road it has totally collapsed. At the lower end of the back wall of the furnace shop there is the base of a chimney, probably belonging to the roasting furnace. The leat bringing water from the beck can be easily traced to the road and for some distance upstream from there.

All along the banks of the stream are heaps of slag or dross, where it was tipped, and here and there fragments of black glassy slag can be found suggesting that the mill reworked some of the dross to recover the lead it still contained. There was a very large peat store a little distance away which, apart from the end walls, was entirely built of pillars. Because of this lightweight construction it had a thatched roof: a design that allowed the peat to dry out. Just enough is left today to see this construction.

These two smelt mills were only two of the eighteen or so that were at work in the hey-day of the mining industry. It is estimated that between them they produced 250,000 tons of lead between 1790 and 1890 when many of them closed.

11.7   Great Shunner Fell 2,340 feet (716 metres), and Lovely Seat 2,213 feet (675 metres) from Thwaite

Great Shunner by the Pennine Way path is a very short trip, 2 $\frac{1}{2}$-3 hours return, and it may be conveniently lengthened by adding Lovely Seat. At around 5 hours it is still a short day, but is given Category A because of the rough and trackless going in parts. Not recommended except on a clear day. Lovely Seat itself is worth doing from the top of the Butter Tubs Pass and takes around an hour for the trip. It is a good viewpoint. Both Lovely Seat and Great Shunner separately would be Category B, but note that Great Shunner is apt to be wet despite the 'carpet' of now decrepit chestnut palings laid in the worst places - though that's still a big improvement. Maps: 1:25,000 Outdoor Leisure Series No. 30, Northern and Central Areas. Park in Thwaite. There is room at the junction of the road from Hawes and this is particularly convenient for the return. There is room to park at the right place at the top of the Butter Tubs for Lovely Seat.

Muker with its new car park is a better starting point than the road end. Field paths take you to Thwaite and a direct return to it is easy. In addition it is the best place to park if you want to do the extension and make a full day of it. Add 1 $\frac{1}{2}$ to 2 hours.

Muker Start

Turn right in the village between the Farmers' Arms and the Literary Institute, turn second left and the stile is at the end of this short lane. The path leads unmistakably to Usher Gap Farm where you join the road as far as the bridge. The stile is in the first corner and again, the path to

The Butter Tubs

Thwaite is unmistakable. In Thwaite simply continue up the road where you join the route from Thwaite.

Go along the Keld road until you come to a rough lane[1] on the left with a finger post 'The Pennine Way'. From here a very well marked track leads all the way to the top and takes about 1 1/2hrs. Now the tricky bit starts. To hit off the right point on the Butter Tubs requires care, for Fossdale Beck is in the way and it cuts high - and deep - into Great Shunner. First aim for a collection of small cairns just to the left of a small pool. From here go quite a bit to the left to get round the beck then straighten your course again. You will come to a fence in due course when you are nearly down, just follow it to the road. The easy but circuitous way is to cross the stile over the summit fence, and turn right. Follow the fence all the way to the road. It is circuitous in the extreme but very easy, and on a cold windy day has the advantage of passing a good sheltering wall where lunch might be eaten.

From the top of the pass follow the fence by the cattle grid on its left, picking up a faint path in due course. It will bring you to the true top, not the cairns that are so compelling from the road. The view is wide. The flat top of Ingleborough in the distance identifies it easily. To its right is Whernside and right again the fells of Mallerstang are masked by Great Shunner; leftwards the view is open and of the lesser heights across Wensleydale. So far you have not been looking the way you are to go. Now carefully locate the top of Kisdon Pike and the gorge of the Swale to its right, for you must walk the moor, trackless, rough and with a few patches of incipient peat hags, until you are square on to Kisdon Pike in order to locate the stream you want, Greensett Beck, which is directly in line with it. Keep towards the left of the moor well below the line of the fence until you see its many tributaries below. Follow any one of them to the deep-cut stream below and follow this down to the intake wall. Then if you've got it right you will see a gate from which a grassy cart track takes you down to a walled lane. Turn left here and almost at once turn right.² At the barn at the bottom turn left through a gate into the field. The grassy cart track soon reappears, follow it down to the stream where a stile on the right leads you to a tiny packhorse-type bridge at a delightful spot. Continue in the same direction to find the main road in a couple of hundred yards.

Muker finish

When you reach the walled lane turn right. Take the left fork after a short half mile and after about 400 yards keep a look-out for a stile over the fence on the left. The ladder stile is directly below at the bottom of a very steep field. Then make for the barn to find the slit stile in the wall. From here a cart track leads you back direct to the car park.

Extension: Muker via Oxnop Gill

At the intake wall you have reached a band of Yoredale limestone which gives pleasant easy going with good views. Follow the line of the wall for a good two miles passing a building (where you make a little height) near Routin Gill. Towards the end the wall winds its way down a steep-sided valley between two sizeable hillocks, quite a surprise, and joins the fenced road at a barn. Turn left and walk down the road for about 15 minutes.

When you reach the start of the final steep bit look out for a slit stile on the left. Continue to the barn and turn left above it. From the next stile keep above the decrepit wall to reach a fine house above the lower part of Routin Gill. Go down the road to the obvious fork and turn left. Just above the house go through the gate and turn right following the top of the wall all the way to a walled lane that leads you into the car park at Muker in a few minutes. The whole of this path has exceptionally pleasing views of the valley and Muker.

Things of Interest

1. Coal was mined in the Yoredale series of rocks in several places on

Great Shunner Fell up to the 1880s when the advent of the railway to Hawes made better quality coal cheaply available. The lane at the start of this walk leads to one of these pits whose spoil heaps of black shale you walk over soon after the end of the lane.

2. Even in late summer this lane boasts a good show of flowers - hawksbit/weeds, devil's scabious, harebells, foxgloves - to name but a few.

AROUND REETH AND ARKENGARTHDALE

Just as Grassington may be called the capital of upper Wharfedale, so may Reeth be called the capital of upper Swaledale. Both villages were radically changed by the eighteenth and nineteenth century lead mining and smelting industry, both still share a parish church with another village and today both are dependent on tourism to make a living. Reeth's green, fringed by the well set-up pubs and shops of High Row, smacks of prosperity, derived from the mining industry of 150 years ago. Reeth was then the market town for the whole of the upper dale and for Arkengarthdale as well, which was the centre of the lead industry. As the lead industry prospered, so did Reeth. In those days it had three times the population it has today. Arkengarthdale is almost big enough to rank as a Yorkshire dale in its own right, though it is but a branch of Swaledale. The valley is delightfully pastoral and well wooded with Langthwaite as its principal village.

Lead mine adit

11.8   From Reeth to Langthwaite

This walk goes up one side of Arkengarthdale and down the other and
has a great variety of scenery - woodland, riverside pasture and hay
meadows as well as excellent views in both directions. The outer leg
may be very wet in places but the return is pleasantly dry, and the worst
of the wet is avoided by the short version. The whole route is now fairly
well trodden and easy to follow. Category C. Time: 3 hours for the
whole, 1 ¹/₂ hours for the short version. Map: 1:25,000 Outdoor Leisure
Series No. 30, Northern and Central Areas.

Park by the green in Reeth (parking charge) and go down the main
Richmond road until you have crossed Arkle Beck, a large stream
which could be mistaken for the Swale. There you will see a double
finger post, one to the left, one to the right. Follow the left-hand one
through a line of waymarked stiles, at first by the river, then bear right
and climb up past a barn to join the bridleway from Fremlington where
you turn left. There are fine views up the dale from there and from many
places along this side. Follow the bridleway past a deserted farm and
go on to the next one, Castle Farm House, being restored in 1991.
Assuming that you are doing the entire walk, as you approach the farm,
look out for a finger post on the right at the corner of the first building
and follow the waymarked slit stiles from there down to the river. (If
you are doing the short walk, go through the yard and turn left when you
meet the gravel road. It takes you down to the bridge and you simply
follow it up the hill to join the return at*.) Note that diversions to these
paths may be made when the house is occupied again, so look out for
waymarks. The path along the riverside pastures can be exceedingly
wet and muddy and is quite complex to follow. It is however,well
waymarked, and gives you time to enjoy the riverside, its birds and
flowers. The path improves on the approaches to Slei Gill, crossed by
a good footbridge, and becomes a bridleway for the last mile into
Langthwaite, where it arrives in the village square complete with pub
and village shop, a most pleasant corner.

On the return retrace your steps to the first bridge, cross it and turn
left. Almost at once there's a tricky bit where a stream comes in on your
right: go down to the river bed to cross it easily. The path continues
easily by the river and then crosses a stile into a field on the right. Now
climb up towards the wooden electricity pole and you'll find a line of
marked stiles that bring you to a finger post. Follow the direction it

The Old Powder House, Arkengarthdale

gives to the wall corner, then the wall to West Raw Croft Farm which you bypass on its right climbing up to find the slit stile above. Now follow the green tractor marks through three long fields until you meet the gravelled track* from the bridge used on the short walk. Go up it a little way then bear left through a gate. A set of waymarked slit stiles leads you to a kind of green ramp that curves up the hillside. Keep a look-out for an electricity pole with a waymark on it and bear left there crossing a little stream and continue through more hay fields to reach the Arkengarth road just to the right of a large house about 5 minutes from Reeth.

Things of Interest
The flowers along the edge of the stream are worth a look, especially in the month of June. If you spot a great clump of yellow it is probably monkey musk, which is not all that common, partly because it is an annual, so isn't found in the same place year after year. You may find ragged robin, forget-me-not, brook lime and scurvy grass in flower as well as the more usual May flowers and marsh marigolds. With luck you may see that gorgeous canary-like bird, the cock grey wagtail as well as the pied wagtail and dippers.

Langthwaite is the main village of the dale and the centre of the former lead mining industry. Apart from its typically crowded houses the village retains no sign of this. The mines are scattered on the moors and the remains of its smelt mills lie a good half mile up the road past the church and the C.B. Inn. The church is not the original one but a rather austere Georgian building, its interior reminiscent of a Methodist chapel. The initial C.B. stands for Charles Bathurst, one of the family that owned the dale for almost 300 years. Just beyond the C.B. Inn is a terrace of houses, once the offices of the mines and the mills. The remains of one of the mills, Langthwaite Old Mill, is opposite, but scarcely anything can be identified except the wheel pit and the flues. The new or Octagon Mill was in the field below the road, but there's nothing left except the foundations and the great slag heaps by the beck. The old powder house is in the middle of a field above the church.

11.9   Around Slei Gill from Langthwaite

Parking in Langthwaite is not easy. There is space for a very few cars in the tiny square opposite the Red Lion. There are toilets opposite the chapel on the main road. Category B. Map: 1:25,000 Outdoor Leisure series No. 30, Northern and Central Areas. Time: About 3 hours.

The gill itself gives easy walking although pulling out at its head onto the old bridleway gives a short spell of hard going. There are quite exceptionally wide and good views during the whole of the descent as compensation.

The way starts beyond the first building by the river bridge and is a very obvious bridle track on the river bank. Follow it through the field and bear left at the fork and climb up to a gate. Here it becomes a beautiful grass track wending its way up the gill. At the spoil heaps bear left to get through them most easily. Higher up at a fork in the gill where there is a large spoil heap and what looks like a limekiln, this excellent track ends, though the map shows a right of way track continuing up the moor. Go to the right round the back of the spoil heaps to a cairn and strike off left up a tiny track from there. It soon peters out and leaves you with some rough going which is somewhat better nearer the stream. In due course you will come to the end of a line of shooting butts. From here you will see two wide streaks of white stones down the hillside, the second one ending in a broad expanse of grass. Make for this and climb up to reach a Land-Rover shooting track. Here on the left you should see a tiny track through the heather, marked by a small cairn in 1990. This tiny track is all that is left of the once wide bridleway that is marked on the map. It traverses the headwaters of Slei Gill giving excellent views of Calver and the moors behind Grinton. In places it is faint but is not difficult to follow, and leads you to a new large shooting hut where you join the Land-Rover track. Turn left and follow a pleasant green branch of it up the side of a deep cutting in the hillside. It swings left and eventually joins the Land-Rover track which you follow, enjoying the fine views until it swings sharply to the right. Here you turn left onto a peaty cart track through the heather and follow it gently down the moor bearing left, eventually reaching a gate. Turn left here and right at the wall corner to find the stile in the next corner. From here a fine green track, faint at first then well marked and giving splendid views, runs down to the road just below the hamlet of Booze. When you reach the road turn right to return to Langthwaite.

A Note on the Lead Mining remains in Slei Gill
All the way up Slei Gill is a series of deep cut gullies. These were 'hushes' made in the relatively early days of mining. Low down by the bed of the stream you will see a tunnel. This is probably a drainage level rather than a mine entrance. The building that looks like a limekiln at the foot of the upper spoil heaps is in fact the wheel pit of one of the waterwheels that powered the pumping and hauling machinery of the mines. Power could be transmitted quite long distances. It is not clear how this one received its water supply, but no doubt the spoil heap has shuttered down and covered the leat. The remains of one of the bearings of the wheel can be seen and the small tunnel is where the tail race came out. Higher up on the moor is another long hush and beside it is a row of old shafts, easily recognised as they are now smooth green mounds in the heather.

In June and July the lower spoil heaps are covered with a starry white flower, spring sandwort, very characteristic of old spoil heaps.

11.10 Cogden Gill and Grinton Smelt Mill
A walk with a good deal of variety - woodland, stream and moor, and good views into Swaledale. Just about the only place to park in Grinton is the car park of the Bridge Inn, but it doesn't add a lot on if you walk from Reeth. Simply walk down the road, cross the bridge and go over a stile on the right. Then follow the path to the bridge at Grinton. Category B. Map: 1:25,000 Outdoor Leisure No. 30, Yorkshire Dales Northern and Central Areas.

From Grinton go along the Richmond road and in about ³/₄ mile you will come to the entrance to Cogden Hall. Turn up this drive and in about 100 yards you will see a stile on the right into the wood. Cross it and follow the path up the stream. When you are just below Grinton Hall which is a youth hostel, the path swings left across a muddy patch to a stile and then to the edge of a water leat. It then continues to the road on the right, but you follow the leat left to the stream and then follow the stream all the way up to the road bridge. It's not a right of way but there's a little path all the way.

At the road cross the bridge and take the cart track immediately on the right which will bring you in 10 minutes' walk to the two remaining buildings of Grinton Smelt Mill.[1] Take time to have a good look round, few are as well preserved. (You can of course drive to the road bridge if all you want to do is have a look at the smelt mill.) Then retrace your steps to the road, or as a variation, after about 100 yards drop down to the stream on a little path, cross it and follow it down to the road. Now go left along the road, and 100 yards or so past the road sign look carefully for the start of a grassy track on the left. It isn't well marked but runs as a distinct grass strip 3-6 feet wide through the heather down to a little gully, out of it, and across the moor to a road. The track continues straight across the road but starts to disappear as you come in sight of Grinton Gill and a line of shooting butts. Just keep in the

The remains of the flue, Grinton Smelt Mill

311

Grinton Smelt Mill and Peat Store

same direction and it will take you on to a broad green track that goes up the gill to a shooting hut. Turn left on it and keep a look-out for another green strip through the heather on the right that goes down to the stream. You'll cross the stream without any difficulty and climb up the other side onto a path that goes to a gap in one of the many long earthworks[2] that are found in this part of Swaledale. Go straight ahead and follow this same green strip - hardly a path - down to the intake wall. Turn right here and follow a narrow walled lane onto the road, then this down to the main road.

Things of Interest

1. Grinton Smelt Mill is the lower of the two buildings; the upper one was the peat store, now modified for agricultural usage. It is thought from the records that this mill was built between 1820 and 1822, when the Grinton mines were in full production. Originally the main room of the mill had three ore hearths but they were later converted to the reverberatory type by the London Lead Co. There have been many later alterations in this room that make it difficult to see what this lay-out was. Behind the main room a smaller one housed a water-wheel and bellows. The wooden chute or launder that supplied it with water is still in position today and from it we can see that the wheel was roughly 18 feet diameter. Only fragments of the hearths are left but the great curve of their upper structure and flues is very impressive. The flue - still intact - runs out of the building and a long way up the moor to the site

of the chimney, now demolished. No trace of the wheel or bellows remains - indeed, Raistrick states that a blowing machine was installed in 1860 or 1870 and it is its massive wooden framework that remains in the wheel room today. A blowing machine gave a smoother air supply than the bellows, and like them was worked by a crank from the water-wheel. The mill was worked until 1893.

2.   The earthwork is one of many similar ones to be seen in this part of Swaledale. There's one by the river near Marrick Priory and Maiden Castle on the flanks of Harkerside Moor is yet another. They are probably of Iron Age origin, say around 500 BC, but little seems to be known about them.

11.11   Apedale and Harkerside Moor

Apedale really belongs to Wensleydale but forms a goodly part of this walk taking in Harkerside Moor. Category B, but route finding on Harkerside is not easy in parts and the heather gives hard going if you lose the path. Time: 3½-4hrs. Map: 1:25,000 Outdoor Leisure No. 30, Yorkshire Dales Northern and Central Areas. Drive up the road to Redmire from Grinton until, not far from the top, you see a finger post 'Bridleway to Castle Bolton 3M'. Park there.

Follow the direction indicated by the finger post - there's no path at first - to the first cairn. There you'll find an obvious length of greensward between heather and stony ground that will lead you to the fence on the top of Greets Hill. From it a bridletrack leads down to the shooting hut in Apedale. It takes you away from your general direction but don't try to cut the corner until the track branches. Then it's worth while. Now follow the cart track right up the little dale, climbing steeply out of it onto the moor above. As you come towards the fence turn sharp left towards a fenced spoil heap to find the gate and continuation of the path. There are good views of Swaledale. More or less straight ahead is Gunnerside Gill identified by the wide rough road running up it almost to the top of Rogan's Seat. The village is below, hidden, like all the others by the curve of the fell. The fell quite close to hand with the dark flat cap is Blea Barf. Behind it to the left is Lovely Seat and to its right is Great Shunner Fell.

From the gate follow the main track past the finger post to the biggish stream that crosses the path. It's marked by a small cairn and

Ancient earthworks on Harkerside Moor

two shooting butts are just visible. Turn down the stream following the greensward on the left-hand side until you are forced to cross the stream. There you will find a little path in the heather. Follow it downstream for a short distance. It soon pulls away to the right, dropping steadily until you come in sight of a large well-built cairn on a patch of good green grass. The track is faint, but just keep along this stretch of grass below the heather, dropping gently the while, but not going down through the intake wall, quite close in places. Eventually you come to a shooting hut. Follow its Land Rover track until that turns left into the valley. From its bend a faint track goes up on the right and climbs to the brow of the hill along the side of a huge 'hush'. Then tracks become confused. The way with the best views, but not the quickest, keeps left of the hush that drops into Grinton Gill and goes along the ridge ahead to a row of cairns. Then go right off the end of the ridge taking the right fork down to the stream. Cross the stream and follow a little path to a good cart track. Turn left and a few minutes' walk see you on the road. Turn right and a few more minutes will see you at your car. The quickest way from the top of the 'hush' is to follow the little path down to the stream, follow it and cross it where convenient and cut across to yet another shooting hut. Follow its Land-Rover track to the road, it's the one you join on the other route.

Things of Interest

See the notes to Walk 9.6 for something about Apedale.

Harkerside Moor is full of old lead mining remains, though there is nothing so good as in Apedale. There are also a number of earthworks, thought to be of Iron Age origin.

Notes

CICERONE GUIDES

Cicerone publish a wide range of reliable guides to walking and climbing in Britain - and other general interest books

LAKE DISTRICT - General Books
LAKELAND VILLAGES
WORDSWORTH'S DUDDON REVISITED
THE REGATTA MEN
REFLECTIONS ON THE LAKES
OUR CUMBRIA
PETTIE
THE HIGH FELLS OF LAKELAND
CONISTON COPPER A History
LAKELAND - A taste to remember (Recipes)
THE LOST RESORT?
CHRONICLES OF MILNTHORPE
LOST LANCASHIRE

LAKE DISTRICT - Guide Books
CASTLES IN CUMBRIA
WESTMORLAND HERITAGE WALK
IN SEARCH OF WESTMORLAND
CONISTON COPPER MINES
SCRAMBLES IN THE LAKE DISTRICT
MORE SCRAMBLES IN THE LAKE DISTRICT
WINTER CLIMBS IN THE LAKE DISTRICT
WALKS IN SILVERDALE/ARNSIDE
BIRDS OF MORECAMBE BAY
THE EDEN WAY

NORTHERN ENGLAND (outside the Lakes
THE YORKSHIRE DALES A walker's guide
WALKING IN THE SOUTH PENNINES
LAUGHS ALONG THE PENNINE WAY
WALKS IN THE YORKSHIRE DALES (2 VOL)
WALKS TO YORKSHIRE WATERFALLS
NORTH YORK MOORS Walks
THE CLEVELAND WAY & MISSING LINK
DOUGLAS VALLEY WAY
THE RIBBLE WAY
WALKING NORTHERN RAILWAYS EAST
WALKING NORTHERN RAILWAYS WEST
HERITAGE TRAILS IN NW ENGLAND
BIRDWATCHING ON MERSEYSIDE
THE LANCASTER CANAL
FIELD EXCURSIONS IN NW ENGLAND
ROCK CLIMBS LANCASHIRE & NW
THE ISLE OF MAN COASTAL PATH

DERBYSHIRE & EAST MIDLANDS
WHITE PEAK WALKS - 2 Vols
HIGH PEAK WALKS
WHITE PEAK WAY
KINDER LOG
THE VIKING WAY
THE DEVIL'S MILL (Novel)
WHISTLING CLOUGH (Novel)
WALES & WEST MIDLANDS
THE RIDGES OF SNOWDONIA
HILLWALKING IN SNOWDONIA
ASCENT OF SNOWDON
WELSH WINTER CLIMBS
SNOWDONIA WHITE WATER SEA & SURF
SCRAMBLES IN SNOWDONIA
ROCK CLIMBS IN WEST MIDLANDS
THE SHROPSHIRE HILLS A Walker's Guide

SOUTH & SOUTH WEST ENGLAND
WALKS IN KENT
THE WEALDWAY & VANGUARD WAY
SOUTH DOWNS WAY & DOWNS LINK
COTSWOLD WAY
WALKING ON DARTMOOR
SOUTH WEST WAY - 2 Vol

SCOTLAND
SCRAMBLES IN LOCHABER
SCRAMBLES IN SKYE
THE ISLAND OF RHUM
CAIRNGORMS WINTER CLIMBS
WINTER CLIMBS BEN NEVIS & GLENCOE
SCOTTISH RAILWAY WALKS
TORRIDON A Walker's Guide
SKI TOURING IN SCOTLAND

THE MOUNTAINS OF ENGLAND & WALES
VOL 1 WALES
VOL 2 ENGLAND

Also a full range of guidebooks to walking, scrambling, ice-climbing, rock climbing, and other adventurous pursuits in Europe

Other guides are constantly being added to the Cicerone List.
Available from bookshops, outdoor equipment shops or direct (send for price list)
from CICERONE, 2 POLICE SQUARE, MILNTHORPE, CUMBRIA, LA7 7PY

CICERONE GUIDES

Cicerone publish a wide range of reliable guides to walking and climbing in Europe

FRANCE
TOUR OF MONT BLANC
CHAMONIX MONT BLANC - A Walking Guide
TOUR OF THE OISANS: GR54
WALKING THE FRENCH ALPS: GR5
THE CORSICAN HIGH LEVEL ROUTE: GR20
THE WAY OF ST JAMES: GR65
THE PYRENEAN TRAIL: GR10
THE RLS (Stevenson) TRAIL
TOUR OF THE QUEYRAS
ROCK CLIMBS IN THE VERDON
WALKS IN VOLCANO COUNTRY (Auvergne)

FRANCE / SPAIN
WALKS AND CLIMBS IN THE PYRENEES
ROCK CLIMBS IN THE PYRENEES

SPAIN
WALKS & CLIMBS IN THE PICOS DE EUROPA
WALKING IN MALLORCA
BIRDWATCHING IN MALLORCA
COSTA BLANCA CLIMBS

FRANCE / SWITZERLAND
THE JURA - Walking the High Route and Winter Ski Traverses
CHAMONIX TO ZERMATT The Walker's Haute Route

SWITZERLAND
WALKING IN THE BERNESE ALPS
WALKS IN THE ENGADINE
THE VALAIS - A Walking Guide
THE ALPINE PASS ROUTE

GERMANY / AUSTRIA
THE KALKALPEN TRAVERSE
KLETTERSTEIG - Scrambles
WALKING IN THE BLACK FOREST
MOUNTAIN WALKING IN AUSTRIA
WALKING IN THE SALZKAMMERGUT
KING LUDWIG WAY

ITALY
ALTA VIA - High Level Walkis in the Dolomites
VIA FERRATA - Scrambles in the Dolomites
ITALIAN ROCK - Selected Rock Climbs in Northern Italy
CLASSIC CLIMBS IN THE DOLOMITES
WALKING IN THE DOLOMITES

OTHER AREAS
THE MOUNTAINS OF GREECE - A Walker's Guide
CRETE: Off the beaten track
Treks & Climbs in the mountains of RHUM & PETRA, JORDAN
THE ATLAS MOUNTAINS

GENERAL OUTDOOR BOOKS
LANDSCAPE PHOTOGRAPHY
FIRST AID FOR HILLWALKERS
MOUNTAIN WEATHER
MOUNTAINEERING LITERATURE
THE ADVENTURE ALTERNATIVE
MODERN ALPINE CLIMBING
MODERN ROPE TECHNIQUES
MODERN SNOW & ICE TECHNIQUES
LIMESTONE -100 BEST CLIMBS IN BRITAIN

CANOEING
SNOWDONIA WILD WATER, SEA & SURF
WILDWATER CANOEING
CANOEIST'S GUIDE TO THE NORTH EAST

CARTOON BOOKS
ON FOOT & FINGER
ON MORE FEET & FINGERS
LAUGHS ALONG THE PENNINE WAY
BLACKNOSE THE PIRATE

Also a full range of guidebooks to walking, scrambling, ice-climbing, rock climbing, and other adventurous pursuits in Britain and abroad

Other guides are constantly being added to the Cicerone List. Available from bookshops, outdoor equipment shops or direct (send for price list) from CICERONE, 2 POLICE SQUARE, MILNTHORPE, CUMBRIA, LA7 7PY

Printed by
Carnmor Print & Design, London Road, Preston